Year 2C
A Guide to Teaching for Mastery

Series Editor: Tony Staneff

Contents

Introduction

Foreword by the series editor and author, Tony Staneff

For far too long in the UK, maths has been feared by learners – and by many teachers, too. As a result, most learners consistently underachieve. More crucially, negative beliefs about ability, aptitude and the nature of maths are entrenched in children's thinking from an early age.

Yet, as someone who has loved maths all my life, I've always believed that every child has the capacity to succeed in maths. I've also had the great pleasure of leading teams and departments who share that belief and passion. Teaching for mastery, as practised in China and other South-East Asian jurisdictions since the 1980s, has confirmed my conviction that maths really is for everyone and not just those who have a special talent. In recent years my team and I at Trinity Academy, Halifax, have had the privilege of researching with and working with some of the finest mastery practitioners from the UK and beyond, whose impact on learners' confidence, achievement and attitude is an inspiration.

The mastery approach recognises the value of developing the power to think rather than just do. It also recognises the value of making a coherent journey in which whole-class groups tackle concepts in very small steps, one by one. You cannot build securely on loose foundations – and it is just the same with maths: by creating a solid foundation of deep understanding, our children's skills and confidence will be strong and secure. What's more, the mindset of learner and teacher alike is fundamental: everyone can do maths… EVERYONE CAN!

I am proud to have been part of the extensive team responsible for turning the best of the world's practice, research, insights, and shared experiences into *Power Maths*, a unique teaching and learning resource developed especially for UK classrooms. *Power Maths* embodies our vision to help and support primary maths teachers to transform every child's mathematical and personal development. 'Everyone can!' has become our mantra and our passion, and we hope it will be yours, too.

Now, explore and enjoy all the resources you need to teach for mastery, and please get back to us with your *Power Maths* experiences and stories!

What is *Power Maths*?

Created especially for UK primary schools, and aligned with the new National Curriculum, *Power Maths* is a whole-class, textbook-based mastery resource that empowers every child to understand and succeed. *Power Maths* rejects the notion that some people simply 'can't do' maths. Instead, it develops growth mindsets and encourages hard work, practice and a willingness to see mistakes as learning tools.

Best practice consistently shows that mastery of small, cumulative steps builds a solid foundation of deep mathematical understanding. *Power Maths* combines interactive teaching tools, high-quality textbooks and continuing professional development (CPD) to help you equip children with a deep and long lasting understanding. Based on extensive evidence, and developed in partnership with practising teachers, *Power Maths* ensures that it meets the needs of children in the UK.

Power Maths and Mastery

Power Maths makes mastery practical and achievable by providing the structures, pathways, content, tools and support you need to make it happen in your classroom.

To develop mastery in maths children must be enabled to acquire a deep understanding of maths concepts, structures and procedures, step by step. Complex mathematical concepts are built on simpler conceptual components and when children understand every step in the learning sequence, maths becomes transparent and makes logical sense. Interactive lessons establish deep understanding in small steps, as well as effortless fluency in key facts such as tables and number bonds. The whole class works on the same content and no child is left behind.

Power Maths

- Builds every concept in small, progressive steps
- Is built with interactive, whole-class teaching in mind
- Provides the tools you need to develop growth mindsets
- Helps you check understanding and ensure that every child is keeping up
- Establishes core elements such as intelligent practice and reflection

The *Power Maths* approach

Everyone can!

Founded on the conviction that every child can achieve, *Power Maths* enables children to build number fluency, confidence and understanding, step by step.

Child-centred learning

Children master concepts one step at a time in lessons that embrace a concrete-pictorial-abstract (C-P-A) approach, avoid overload, build on prior learning and help them see patterns and connections. Same-day intervention ensures sustained progress.

Continuing professional development

Embedded teacher support and development offer every teacher the opportunity to continually improve their subject knowledge and manage whole-class teaching for mastery.

Whole-class teaching

An interactive, whole-class teaching model encourages thinking and precise mathematical language and allows children to deepen their understanding as far as they can.

Introduction to the author team

Power Maths arises from the work of maths mastery experts who are committed to proving that, given the right mastery mindset and approach, **everyone can do maths**. Based on robust research and best practice from around the world, *Power Maths* was developed in partnership with a group of UK teachers to make sure that it not only meets our children's wide-ranging needs but also aligns with the National Curriculum in England.

Tony Staneff, Series Editor and author

Vice Principal at Trinity Academy, Halifax, Tony also leads a team of mastery experts who help schools across the UK to develop teaching for mastery via nationally recognised CPD courses, problem-solving and reasoning resources, schemes of work, assessment materials and other tools.

A team of experienced authors, including:

- **Josh Lury** – a specialist maths teacher, author and maths consultant with a passion for innovative and effective maths education
- **Jenny Lewis, Stephen Monaghan, Beth Smith and Kelsey Brown** – skilled maths teachers and mastery experts
- **Cherri Moseley** – a maths author, former teacher and professional development provider
- **Paul Wrangles** – a maths author and former teacher, Paul's goal is to "ignite creative thought in teachers and pupils by providing creative teaching resources".

Professor Liu Jian, Series Consultant and author, and his team of mastery expert authors:

- **Hou Huiying, Huang Lihua, Wang Mingming, Yin Lili, Zhang Dan, Zhang Hong and Zhou Da**

Used by over 20 million children, Professor Liu Jian's textbook programme is one of the most popular in China. He and his author team are highly experienced in intelligent practice and in embedding key maths concepts using a C-P-A approach.

A group of 15 teachers and maths co-ordinators

We have consulted our teacher group throughout the development of *Power Maths* to ensure we are meeting their real needs in the classroom.

Your *Power Maths* resources

To help you teach for mastery, *Power Maths* comprises a variety of high-quality resources.

Pupil Textbooks

Discover, Share, and Think together sections promote discussion and introduce mathematical ideas logically, so that children understand more easily.

Using a Concrete-Pictorial-Abstract approach, clear mathematical models help children to make connections and grasp concepts.

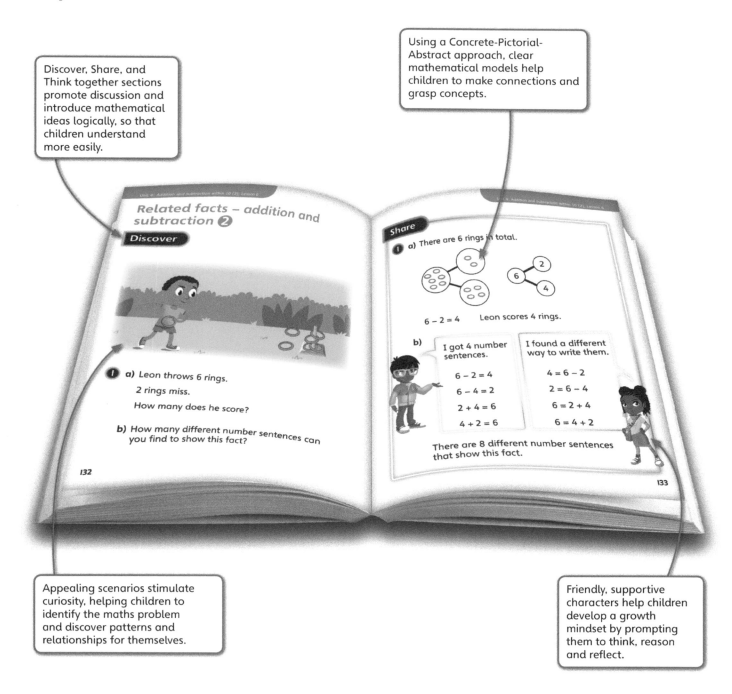

Related facts – addition and subtraction ❷

Discover

❶ a) Leon throws 6 rings.

2 rings miss.

How many does he score?

b) How many different number sentences can you find to show this fact?

132

Share

❶ a) There are 6 rings in total.

6 – 2 = 4   Leon scores 4 rings.

b) I got 4 number sentences.

6 – 2 = 4
6 – 4 = 2
2 + 4 = 6
4 + 2 = 6

I found a different way to write them.

4 = 6 – 2
2 = 6 – 4
6 = 2 + 4
6 = 4 + 2

There are 8 different number sentences that show this fact.

133

Appealing scenarios stimulate curiosity, helping children to identify the maths problem and discover patterns and relationships for themselves.

Friendly, supportive characters help children develop a growth mindset by prompting them to think, reason and reflect.

The coherent *Power Maths* lesson structure carries through into the vibrant, high-quality textbooks. Setting out the core learning objectives for each class, the lesson structure follows a carefully mapped journey through the curriculum and supports children on their journey to deeper understanding.

Pupil Practice Books

The Practice Books offer just the right amount of intelligent practice for children to complete independently in the final section of each lesson.

The practice questions are for everyone – each question varies one small element to move children on in their thinking. Look at the different parts in question ❶!

Calculations are connected so that children think about the underlying concept. In question ❸ , children have to write out the calculation to find the answer. Concepts are presented differently again in question ❹ to challenge children.

Practice questions are finely tuned to move children forward in their thinking and to reveal misconceptions.

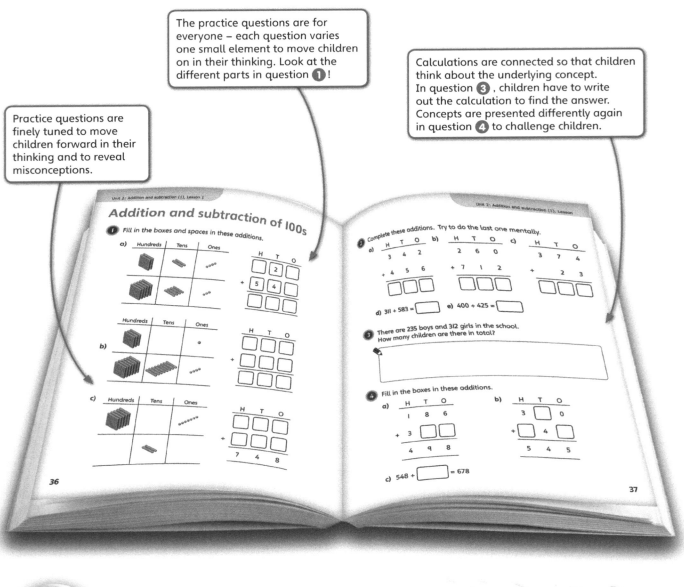

Challenge questions allow children to delve deeper into a concept.

Reflect questions reveal the depth of each child's understanding before they move on.

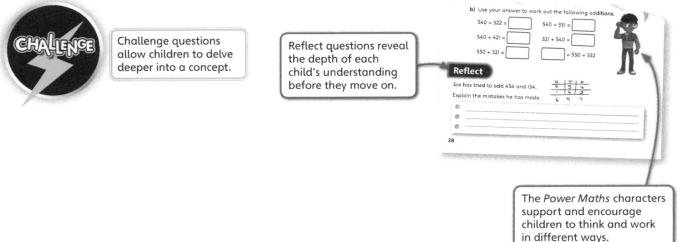

The *Power Maths* characters support and encourage children to think and work in different ways.

Online subscriptions

The online subscription will give you access to additional resources.

eTextbooks

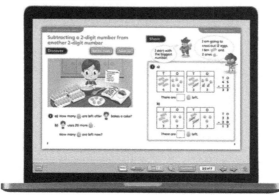

Digital versions of *Power Maths* Textbooks allow class groups to share and discuss questions, solutions and strategies. They allow you to project key structures and representations at the front of the class, to ensure all children are focusing on the same concept.

Teaching tools

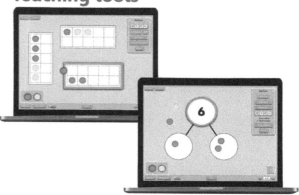

Here you will find interactive versions of key *Power Maths* structures and representations.

Power Ups

Use this series of daily activities to promote and check number fluency.

Online versions of Teacher Guide pages

PDF pages give support at both unit and lesson levels. You will also find help with key strategies and templates for tracking progress.

Unit videos

Watch the professional development videos at the start of each unit to help you teach with confidence. The videos explore common misconceptions in the unit, and include intervention suggestions as well as suggestions on what to look out for when assessing mastery in your students.

End of unit Strengthen and Deepen materials

Each Strengthen activity at the end of every unit addresses a key misconception and can be used to support children who need it. The Deepen activities are designed to be low ceiling / high threshold and will challenge those children who can understand more deeply. These resources will help you ensure that every child understands and will help you keep the class moving forward together. These printable activities provide an optional resource bank for use after the assessment stage.

Underpinning all of these resources, *Power Maths* is infused throughout with continual professional development, supporting you at every step.

The *Power Maths* teaching model

At the heart of *Power Maths* is a clearly structured teaching and learning process that helps you make certain that every child masters each maths concept securely and deeply. For each year group, the curriculum is broken down into core concepts, taught in units. A unit divides into smaller learning steps – lessons. Step by step, strong foundations of cumulative knowledge and understanding are built.

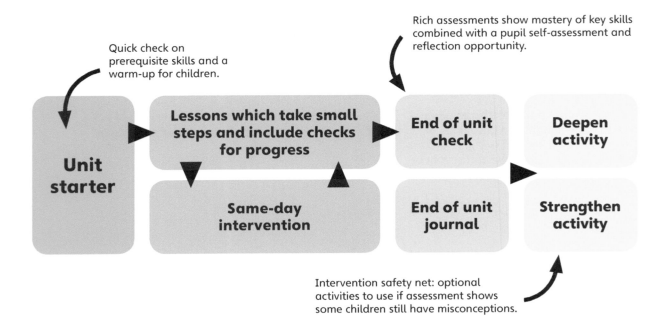

Quick check on prerequisite skills and a warm-up for children.

Rich assessments show mastery of key skills combined with a pupil self-assessment and reflection opportunity.

Unit starter → **Lessons which take small steps and include checks for progress** → **End of unit check** → **Deepen activity**

Same-day intervention   **End of unit journal**   **Strengthen activity**

Intervention safety net: optional activities to use if assessment shows some children still have misconceptions.

Unit starter

Each unit begins with a unit starter, which introduces the learning context along with key mathematical vocabulary and structures and representations.

- The Pupil Textbooks include a check on readiness and a warm-up task for children to complete.

- Your Teacher Guide gives support right from the start on important structures and representations, mathematical language, common misconceptions and intervention strategies.

- Unit-specific videos develop your subject knowledge and insights so you feel confident and fully equipped to teach each new unit. These are available via the online subscription.

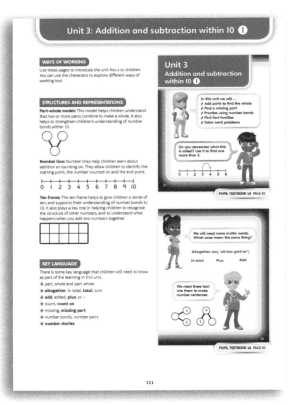

Lesson

Once a unit has been introduced, it is time to start teaching the series of lessons.

- Each lesson is scaffolded with Pupil Textbook and Practice Book activities and always begins with a Power Up activity (available via online subscription).

- *Power Maths* identifies lesson by lesson what concepts are to be taught.

- Your Teacher Guide offers lots of support for you to get the most from every child in every lesson. As well as highlighting key points, tricky areas and how to handle them, you will also find question prompts to check on understanding and clarification on why particular activities and questions are used.

Same-day intervention

Same-day interventions are vital in order to keep the class progressing together. Therefore, *Power Maths* provides plenty of support throughout the journey.

- Intervention is focused on keeping up now, not catching up later, so interventions should happen as soon as they are needed.

- Practice section questions are designed to bring misconceptions to the surface, allowing you to identify these easily as you circulate during independent practice time.

- Child-friendly assessment questions in the Teacher Guide help you identify easily which children need to strengthen their understanding.

End of unit check and journal

At the end of a unit, summative assessment tasks reveal essential information on each child's understanding. An End of unit check in the Pupil Textbook lets you see which children have mastered the key concepts, which children have not and where their misconceptions lie. The Practice Book also includes an End of unit journal in which children can reflect on what they have learned. Each unit also offers Strengthen and Deepen activities, available via the online subscription.

The Teacher Guide offers different ways of managing the End of unit assessments as well as giving support with handling misconceptions.

The End of unit check presents four multiple-choice questions. Children think about their answer, decide on a solution and explain their choice.

Unit 1: Numbers to 10 — Textbook 1A p56

End of unit check

My journal

Bea has 5 red ◯ and 1 yellow ◯ . Colour them in.

◯◯◯◯◯◯

Seth has 3 red ◯ and 3 yellow ◯ . Colour them in.

◯◯◯◯◯◯

What is the same? _____

_____

What is different? _____

_____

These words might help you.

balloon	1	one
less	3	three
more	5	five

42

The End of unit journal is an opportunity for children to test out their learning and reflect on how they feel about it. Tackling the 'journal' problem reveals whether a child understands the concept deeply enough to move on to the next unit.

Unit 1: Numbers to 10

End of unit check

Your teacher will ask you these questions.

1 What is the missing number?

____ 1   2   3

A 4   B 1   C 0   D 5

2 What is the number?

A 3   B 4   C 5   D 7

3 Demi is counting from 1 to 10. She says, 'four'. What numbers come next?

A 3, 2, 1   C 5, 6, 7
B 5, 7, 6   D 4, 5, 6

56

The *Power Maths* lesson sequence

At the heart of *Power Maths* is a unique lesson sequence designed to empower children to understand core concepts and grow in confidence. Embracing the National Centre for Excellence in the Teaching of Mathematics' (NCETM's) definition of mastery, the sequence guides and shapes every *Power Maths* lesson you teach.

Flexibility is built into the *Power Maths* programme so there is no one-to-one mapping of lessons and concepts meaning you can pace your teaching according to your class. While some children will need to spend longer on a particular concept (through interventions or additional lessons), others will reach deeper levels of understanding. However, it is important that the class moves forward together through the termly schedules.

Power Up ⏲ 5 minutes

Each lesson begins with a Power Up activity (available via the online subscription) which supports fluency in key number facts.

The whole-class approach depends on fluency, so the Power Up is a powerful and essential activity.

TOP TIP
If the class is struggling with the task, revisit it later and check understanding.

Power Ups reinforce the two key things that are essential for success: times-tables and number bonds.

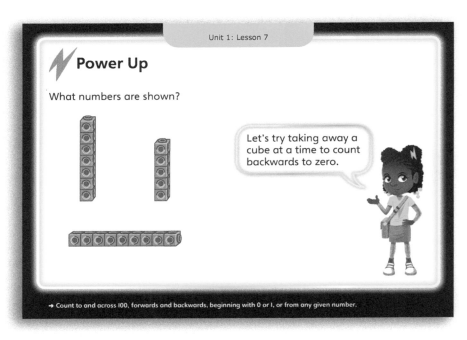

Discover ⏲ 10 minutes

A practical, real-life problem arouses curiosity. Children find the maths through story-telling.

TOP TIP
Discover works best when run at tables, in pairs with concrete objects.

Question ❶ a) tackles the key concept and question ❶ b) digs a little deeper. Children have time to explore, play and discuss possible strategies.

Share ⏱ 10 minutes

Teacher-led, this interactive section follows the Discover activity and highlights the variety of methods that can be used to solve a single problem.

TOP TIP
Bring children to the front or onto the carpet to discuss their methods. Pairs sharing a textbook is a great format for this!

Your Teacher Guide gives target questions for children. The online toolkit provides interactive structures and representations to link concrete and pictorial to abstract concepts.

Bring children to the front to share and celebrate their solutions and strategies.

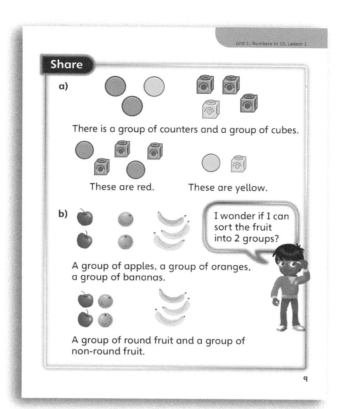

Share

a) There is a group of counters and a group of cubes.

These are red.   These are yellow.

b) I wonder if I can sort the fruit into 2 groups?

A group of apples, a group of oranges, a group of bananas.

A group of round fruit and a group of non-round fruit.

9

Think together

⏱ 10 minutes

Children work in groups on the carpet or at tables, using their textbooks or eBooks.

TOP TIP
Make sure children have mini whiteboards or pads to write on if they are not at their tables.

Using the Teacher Guide, model question ❶ for your class.

Question ❷ is less structured. Children will need to think together in their groups, then discuss their methods and solutions as a class.

Question ❸ – the openness of the Challenge question helps to check depth of understanding.

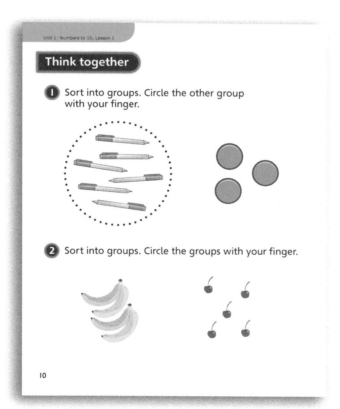

Think together

❶ Sort into groups. Circle the other group with your finger.

❷ Sort into groups. Circle the groups with your finger.

10

Practice ⏱ 15 minutes

Using their Practice Books, children work independently while you circulate and check on progress.

Questions follow small steps of progression to deepen learning.

TOP TIP
Some children could work separately with a teacher or assistant.

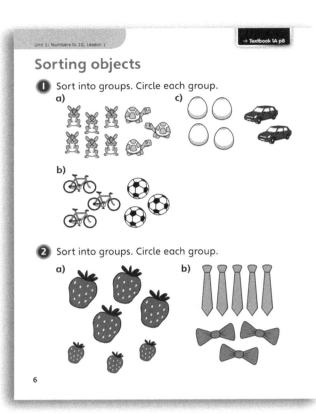

Are some children struggling? If so, work with them as a group, using mathematical structures and representations to support understanding as necessary.

There are no set routines: for real understanding, children need to think about the problem in different ways.

Reflect ⏱ 5 minutes

'Spot the mistake' questions are great for checking misconceptions.

The Reflect section is your opportunity to check how deeply children understand the target concept.

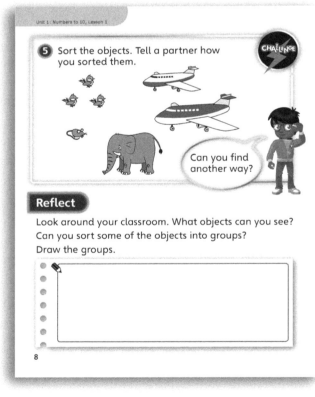

The Practice Books use various approaches to check that children have fully understood each concept.

Looking like they understand is not enough! It is essential that children can show they have grasped the concept.

Using the *Power Maths* Teacher Guide

Think of your Teacher Guides as *Power Maths* handbooks that will guide, support and inspire your day-to-day teaching. Clear and concise, and illustrated with helpful examples, your Teacher Guides will help you make the best possible use of every individual lesson. They also provide wrap-around professional development, enhancing your own subject knowledge and helping you to grow in confidence about moving your children forward together.

There is a Teacher Guide per year group for every term with unit and lesson level guidance and support.

Tips and advice on key elements such as C-P-A approaches, misconceptions, language, modelling growth mindsets and same-day intervention.

Annotations for every Pupil Textbook and Practice Book page, providing prompts for key questions to ask to expose understanding and explanations as to why key questions have been chosen.

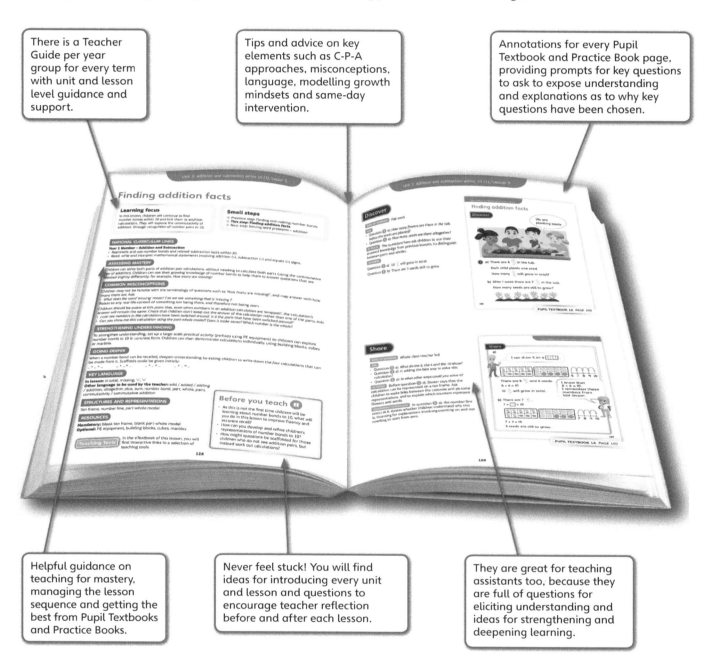

Helpful guidance on teaching for mastery, managing the lesson sequence and getting the best from Pupil Textbooks and Practice Books.

Never feel stuck! You will find ideas for introducing every unit and lesson and questions to encourage teacher reflection before and after each lesson.

They are great for teaching assistants too, because they are full of questions for eliciting understanding and ideas for strengthening and deepening learning.

At the end of each unit, your Teacher Guide helps you identify who has fully grasped the concept, who has not and how to move every child forward. This is covered later in the Assessment strategies section.

Power Maths Year 2, yearly overview

Textbook	Strand	Unit	Number of Lessons	
Textbook A / Practice Book A	Number – number and place value	1	Numbers to 100	10
	Number – addition and subtraction	2	Addition and subtraction (1)	12
(Term 1)	Number – addition and subtraction	3	Addition and subtraction (2)	9
	Measurement	4	Money	9
	Number – multiplication and division	5	Multiplication and division (1)	9
Textbook B / Practice Book B	Number – multiplication and division	6	Multiplication and division (2)	9
	Statistics	7	Statistics	7
(Term 2)	Measurement	8	Length and height	5
	Geometry – properties of shape	9	Properties of shapes	12
	Number – fractions	10	Fractions	14
Textbook C / Practice Book C	Geometry – position and direction	11	Position and direction	4
	Number – addition and subtraction	12	Problem solving and efficient methods	12
(Term 3)	Measurement	13	Time	9
	Measurement	14	Weight, volume and temperature	10

Power Maths Year 2, Textbook 2C (Term 3) overview

Strand 1	Strand 2	Unit		Lesson number	Lesson title	NC Objective 1	NC Objective 2	NC Objective 3
Geometry – position and direction		Unit 11	Position and direction	1	Describing movement	Use mathematical vocabulary to describe position, direction and movement, including movement in a straight line and distinguishing between rotation as a turn and in terms of right angles for quarter, half and three-quarter turns (clockwise and anti-clockwise)		
Geometry – position and direction		Unit 11	Position and direction	2	Describing turns	Use mathematical vocabulary to describe position, direction and movement, including movement in a straight line and distinguishing between rotation as a turn and in terms of right angles for quarter, half and three-quarter turns (clockwise and anti-clockwise)		
Geometry – position and direction		Unit 11	Position and direction	3	Describing movement and turns	Use mathematical vocabulary to describe position, direction and movement, including movement in a straight line and distinguishing between rotation as a turn and in terms of right angles for quarter, half and three-quarter turns (clockwise and anti-clockwise)		
Geometry – position and direction		Unit 11	Position and direction	4	Making patterns with shapes	Use mathematical vocabulary to describe position, direction and movement, including movement in a straight line and distinguishing between rotation as a turn and in terms of right angles for quarter, half and three-quarter turns (clockwise and anti-clockwise)	Order and arrange combinations of mathematical objects in patterns and sequences	
Number – number and place value	Number – addition and subtraction	Unit 12	Problem-solving and efficient methods	1	My way, your way!	Use place value and number facts to solve problems	Recognise and use the inverse relationship between addition and subtraction and use this to check calculations and solve missing number problems	
Number – number and place value		Unit 12	Problem-solving and efficient methods	2	Using number facts	Use place value and number facts to solve problems	Recognise and use the inverse relationship between addition and subtraction and use this to check calculations and solve missing number problems	
Number – number and place value	Number – addition and subtraction	Unit 12	Problem-solving and efficient methods	3	Using number facts and equivalence	Use place value and number facts to solve problems	Recognise and use the inverse relationship between addition and subtraction and use this to check calculations and solve missing number problems	
Number – number and place value	Number – addition and subtraction	Unit 12	Problem-solving and efficient methods	4	Using a 100 square	Use place value and number facts to solve problems	Solve problems with addition and subtraction: using concrete objects and pictorial representations, including those involving numbers, quantities and measures	
Number – number and place value	Number – addition and subtraction	Unit 12	Problem-solving and efficient methods	5	Getting started	Recognise and use the inverse relationship between addition and subtraction and use this to check calculations and solve missing number problems		
Number – addition and subtraction		Unit 12	Problem-solving and efficient methods	6	Missing numbers	Use place value and number facts to solve problems	Recognise and use the inverse relationship between addition and subtraction and use this to check calculations and solve missing number problems	

Strand 1	Strand 2	Unit		Lesson number	Lesson title	NC Objective 1	NC Objective 2	NC Objective 3
Number – number and place value	Number – addition and subtraction	Unit 12	Problem-solving and efficient methods	7	Mental addition and subtraction (1)	Solve problems with addition and subtraction: using concrete objects and pictorial representations, including those involving numbers, quantities and measures		
Number – addition and subtraction		Unit 12	Problem-solving and efficient methods	8	Mental addition and subtraction (2)	Solve problems with addition and subtraction: using concrete objects and pictorial representations, including those involving numbers, quantities and measures		
Number – addition and subtraction		Unit 12	Problem-solving and efficient methods	9	Efficient subtraction	Use place value and number facts to solve problems		
Number – number and place value		Unit 12	Problem-solving and efficient methods	10	Solving problems – addition and subtraction	Recognise and use the inverse relationship between addition and subtraction and use this to check calculations and solve missing number problems	Solve problems with addition and subtraction: using concrete objects and pictorial representations, including those involving numbers, quantities and measures	
Number – addition and subtraction		Unit 12	Problem-solving and efficient methods	11	Solving problems – multiplication and division	Solve problems involving multiplication and division, using materials, arrays, repeated addition, mental methods, and multiplication and division facts, including problems in contexts	Show that multiplication of two numbers can be done in any order (commutative) and division of one number by another cannot	
Number – addition and subtraction		Unit 12	Problem-solving and efficient methods	12	Solving problems using the four operations	Solve problems with addition and subtraction: using concrete objects and pictorial representations, including those involving numbers, quantities and measures	Solve problems involving multiplication and division, using materials, arrays, repeated addition, mental methods, and multiplication and division facts, including problems in contexts	
Measurement		Unit 13	Time	1	Telling and writing time to the hour and the half hour	(Year 1) tell the time to the hour and half past the hour and draw the hands on a clock face to show these times		
Measurement		Unit 13	Time	2	Telling time to the quarter hour	Tell and write the time to five minutes, including quarter past/to the hour and draw the hands on a clock face to show these times		
Measurement		Unit 13	Time	3	Telling time to 5 minutes	Tell and write the time to five minutes, including quarter past/to the hour and draw the hands on a clock face to show these times		
Measurement		Unit 13	Time	4	Minutes in an hour	Know the number of minutes in an hour and the number of hours in a day		
Measurement		Unit 13	Time	5	Finding durations of time	Compare and sequence intervals of time		
Measurement		Unit 13	Time	6	Comparing durations of time	Compare and sequence intervals of time		
Measurement		Unit 13	Time	7	Finding the end time	Know the number of minutes in an hour and the number of hours in a day		
Measurement		Unit 13	Time	8	Finding the start time	Compare and sequence intervals of time		
Measurement		Unit 13	Time	9	Hours in a day	Know the number of minutes in an hour and the number of hours in a day		
Measurement		Unit 14	Weight, volume and temperature	1	Comparing mass	Compare and order lengths, mass, volume/capacity and record the results using >, < and =		

Strand 1	Strand 2	Unit		Lesson number	Lesson title	NC Objective 1	NC Objective 2	NC Objective 3
Measurement		Unit 14	Weight, volume and temperature	2	Measuring mass in grams (1)	Choose and use appropriate standard units to estimate and measure length/height in any direction (m/cm); mass (kg/g); temperature (°C); capacity (litres/ml) to the nearest appropriate unit, using rulers, scales, thermometers and measuring vessels		
Measurement		Unit 14	Weight, volume and temperature	3	Measuring mass in grams (2)	Choose and use appropriate standard units to estimate and measure length/height in any direction (m/cm); mass (kg/g); temperature (°C); capacity (litres/ml) to the nearest appropriate unit, using rulers, scales, thermometers and measuring vessels	Compare and order lengths, mass, volume/capacity and record the results using >, < and =	
Measurement		Unit 14	Weight, volume and temperature	4	Measuring mass in kilograms	Choose and use appropriate standard units to estimate and measure length/height in any direction (m/cm); mass (kg/g); temperature (°C); capacity (litres/ml) to the nearest appropriate unit, using rulers, scales, thermometers and measuring vessels	Compare and order lengths, mass, volume/capacity and record the results using >, < and =	
Measurement		Unit 14	Weight, volume and temperature	5	Comparing volume	Compare and order lengths, mass, volume/capacity and record the results using >, < and =		
Measurement		Unit 14	Weight, volume and temperature	6	Measuring volume in millilitres (1)	Choose and use appropriate standard units to estimate and measure length/height in any direction (m/cm); mass (kg/g); temperature (°C); capacity (litres/ml) to the nearest appropriate unit, using rulers, scales, thermometers and measuring vessels		
Measurement		Unit 14	Weight, volume and temperature	7	Measuring volume in millilitres (2)	Choose and use appropriate standard units to estimate and measure length/height in any direction (m/cm); mass (kg/g); temperature (°C); capacity (litres/ml) to the nearest appropriate unit, using rulers, scales, thermometers and measuring vessels		
Measurement		Unit 14	Weight, volume and temperature	8	Measuring volume in litres	Choose and use appropriate standard units to estimate and measure length/height in any direction (m/cm); mass (kg/g); temperature (°C); capacity (litres/ml) to the nearest appropriate unit, using rulers, scales, thermometers and measuring vessels		
Measurement		Unit 14	Weight, volume and temperature	9	Measuring temperature using a thermometer	Choose and use appropriate standard units to estimate and measure length/height in any direction (m/cm); mass (kg/g); temperature (°C); capacity (litres/ml) to the nearest appropriate unit, using rulers, scales, thermometers and measuring vessels		
Measurement		Unit 14	Weight, volume and temperature	10	Reading thermometers	Choose and use appropriate standard units to estimate and measure length/height in any direction (m/cm); mass (kg/g); temperature (°C); capacity (litres/ml) to the nearest appropriate unit, using rulers, scales, thermometers and measuring vessels		

Mindset: an introduction

Global research and best practice deliver the same message: learning is greatly affected by what learners perceive they can or cannot do. What is more, it is also shaped by what their parents, carers and teachers perceive they can do. Mindset – the thinking that determines our beliefs and behaviours – therefore has a fundamental impact on teaching and learning.

Everyone can!

Power Maths and mastery methods focus on the distinction between 'fixed' and 'growth' mindsets (Dweck, 2007).[1] Those with a fixed mindset believe that their basic qualities (for example, intelligence, talent and ability to learn) are pre-wired or fixed: 'If you have a talent for maths, you will succeed at it. If not, too bad!' By contrast, those with a growth mindset believe that hard work, effort and commitment drive success and that 'smart' is not something you are or are not, but something you become. In short, everyone can do maths!

Key mindset strategies

A growth mindset needs to be actively nurtured and developed. *Power Maths* offers some key strategies for fostering healthy growth mindsets in your classroom.

It is okay to get it wrong

Mistakes are valuable opportunities to re-think and understand more deeply. Learning is richer when children and teachers alike focus on spotting and sharing mistakes as well as solutions.

Praise hard work

Praise is a great motivator, and by focusing on praising effort and learning rather than success, children will be more willing to try harder, take risks and persist for longer.

Mind your language!

The language we use around learners has a profound effect on their mindsets. Make a habit of using growth phrases, such as, 'Everyone can!', 'Mistakes can help you learn' and 'Just try for a little longer'. The king of them all is one little word, 'yet… I can't solve this…yet!' Encourage parents and carers to use the right language too.

Build in opportunities for success

The step-by-small-step approach enables children to enjoy the experience of success. In addition, avoid ability grouping and encourage every child to answer questions and explain or demonstrate their methods to others.

[1] Dweck, C (2007) The New Psychology of Success, Ballantine Books: New York

The *Power Maths* characters

The *Power Maths* characters model the traits of growth mindset learners and encourage resilience by prompting and questioning children as they work. Appearing frequently in the Textbooks and Practice Books, they are your allies in teaching and discussion, helping to model methods, alternatives and misconceptions, and to pose questions. They encourage and support your children, too: they are all hardworking, enthusiastic and unafraid of making and talking about mistakes.

Meet the team!

Creative Flo is open-minded and sometimes indecisive. She likes to think differently and come up with a variety of methods or ideas.

Determined Dexter is resolute, resilient and systematic. He concentrates hard, always tries his best and he'll never give up – even though he doesn't always choose the most efficient methods!

'Let's try again.'

'Mistakes are cool!'

'Have I found all of the solutions?'

'Let's try it this way…'

'Can we do it differently?'

'I've got another way of doing this!'

'I'm going to try this!'

'I know how to do that!'

'Want to share my ideas?'

Curious Ash is eager, interested and inquisitive, and he loves solving puzzles and problems. Ash asks lots of questions but sometimes gets distracted.

'What if we tried this…?'

'I wonder…'

'Is there a pattern here?'

Sparks the Cat

Miaow!

Brave Astrid is confident, willing to take risks and unafraid of failure. She's never scared to jump straight into a problem or question, and although she often makes simple mistakes she's happy to talk them through with others.

Mathematical language

Traditionally, we in the UK have tended to try simplifying mathematical language to make it easier for young children to understand. By contrast, evidence and experience show that by diluting the correct language, we actually mask concepts and meanings for children. We then wonder why they are confused by new and different terminology later down the line! *Power Maths* is not afraid of 'hard' words and avoids placing any barriers between children and their understanding of mathematical concepts. As a result, we need to be planned, precise and thorough in building every child's understanding of the language of maths. Throughout the Teacher Guides you will find support and guidance on how to deliver this, as well as individual explanations throughout the Pupil Textbooks.

Use the following key strategies to build children's mathematical vocabulary, understanding and confidence.

Precise and consistent

Everyone in the classroom should use the correct mathematical terms in full, every time. For example, refer to 'equal parts', not 'parts'. Used consistently, precise maths language will be a familiar and non-threatening part of children's everyday experience.

Full sentences

Teachers and children alike need to use full sentences to explain or respond. When children use complete sentences, it both reveals their understanding and embeds their knowledge.

Stem sentences

These important sentences help children express mathematical concepts accurately, and are used throughout the *Power Maths* books. Encourage children to repeat them frequently, whether working independently or with others. Examples of stem sentences are:

'4 is a part, 5 is a part, 9 is the whole.'

'There are … groups. There are … in each group.'

Key vocabulary

The unit starters highlight essential vocabulary for every lesson. In the Pupil Textbooks, characters flag new terminology and the Teacher Guide lists important mathematical language for every unit and lesson. New terms are never introduced without a clear explanation.

Symbolic language

Symbols are used early on so that children quickly become familiar with them and their meaning. Often, the *Power Maths* characters will highlight the connection between language and particular symbols.

The role of talk and discussion

When children learn to talk purposefully together about maths, barriers of fear and anxiety are broken down and they grow in confidence, skills and understanding. Building a healthy culture of 'maths talk' empowers their learning from day one.

Explanation and discussion are integral to the *Power Maths* structure, so by simply following the books your lessons will stimulate structured talk. The following key 'maths talk' strategies will help you strengthen that culture and ensure that every child is included.

Sentences, not words

Encourage children to use full sentences when reasoning, explaining or discussing maths. This helps both speaker and listeners to clarify their own understanding. It also reveals whether or not the speaker truly understands, enabling you to address misconceptions as they arise.

Working together

Working with others in pairs, groups or as a whole class is a great way to support maths talk and discussion. Use different group structures to add variety and challenge. For example, children could take timed turns for talking, work independently alongside a 'discussion buddy', or perhaps play different *Power Maths* character roles within their group.

Think first – then talk

Provide clear opportunities within each lesson for children to think and reflect, so that their talk is purposeful, relevant and focused.

Give every child a voice

Where the 'hands up' model allows only the more confident child to shine, *Power Maths* involves everyone. Make sure that no child dominates and that even the shyest child is encouraged to contribute – and praised when they do.

Assessment strategies

Teaching for mastery demands that you are confident about what each child knows and where their misconceptions lie: therefore, practical and effective assessment is vitally important.

Formative assessment within lessons

The **Think together** section will often reveal any confusions or insecurities: try ironing these out by doing the first Think together question as a class. For children who continue to struggle, you or your teaching assistant should provide support and enable them to move on.

Performance in **Practice** can be very revealing: check Practice Books and listen out both during and after practice to identify misconceptions.

The **Reflect** section is designed to check on the all-important depth of understanding. Be sure to review how the children performed in this final stage before you teach the next lesson.

End of unit check – Textbook

Each unit concludes with a summative check to help you assess quickly and clearly each child's understanding, fluency, reasoning and problem-solving skills. Your Teacher Guide will suggest ideal ways of organising a given activity and offer advice and commentary on what children's responses mean. For example, 'What misconception does this reveal?'; 'How can you reinforce this particular concept?'

For Year 1 and Year 2 children, assess in small, teacher-led groups, giving each child time to think and respond while also consolidating correct mathematical language. Assessment with young children should always be an enjoyable activity, so avoid one-to-one individual assessments, which they may find threatening or scary. If you prefer, the End of unit check can be carried out as a whole-class group using whiteboards and Practice Books.

End of unit check – Practice Book

The Practice Book contains further opportunities for assessment, and can be completed by children independently whilst you are carrying out diagnostic assessment with small groups. Your Teacher Guide will advise you on what to do if children struggle to articulate an explanation – or perhaps encourage you to write down something they have explained well. It will also offer insights into children's answers and their implications for next learning steps. It is split into three main sections, outlined below.

My journal and Think!

My journal is designed to allow children to show their depth of understanding of the unit. It can also serve as a way of checking that children have grasped key mathematical vocabulary. The question children should answer is first presented in the Pupil Textbook in the Think! section. This provides an opportunity for you to discuss the question first as a class to ensure children have understood their task. Children should have some time to think about how they want to answer the question, and you could ask them to talk to a partner about their ideas. Then children should write their answer in their Practice Book, using the word bank provided to help them with vocabulary.

Power check

The Power check allows pupils to self-assess their level of confidence on the topic by colouring in different smiley faces. You may want to introduce the faces as follows:

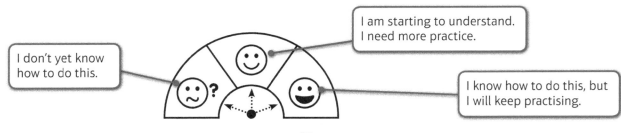

I am starting to understand. I need more practice.

I don't yet know how to do this.

I know how to do this, but I will keep practising.

Power play or Power puzzle

Each unit ends with either a Power play or a Power puzzle. This is an activity, puzzle or game that allows children to use their new knowledge in a fun, informal way.

How to ask diagnostic questions

The diagnostic questions provided in children's Practice Books are carefully structured to identify both understanding and misconceptions (if children answer in a particular way, you will know why). The simple procedure below may be helpful:

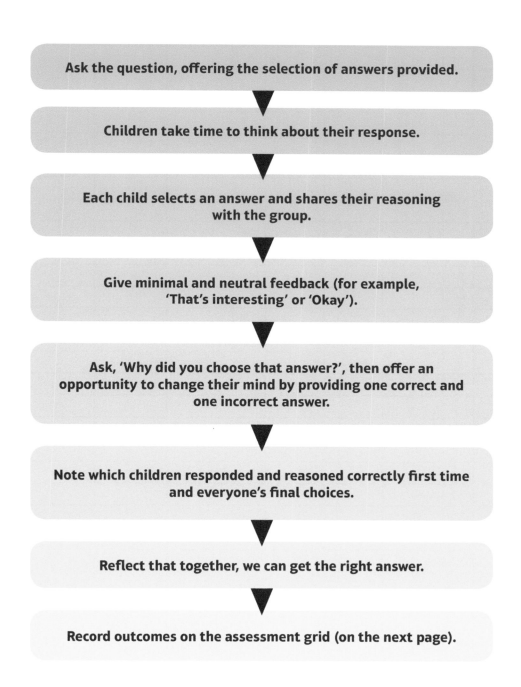

Ask the question, offering the selection of answers provided.

Children take time to think about their response.

Each child selects an answer and shares their reasoning with the group.

Give minimal and neutral feedback (for example, 'That's interesting' or 'Okay').

Ask, 'Why did you choose that answer?', then offer an opportunity to change their mind by providing one correct and one incorrect answer.

Note which children responded and reasoned correctly first time and everyone's final choices.

Reflect that together, we can get the right answer.

Record outcomes on the assessment grid (on the next page).

Power Maths unit assessment grid

Year ___   **Unit** ___ _____

Record only as much information as you judge appropriate for your assessment of each child's mastery of the unit and any steps needed for intervention.

Name	Q1	Q2	Q3	Q4	Q5	My journal	Power check	Power play/puzzle	Mastery	Intervention/ Strengthen

Keeping the class together

Traditionally, children who learn quickly have been accelerated through the curriculum. As a consequence, their learning may be superficial and will lack the many benefits of enabling children to learn with and from each other.

By contrast, *Power Maths'* mastery approach values real understanding and richer, deeper learning above speed. It sees all children learning the same concept in small, cumulative steps, each finding and mastering challenge at their own level. Remember that when you teach for mastery, EVERYONE can do maths! Those who grasp a concept easily have time to explore and understand that concept at a deeper level. The whole class therefore moves through the curriculum at broadly the same pace via individual learning journeys.

For some teachers, the idea that a whole class can move forward together is revolutionary and challenging. However, the evidence of global good practice clearly shows that this approach drives engagement, confidence, motivation and success for all learners, and not just the high flyers. The strategies below will help you keep your class together on their maths journey.

Mix it up

Do not stick to set groups at each table. Every child should be working on the same concept, and mixing up the groupings widens children's opportunities for exploring, discussing and sharing their understanding with others.

Recycling questions

Reuse the Pupil Textbook and Practice Book questions with concrete materials to allow children to explore concepts and relationships and deepen their understanding. This strategy is especially useful for reinforcing learning in same-day interventions.

Strengthen at every opportunity

The next lesson in a *Power Maths* sequence always revises and builds on the previous step to help embed learning. These activities provide golden opportunities for individual children to strengthen their learning with the support of teaching assistants.

Prepare to be surprised!

Children may grasp a concept quickly or more slowly. The 'fast graspers' won't always be the same individuals, nor does the speed at which a child understands a concept predict their success in maths. Are they struggling or just working more slowly?

Depth and breadth

Just as prescribed in the National Curriculum, the goal of *Power Maths* is never to accelerate through a topic but rather to gain a clear, deep and broad understanding.

"Pupils who grasp concepts rapidly should be challenged through being offered rich and sophisticated problems before any acceleration through new content. Those who are not sufficiently fluent with earlier material should consolidate their understanding, including through additional practice, before moving on."

National Curriculum: Mathematics programmes of study: KS1 & 2, 2013

The lesson sequence offers many opportunities for you to deepen and broaden children's learning, some of which are suggested below.

Discover

As well as using the questions in the Teacher Guide, check that children are really delving into why something is true. It is not enough to simply recite facts, such as '6 + 3 = 9'. They need to be able to see why, explain it, and to demonstrate the solution in several ways.

Share

Make sure that every child is given chances to offer answers and expand their knowledge and not just those with the greatest confidence.

Think together

Encourage children to think about how they solved the problem and explain it to their partner. Be sure to make concrete materials available on group tables throughout the lesson to support and reinforce learning.

Practice

Avoid any temptation to select questions according to your assessment of ability: practice questions are presented in a logical sequence and it is important that each child works through every question.

Reflect

Open-ended questions allow children to deepen their understanding as far as they can by finding new ways of finding answers. For example, *Give me another way of working out how high the wall is... And another way?*

Online materials

For each unit you will find additional strengthening activities to support those children who need it and to deepen the understanding of those who need the additional challenge.

Same-day intervention

Since maths competence depends on mastering concepts one by one in a logical progression, it is important that no gaps in understanding are ever left unfilled. Same-day interventions – either within or after a lesson – are a crucial safety net for any child who has not fully made the small step covered that day. In other words, intervention is always about keeping up, not catching up, so that every child has the skills and understanding they need to tackle the next lesson. That means presenting the same problems used in the lesson, with a variety of concrete materials to help children model their solutions.

We offer two intervention strategies below, but you should feel free to choose others if they work better for your class.

Within-lesson intervention

The Think together activity will reveal those who are struggling, so when it is time for Practice, bring these children together to work with you on the first practice questions. Observe these children carefully, ask questions, encourage them to use concrete models and check that they reach and can demonstrate their understanding.

After-lesson intervention

You might like to use Think together before an assembly, giving you or teaching assistants time to recap and expand with slow graspers during assembly time. Teaching assistants could also work with strugglers at other convenient points in the school day.

The role of practice

Practice plays a pivotal role in the *Power Maths* approach. It takes place in class groups, smaller groups, pairs, and independently, so that children always have the opportunities for thinking as well as the models and support they need to practise meaningfully and with understanding.

Intelligent practice

In *Power Maths*, practice never equates to the simple repetition of a process. Instead we embrace the concept of intelligent practice, in which all children become fluent in maths through varied, frequent and thoughtful practice that deepens and embeds conceptual understanding in a logical, planned sequence. To see the difference, take a look at the following examples.

Traditional practice

- Repetition can be rote – no need for a child to think hard about what they are doing

- Praise may be misplaced

- Does this prove understanding?

Intelligent practice

- Varied methods – concrete, pictorial and abstract

- Calculations expressed in different ways, requiring thought and understanding

- Constructive feedback

All practice questions are designed to move children on and reveal misconceptions.

Simple, logical steps build onto earlier learning.

C-P-A runs throughout – different ways of modelling and understanding the same concept.

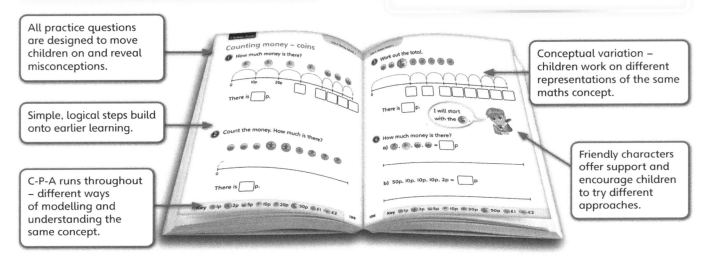

Conceptual variation – children work on different representations of the same maths concept.

Friendly characters offer support and encourage children to try different approaches.

A carefully designed progression

The Pupil Practice Books provide just the right amount of intelligent practice for children to complete independently in the final sections of each lesson. It is really important that all children are exposed to the practice questions, and that children are not directed to complete different sections. That is because each question is different and has been designed to challenge children to think about the maths they are doing. The questions become more challenging so children grasping concepts more quickly will start to slow down as they progress. Meanwhile, you have the chance to circulate and spot any misconceptions before they become barriers to further learning.

Homework and the role of carers

While *Power Maths* does not prescribe any particular homework structure, we acknowledge the potential value of practice at home. For example, practising fluency in key facts, such as number bonds and times tables, is an ideal homework task for Key Stage 1 children, and carers could work through uncompleted Practice Book questions with children at either primary stage.

However, it is important to recognise that many parents and carers may themselves lack confidence in maths, and few, if any, will be familiar with mastery methods. A Parents' and Carers' Evening that helps them understand the basics of mindsets, mastery and mathematical language is a great way to ensure that children benefit from their homework. It could be a fun opportunity for children to teach their families that everyone can do maths!

Structures and representations

Unlike most other subjects, maths comprises a wide array of abstract concepts – and that is why children and adults so often find it difficult. By taking a concrete-pictorial-abstract (C-P-A) approach, *Power Maths* allows children to tackle concepts in a tangible and more comfortable way.

Non-linear stages

Concrete

Replacing the traditional approach of a teacher working through a problem in front of the class, the concrete stage introduces real objects that children can use to 'do' the maths – any familiar object that a child can manipulate and move to help bring the maths to life. It is important to appreciate, however, that children must always understand the link between models and the objects they represent. For example, children need to first understand that three cakes could be represented by three pretend cakes, and then by three counters or bricks. Frequent practice helps consolidate this essential insight. Although they can be used at any time, good concrete models are an essential first step in understanding.

Pictorial

This stage uses pictorial representations of objects to let children 'see' what particular maths problems look like. It helps them make connections between the concrete and pictorial representations and the abstract maths concept. Children can also create or view a pictorial representation together, enabling discussion and comparisons. The *Power Maths* teaching tools are fantastic for this learning stage, and bar modelling is invaluable for problem solving throughout the primary curriculum.

Abstract

Our ultimate goal is for children to understand abstract mathematical concepts, symbols and notation and, of course, some children will reach this stage far more quickly than others. To work with abstract concepts, a child must be comfortable with the meaning of, and relationships between, concrete, pictorial and abstract models and representations. The C-P-A approach is not linear, and children may need different types of models at different times. However, when a child demonstrates with concrete models and pictorial representations that they have grasped a concept, we can be confident that they are ready to explore or model it with abstract symbols such as numbers and notation.

Use at any time and with any age to support understanding

Variation helps visualisation

Children find it much easier to visualise and grasp concepts if they see them presented in a number of ways, so be prepared to offer and encourage many different representations.

For example, the number six could be represented in various ways:

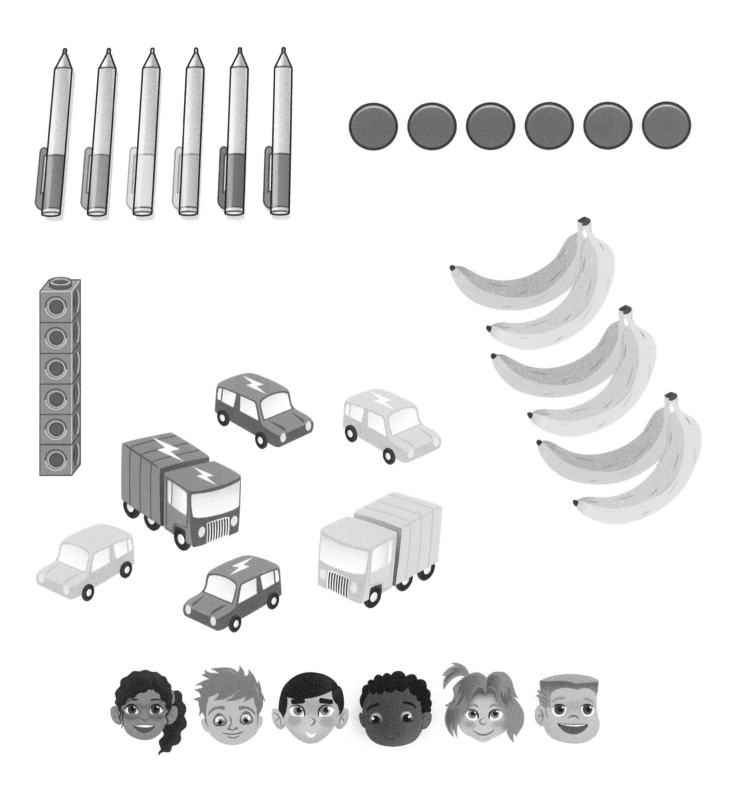

Getting started with *Power Maths*

As you prepare to put *Power Maths* into action, you might find the tips and advice below helpful.

STEP 1: Train up!

A practical, up-front full-day professional development course will give you and your team a brilliant head-start as you begin your *Power Maths* journey. You will learn more about the ethos, how it works and why.

STEP 2: Check out the progression

Take a look at the yearly and termly overviews. Next take a look at the unit overview for the unit you are about to teach in your Teacher Guide, remembering that you can match your lessons and pacing to your class.

STEP 3: Explore the context

Take a little time to look at the context for this unit: what are the implications for the unit ahead? (Think about key language, common misunderstandings and intervention strategies, for example.) If you have the online subscription, don't forget to watch the corresponding unit video.

STEP 4: Prepare for your first lesson

Familiarise yourself with the objectives, essential questions to ask and the resources you will need. The Teacher Guide offers tips, ideas and guidance on individual lessons to help you anticipate children's misconceptions and challenge those who are ready to think more deeply.

STEP 5: Teach and reflect

Deliver your lesson – and enjoy!

Afterwards, reflect on how it went... Did you cover all five stages? Does the lesson need more time? How could you improve it?

Unit 11
Position and direction

Mastery Expert tip! "Finding opportunities for practical application both in and outside the lessons really helped me to secure children's understanding. When children were able to carry out the movements themselves, they were able to think more deeply about the questions and problems."

Don't forget to watch the Unit 11 video!

WHY THIS UNIT IS IMPORTANT

This unit focuses on describing position in relation to other objects, describing lateral and rotational movement and describing and completing repeating patterns. Children will apply their previous learning about fractions to describe degrees of turn and their knowledge of 2D shapes.

This unit also helps children to develop their logical and computational thinking in order to follow and describe sequences relating to movement, which prepares them for the following unit.

WHERE THIS UNIT FITS

→ Unit 10: Fractions

→ **Unit 11: Position and direction**

→ Unit 12: Problem solving and efficient methods

Before they start this unit, it is expected that children:
- know how to describe the position of an object in relation to one or more other objects
- understand halves and quarters and the relationship between them
- know positional and directional language such as forwards, backwards, left, right, between, above, below.

ASSESSING MASTERY

Children who have mastered this unit will be able to use correct mathematical language to describe position and lateral and rotational movement. Children will be able to follow a series of instructions related to movement and they will be able to plan a series of instructions to arrive at a desired goal.

COMMON MISCONCEPTIONS	STRENGTHENING UNDERSTANDING	GOING DEEPER
Children may confuse left and right, particularly when the orientation of the object is different to their own orientation.	Provide practical opportunities for children to either turn themselves or objects left and right, labelling the left and right sides if necessary. Ask children to raise their left or right hand and then point to the left or right hand of a partner who is facing them. What do they notice? Can they explain this?	Encourage children to create their own problems using various sizes of grids, such as on paper or outside in the playground. Children could design a treasure hunt with obstacles to avoid and ask a partner to work out a possible route. Children could use programmable toys to devise and solve their own problems.
Children may struggle to identify quarter, half and three-quarter turns around a point.	Provide children with a paper circle and demonstrate how to fold it in half and then in half again to divide it into quarters. Children can label one quarter, one half and three quarters, and refer to this paper circle during the lessons in this unit.	

Unit II: Position and direction

WAYS OF WORKING

Use Astrid's comment to introduce the unit and ask children what they already know about these things. Discuss with children what Ash might mean and ask whether they can demonstrate a half turn. Question children to find out whether they know any of the key language that Flo introduces. Use Dexter's comment to discuss what clockwise and anticlockwise might mean. Does the picture of the clock help children to explain these terms?

STRUCTURES AND REPRESENTATIONS

Using a circle divided into quarters can help the children to visualise quarter, half and three-quarter turns around a point. Using the image of a clock face can help reinforce the direction of clockwise and anticlockwise turns. Curved arrows can also be used to illustrate the direction and fraction of a turn.

KEY LANGUAGE

There is some key language that children will need to know as part of the learning in this unit:

→ quarter turn, half turn, three-quarter turn, whole turn
→ clockwise, anticlockwise
→ forwards, backwards
→ left, right
→ up, down
→ turn
→ middle
→ position
→ pattern
→ above, below
→ top, bottom
→ between
→ cube, cylinder
→ circle, semicircle
→ triangle, rectangle, square

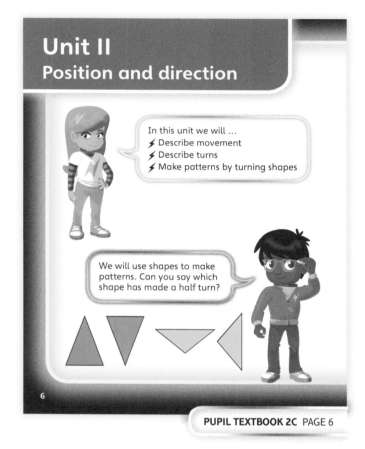

PUPIL TEXTBOOK 2C PAGE 6

PUPIL TEXTBOOK 2C PAGE 7

Describing movement

Learning focus

In this lesson, children will describe movement and follow instructions using the words 'left', 'right', 'forwards' and 'backwards'.

Small steps

→ Previous step: Counting in quarters
→ **This step: Describing movement**
→ Next step: Describing turns

NATIONAL CURRICULUM LINKS

Year 2 Geometry – Position and Direction

Use mathematical vocabulary to describe position, direction and movement, including movement in a straight line and distinguishing between rotation as a turn and in terms of right angles for quarter, half and three-quarter turns (clockwise and anticlockwise).

ASSESSING MASTERY

Children can correctly describe position and movement using the words 'left', 'right', 'forwards' and 'backwards'. Children can systematically follow a series of instructions involving movement.

COMMON MISCONCEPTIONS

Children may confuse which way is forwards when seen on a 2D grid.

Children may confuse where a start point is, for example, counting the square on which they start.

Children may confuse left and right. Ask questions such as:
• *Who can raise their right hand? Who is sitting to the left of you?*

STRENGTHENING UNDERSTANDING

Ask children to follow instructions practically. This could start off as a simple game of 'Simon says' and build towards replicating the problems in the books with themselves or with toys on a grid.

GOING DEEPER

Challenge children to find more than one possible solution to a problem, then ask them to create their own versions of the problems.

KEY LANGUAGE

In lesson: movement, forwards, backwards, left, right, middle, upwards

Other language to be used by the teacher: position, direction, above, below, between

RESOURCES

Optional: laminated copies of the problems, dry-wipe pens and a selection of grids and objects (including 2D and 3D shapes) to model the problems

 In the eTextbook of this lesson, you will find interactive links to a selection of teaching tools.

Before you teach

• What experience have children had with describing position and movement?
• What practical opportunities can you provide to support children's understanding of movement?
• Can you make links to previous work in other curriculum areas such as PE and computing?

Discover

WAYS OF WORKING Pair work

ASK

- *Have you seen this arrangement of signs anywhere else?*
- *What would be the 7th movement?*

IN FOCUS Question ❶ b) requires children to apply vocabulary to the instructions as opposed to following and matching the arrow signs. Encourage children to be clear and concise in their descriptions.

ANSWERS

Question ❶ b): Forwards, backwards, left, forwards, right, forwards.

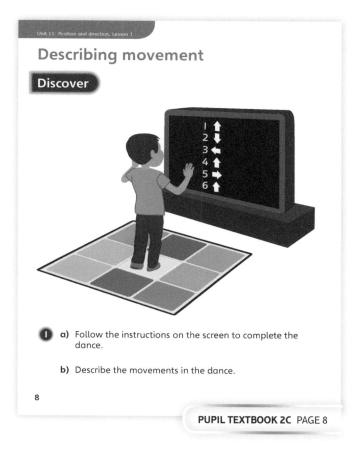

Describing movement

Discover

❶ a) Follow the instructions on the screen to complete the dance.

b) Describe the movements in the dance.

8

PUPIL TEXTBOOK 2C PAGE 8

Share

WAYS OF WORKING Whole class teacher led

ASK

- *How many of each movement were there?*
- *What would the 10th movement be? How do you know?* (N.B. If 6th movement above is forwards then 10th movement would be right.)
- *Do the instructions change if the boy is facing the other way?*

IN FOCUS Question ❶ secures understanding of backwards, forwards, left and right. Ensure children are aware that the boy's left and right hands are opposite to the observer's. Children can test this by looking in a mirror or physically rotating 180 degrees.

Share

a) and b) These are the movements in the dance.

Step 1: forwards

Step 2: backwards

Step 3: left

Step 4: forwards

Step 5: right

Step 6: forwards

I know to use forwards, backwards, left and right to describe movement.

9

PUPIL TEXTBOOK 2C PAGE 9

Think together

WAYS OF WORKING Whole class teacher led (I do, We do, You do)

ASK

- Question **1** : *What different ways can you think of to describe the position of the green spotty flag?*
- Question **2** b): *What other routes can you describe?*
- Question **3** : *How many different solutions can you find?*
- Question **3** : *Where can the mouse not start? Which way is forwards?* (away from the entrance.)

IN FOCUS Question **2** b) introduces the idea that there can be more than one way of describing a route. Discuss with children why they chose the route they did. Prompt children to see more complex routes, not simply the most direct.

STRENGTHEN Strengthen understanding of questions **2** and **3** by providing children with laminated copies of the questions and a dry-wipe pen so they can try out different possibilities. Children can use their laminations to justify why the mouse cannot start at certain points in question **3** .

DEEPEN In question **2** b), ask children if they can get from the star to the sun by entering each empty square only once. Ask them to explain how this is possible. In question **3** , Jake the mouse can only start in four of the nine squares and travels in a square shape. Ask children if they can adapt the instructions so that the mouse still travels in a square shape but can now start at different squares.

ASSESSMENT CHECKPOINT Use questions **1** and **2** to assess whether children are secure with left and right and are able to create a simple set of instructions for movement. Their responses to question **3** will determine if children can reason about different possibilities based on the instructions given.

ANSWERS

Question **1** : The green spotty flag is in the middle.

The green spotty flag is to the left of the blue striped flag.

The blue striped flag is to the right of the green spotty flag.

Question **2** a): To move from the ♥ to the ☀, move 1 square up and 1 square left.

Question **2** b): There are various possibilities. The most direct routes are:

Up 2, right 1

Right 1, up 2

Up 1, right 1, up 1

Question **3** : Jake starts and finishes in the same square. He finishes in the bottom middle, bottom right, middle right or centre square.

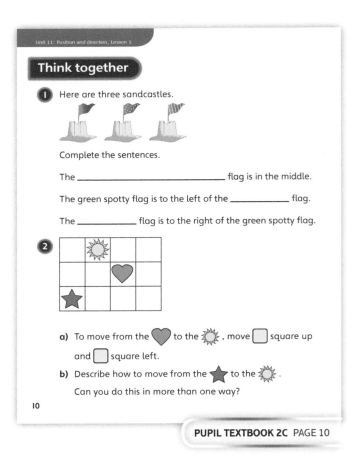

Practice

WAYS OF WORKING Independent work

IN FOCUS Question **5** requires children to follow the instructions to complete the grid. However, they cannot determine the exact position of any shape from the first instruction. Encourage children to look at the first instruction and discuss the possible positions of the square and circle, perhaps using a copy of the grid and 2D shapes. The second instruction enables them to place the square. Ask children how they know where each shape goes and how they went about solving the problem.

STRENGTHEN Provide children with the shapes represented in the problems in question **3** . Ask children to build a tower by giving them instructions. They could then give instructions to each other.

For question **4** , provide children with a laminated version of the problem and dry-wipe markers. This can encourage them to tackle the problem, knowing that they can easily start again.

DEEPEN Provide children with a blank copy of the grid from question **4** . Can children make their own version of the problem, ensuring that they land in every square only once? They can then test it out on a partner.

ASSESSMENT CHECKPOINT Use questions **1** to **3** to assess whether children are confident with the vocabulary of position, and can identify the position of an object in relation to one or two other objects.

ANSWERS Answers for the **Practice** part of the lesson appear in the separate **Practice and Reflect answer guide**.

Reflect

WAYS OF WORKING Pair work

IN FOCUS The **Reflect** activity has more than one possible answer. It highlights the fact that an object's position can be described in relation to more than one other object.

ASSESSMENT CHECKPOINT Assess whether children can give clear and concise descriptions of positions using the correct vocabulary. Can they describe position in different ways?

ANSWERS Answers for the **Reflect** part of the lesson appear in the separate **Practice and Reflect answer guide**.

After the lesson ⏸

- How secure are children using the vocabulary of position, in particular 'left', 'right', 'forwards' and 'backwards'?
- Were children able to reason about the decisions they made when identifying and describing position?

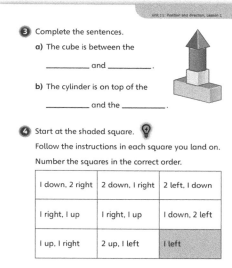

PUPIL PRACTICE BOOK 2C PAGE 6

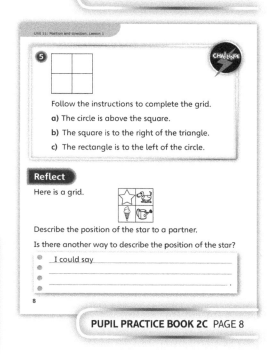

PUPIL PRACTICE BOOK 2C PAGE 7

PUPIL PRACTICE BOOK 2C PAGE 8

Describing turns

Learning focus

In this lesson, children will describe quarter, half and three-quarter turns around a point using the terms 'clockwise' and 'anticlockwise'.

Small steps

→ Previous step: Describing movement
→ **This step: Describing turns**
→ Next step: Describing movement and turns

NATIONAL CURRICULUM LINKS

Year 2 Geometry – Position and Direction

Use mathematical vocabulary to describe position, direction and movement, including movement in a straight line and distinguishing between rotation as a turn and in terms of right angles for quarter, half and three-quarter turns (clockwise and anticlockwise).

ASSESSING MASTERY

Children can describe a turn around a point, using fractions to describe part turns and 'clockwise' and 'anticlockwise' to describe the direction of the turn. Children can describe a pair of turns in opposite directions that result in the same finishing position; for example, a quarter turn clockwise and a three-quarter turn anticlockwise.

COMMON MISCONCEPTIONS

Children may not understand the terms 'clockwise' and 'anticlockwise'. Use clocks to demonstrate and ask:
• *Can you show a clockwise turn? What about an anticlockwise turn?*

Children may also fail to recognise quarter, half and three-quarter turns. Show a whole turn and then focus on fractions of turns. Ask:
• *Can you show a quarter turn clockwise? What about a three-quarter turn anticlockwise?*

STRENGTHENING UNDERSTANDING

Ask children to carry out different turns whilst holding a clock in order to reinforce their understanding of clockwise and anticlockwise. Having objects to physically turn or programmable toys will support them in tackling the problems.

GOING DEEPER

Challenge children to predict the finishing position after two turns; for example, a half turn clockwise followed by a quarter turn anticlockwise. Children could then check their prediction using programmable toys.

KEY LANGUAGE

In lesson: turn, half, quarter, **anticlockwise**, **clockwise**, three-quarter, whole

Other language to be used by the teacher: fraction, part, direction, position, rotation

RESOURCES

Optional: clocks, objects to carry out rotations, programmable toys

 In the eTextbook of this lesson, you will find interactive links to a selection of teaching tools.

Before you teach

• How will you make links to the previous lesson on movement?
• What resources could you provide to support children's understanding of turning clockwise and anticlockwise?
• How will you make the link to children's learning on fractions from previous units?

Discover

Describing turns

Discover

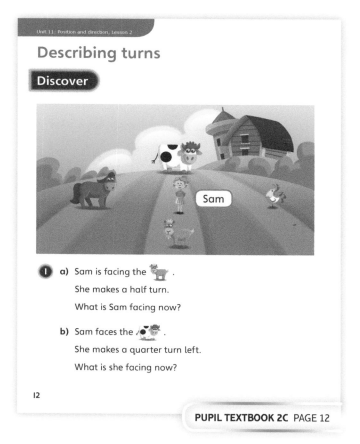

WAYS OF WORKING Pair work

ASK

- Question **1** a): *Does it matter in which direction Sam turns?*
- Question **1** b): *Is there another way Sam could turn and still end up facing the same animal?*

IN FOCUS Question **1** requires children to visualise the turns. In question **1** a), no direction is given as a half turn will produce the same result regardless of the direction. In contrast, question **1** b) requires children to consider the direction of the turn as well. Use this opportunity to discuss direction of rotation and when it is important.

ANSWERS

Question **1** a): Sam is facing the 🐄 now.

Question **1** b): Sam is facing the 🐱 now.

1 a) Sam is facing the 🐐 .
   She makes a half turn.
   What is Sam facing now?

b) Sam faces the 🐄 .
   She makes a quarter turn left.
   What is she facing now?

12

PUPIL TEXTBOOK 2C PAGE 12

Share

WAYS OF WORKING Whole class teacher led

ASK

- *Why do you think we use the terms 'clockwise' and 'anticlockwise'?*
- *If the horse is at 12 on a clock face, what numbers would the other animals be at?*
- *For what size turns does it not matter whether you turn clockwise or anticlockwise?*

IN FOCUS This part of the lesson introduces the terms 'clockwise' and 'anticlockwise', relating them to a pictorial representation of a clock. Provide children with clocks that they can manipulate in order to support them in exploring clockwise and anticlockwise turns. You can then relate what children are doing on the clock to the picture.

Share

a)

Sam is facing the 🐄 now.

b)

Sam turned left. This is **anticlockwise**.

If Sam turned right, this would be **clockwise**.

Sam is facing the 🐱 now.

13

PUPIL TEXTBOOK 2C PAGE 13

Think together

WAYS OF WORKING Whole class teacher led (I do, We do, You do)

ASK

- Question **2** : *Can you describe the turns in more than one way?*
- Question **3** : *How do you know Dai is incorrect?*
- Question **3** : *How else can you describe two quarter turns?*

IN FOCUS Question **2** shows rotations from two different viewpoints. The car is viewed from above, while the frog and bee are viewed from the side. Provide children with concrete representations to support their understanding of the change in viewpoint.

STRENGTHEN Give children objects so that they can carry out the turns practically. Having a clock face as a reference can support their understanding of clockwise and anticlockwise.

DEEPEN Question **3** gives two correct ways to describe a turn from the cow to the horse. Ask children to find combinations of turns with the same result. Challenge them to use both clockwise and anticlockwise; for example, a quarter turn clockwise and a half turn anticlockwise.

ASSESSMENT CHECKPOINT Assess whether children are able to describe fractions of turns and the direction of turns in questions **1** and **2** . Use question **3** to assess whether children understand that the finishing position can be reached by turning in either direction.

ANSWERS

Question **1** a): 🐐 to 🐓 is a quarter turn anticlockwise.

Question **1** b): 🐈 to 🐄 is a three-quarter turn anticlockwise.

Question **1** c): 🐓 to 🐓 is a whole turn clockwise or anticlockwise.

Question **2** : Bee – Quarter turn clockwise.

Frog – Half turn anticlockwise.

Car – Three-quarter turn clockwise.

Question **3** : Harry and Amelia are correct.

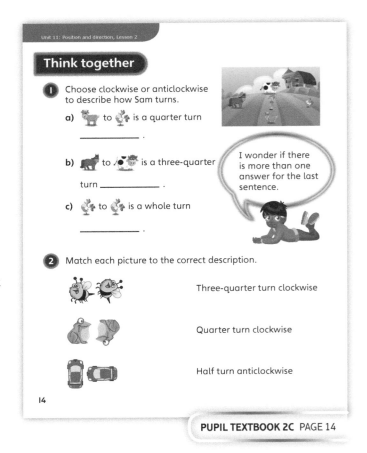

PUPIL TEXTBOOK 2C PAGE 14

PUPIL TEXTBOOK 2C PAGE 15

Practice

WAYS OF WORKING Pair work

IN FOCUS Question **3** highlights the fact that an object can be turned in either direction to reach a given position. 'Quarter turn clockwise' and 'three-quarter turn anticlockwise' are equivalent and each can be used to describe the ladybird. 'Half turn clockwise' and 'half turn anticlockwise' can each be used to describe the bird.

Question **4** illustrates that we cannot determine the direction of the turn simply by observing the start and end position. Although clockwise would be a smaller turn, the fly could have rotated anticlockwise.

STRENGTHEN Provide children with clock faces as a reference and physical objects they can rotate. Ask children to justify their answers to prompt discussion as well as deepen their understanding of rotation.

DEEPEN Give a pair of children a programmable toy. Ask one child to write a series of turns (three or more) and give them to their partner. The partner then has to try to determine which direction the programmable toy will be facing at the end, before trying it out using the toy.

ASSESSMENT CHECKPOINT Questions **1** and **2** will confirm whether children are secure in their understanding of clockwise and anticlockwise, and fractions of turns. Questions **3** and **4** will determine whether children are able to recognise that the finishing position can be reached by turning in either direction.

ANSWERS Answers for the **Practice** part of the lesson appear in the separate **Practice and Reflect answer guide**.

Reflect

WAYS OF WORKING Independent thinking

IN FOCUS This part of the lesson requires children to visualise the final position of the house following the turns described. The final two images will be the same, reinforcing the idea that an object can turn either clockwise or anticlockwise to achieve the same final position.

ASSESSMENT CHECKPOINT Assess whether children are secure in their understanding of clockwise and anticlockwise. Do children understand how the same final position was achieved by rotating a quarter turn clockwise and three-quarter turn anticlockwise?

ANSWERS Answers for the **Reflect** part of the lesson appear in the separate **Practice and Reflect answer guide**.

After the lesson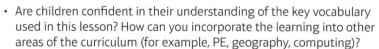

- Are children confident in their understanding of the key vocabulary used in this lesson? How can you incorporate the learning into other areas of the curriculum (for example, PE, geography, computing)?
- Did children justify why there was more than one possible answer to some of the questions?

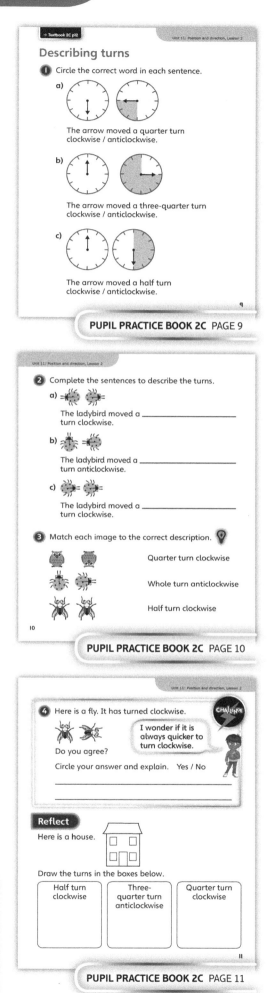

PUPIL PRACTICE BOOK 2C PAGE 9

PUPIL PRACTICE BOOK 2C PAGE 10

PUPIL PRACTICE BOOK 2C PAGE 11

Describing movement and turns

Learning focus

In this lesson, children will combine rotation and linear movement in order to follow or describe a designated path.

Small steps

→ Previous step: Describing turns
→ **This step: Describing movement and turns**
→ Next step: Making patterns with shapes

NATIONAL CURRICULUM LINKS

Year 2 Geometry – Position and Direction

Use mathematical vocabulary to describe position, direction and movement, including movement in a straight line and distinguishing between rotation as a turn and in terms of right angles for quarter, half and three-quarter turns (clockwise and anticlockwise).

ASSESSING MASTERY

Children can follow instructions involving linear movement and rotation in order to follow a desired route. Children can identify a variety of routes to a given goal and describe them using the correct vocabulary for rotation and linear movement.

COMMON MISCONCEPTIONS

Children may not realise that once an object is rotated to face the desired location, it then moves forward. They may still use left and right to describe direction in relation to their perspective as opposed to the object's. Ask:
• *Now the object is facing where it needs to go, what is the next instruction? Does it go left, right or forwards?*

STRENGTHENING UNDERSTANDING

Give children practical opportunities to explore the problems. They could carry out the instructions with themselves or a friend on a grid drawn on the playground. The use of programmable toys will enable children to test and adapt their instructions immediately.

GOING DEEPER

Children could explore finding the most complex routes or create their own versions of the problems to test on a partner. They could design a 'treasure hunt' on the playground, creating their own grid and instructions to land on the 'treasure'.

KEY LANGUAGE

In lesson: movement, turn, forwards, backwards, clockwise, anticlockwise, quarter, three-quarter

Other language to be used by the teacher: position, direction, rotation, route, location, left, right, half, whole

RESOURCES

Optional: laminated copies of grids, dry-wipe pens, physical objects to use on the grids, programmable toys

 In the eTextbook of this lesson, you will find interactive links to a selection of teaching tools.

Before you teach

• How will you provide practical experiences for children to explore rotational and linear movement?
• How could you extend the activities to deepen children's thinking around position and direction?
• What references and prompts can you provide for children to ensure correct use of vocabulary?

Discover

Unit 11: Position and direction, Lesson 3

WAYS OF WORKING Pair work

ASK

- *Which way is the pirate facing? If he moves forward, which direction will he go?*
- Question **1** a): *Is your answer different from anyone else's?*

IN FOCUS Question **1** a) is the first time children are asked to combine turns with moving forwards and backwards. Ensure children understand that in order for the pirate to move in a desired direction, he has to first turn so that he can go forwards; ensure children understand that the pirate's hat points in his direction of travel.

DEEPEN There are several different routes to the treasure. If children find a route other than the fastest, use this as a prompt for a discussion about multiple solutions. Should the correct solution to question **1** a) be the fastest route?

ANSWERS

Question **1** a): The fastest route for the pirate to get to the treasure is forwards 2, quarter turn clockwise, forwards 1.

Question **1** b):

Note that if children found a different answer (assuming the pirate starts on the treasure square but moves left (instead of right) for forwards) , the pirate would be back where he started, but upside down.

Share

WAYS OF WORKING Whole class teacher led

ASK

- Question **1** a): *Is the route you found the same as the one in the book?*
- Question **1** a): *What is the longest route you can create to get the pirate to the treasure without entering a square more than once?*
- Question **1** b): *Can you describe the most direct route back to the start from the pirate's final position?*
- *What route could the snake take to get to the pirate?*
- *Can the snake get to the treasure in fewer moves than the pirate?*

IN FOCUS The diagrams allow children to see the results of each step. Highlight how the pirate needs to turn in order to move in the desired direction. Encourage children to explore alternative routes that the pirate could take.

Describing movement and turns

Discover

1 a) Help the 🐱 reach the treasure safely. Write instructions to get him to the treasure.

Use these words: forwards, backwards, clockwise, anticlockwise, quarter turn.

b) From the treasure, the 🐱 moves forwards 1, quarter turn anticlockwise, forwards 2. Where is he now?

16

Share

a) To get the treasure, the 🐱 needs to move

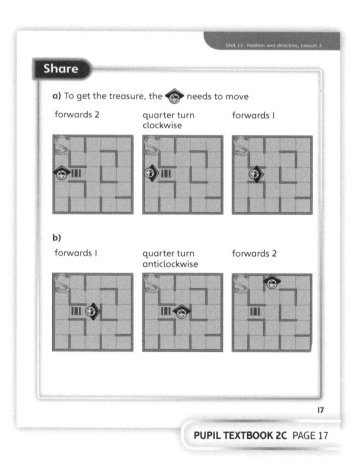

| forwards 2 | quarter turn clockwise | forwards 1 |

b)

| forwards 1 | quarter turn anticlockwise | forwards 2 |

17

Think together

WAYS OF WORKING Whole class teacher led (I do, We do, You do)

ASK

- Questions ❶ and ❷ : *Can you describe an alternative route?*
- Question ❷ : *What happens if you do the instructions in a different order?*
- Question ❸ : *What is the fastest route to the boat, treasure and cannon?*

IN FOCUS Sparks prompts children to come up with their own instructions for question ❸ . Children may fail to realise that a backward movement is possible and may give the unnecessary instruction to rotate a half turn. Asking children to find the fastest route (the one with the fewest instructions) can expose this misconception.

STRENGTHEN Give children laminated copies of each grid and an object such as a toy car that they can physically rotate and move. Children can carry out each movement before describing what they did.

DEEPEN Extend question ❸ by asking children to describe a route that will go to all three objects. What is the fastest route they can find?

ASSESSMENT CHECKPOINT Use question ❷ to assess whether children can link rotational and linear movement to get to a desired goal.

Question ❸ will determine if children are able to follow a series of instructions involving rotational and linear movement.

ANSWERS

Question ❶ : Go forwards 1 space: 1st.

Make a quarter turn anticlockwise: 2nd.

Go forwards 2 spaces: 3rd.

Question ❷ : Go forwards 2 spaces; Make a quarter turn clockwise. Go forward 1 space.

Question ❸ : The ▬▬ .

Think together

❶

Put the sentences in the correct order to show how the ◆ can get to the treasure chest. Use 1st, 2nd, 3rd.

Go forwards 2 spaces ☐

Make a quarter turn anticlockwise ☐

Go forwards 1 space ☐

❷

Complete the sentences to describe how the pirate can get to the treasure chest.

Go _____ ☐ spaces.

Make a _____ turn _____ .

Go _____ ☐ space.

18

PUPIL TEXTBOOK 2C PAGE 18

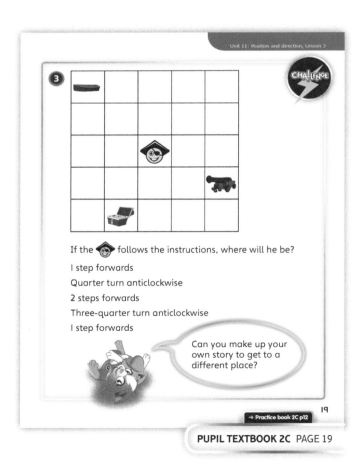

❸

If the ◆ follows the instructions, where will he be?

1 step forwards

Quarter turn anticlockwise

2 steps forwards

Three-quarter turn anticlockwise

1 step forwards

Can you make up your own story to get to a different place?

→ Practice book 2C p12

19

PUPIL TEXTBOOK 2C PAGE 19

Practice

WAYS OF WORKING Pair work

IN FOCUS Question **2** asks children to get the bee to the beehive. Ask children to think of a similar but alternative route to the beehive. Changing the first instruction means children need to think about what else they need to change in the remaining instructions. Encourage them to think about how they can get the bee to the beehive by changing as few instructions as possible.

Question **3** a) requires children to match a set of instructions to a given start and end point. Encourage children to work systematically, trying the instructions on each grid in turn until they find the correct match. Question **3** b) then asks children to describe a simple route using the correct vocabulary. They may identify more than one possible solution.

STRENGTHEN Children could use programmable toys to test their ideas in questions **2** and **3** .

DEEPEN Ask children to create their own challenge using a programmable toy or a grid drawn on the playground. They can place objects to collect, obstacles to avoid and an end position. Encourage them to plan their entire route before testing it out.

ASSESSMENT CHECKPOINT Use questions **1** and **2** to identify any areas of weakness in children's ability to follow or describe a simple route.

Question **3** a) will determine if children can match a set of instructions to a start and end point.

Use question **4** to check whether children remember that a quarter turn in one direction will have the same result as a three-quarter turn in the opposite direction. Can children justify their answer in the context of this lesson?

ANSWERS Answers for the **Practice** part of the lesson appear in the separate **Practice and Reflect answer guide**.

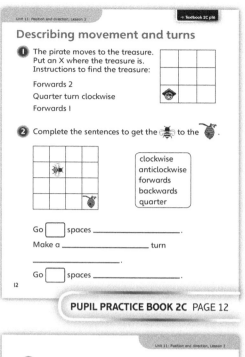

PUPIL PRACTICE BOOK 2C PAGE 12

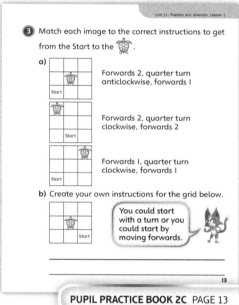

PUPIL PRACTICE BOOK 2C PAGE 13

Reflect

WAYS OF WORKING Pair work

IN FOCUS This part of the lesson secures children's understanding of describing turns in both clockwise and anticlockwise directions. Children need to determine the movement from the end position, based on their knowledge of the starting position.

ASSESSMENT CHECKPOINT Assess whether children can accurately describe rotation using the correct vocabulary.

ANSWERS Answers for the **Reflect** part of the lesson appear in the separate **Practice and Reflect answer guide**.

After the lesson ⏸

- Are children secure in describing the direction of linear movement based on the orientation of the object?
- How secure are children in using the correct vocabulary in order to describe rotational and linear movement?

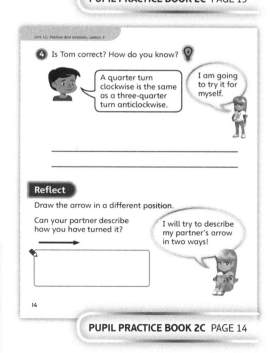

PUPIL PRACTICE BOOK 2C PAGE 14

Making patterns with shapes

Learning focus

In this lesson, children will apply what they have learned about rotation and position in order to complete and describe patterns.

Small steps

→ Previous step: Describing movement and turns
→ **This step: Making patterns with shapes**
→ Next step: My way, your way!

NATIONAL CURRICULUM LINKS

Year 2 Geometry – Position and Direction
- Use mathematical vocabulary to describe position, direction and movement, including movement in a straight line and distinguishing between rotation as a turn and in terms of right angles for quarter, half and three-quarter turns (clockwise and anticlockwise).
- Order and arrange combinations of mathematical objects in patterns and sequences.

ASSESSING MASTERY

Children can use correct mathematical vocabulary to describe position and rotation within a repeating pattern. Children can identify the repeating core of the pattern in order to continue it or identify missing terms.

COMMON MISCONCEPTIONS

When there are more than two shapes within the core of the pattern, children may not look at enough of the pattern in order to determine the missing shapes. Ask:
- *What part of the pattern is being repeated? Can you see where this shape is repeated again?*

Children may fail to draw on their knowledge from previous lessons to describe the rotations. They may use terms such as 'upside down' or 'on its side.' Ask:
- *How has the shape changed?*

STRENGTHENING UNDERSTANDING

Provide children with 2D shapes that are represented in the problems. Children can print or draw round the shapes in order to replicate the patterns. Discuss what they do to the shape in order to create the next term.

GOING DEEPER

Children could create their own patterns and describe the core using vocabulary related to rotation and position. They could explore creating patterns with more than one line.

KEY LANGUAGE

In lesson: pattern, triangle, half, turn, clockwise, anticlockwise

Other language to be used by the teacher: position, rotation, repeating, core, term, quarter, semicircle, three-quarter, rectangle, circle, square

RESOURCES

Optional: variety of 2D shapes

 In the eTextbook of this lesson, you will find interactive links to a selection of teaching tools.

Before you teach

- How will you display the key vocabulary for children to refer to?
- Do children have a secure understanding of 'clockwise' and 'anticlockwise'?
- What questions can you ask to prompt discussion about position and movement?

Discover

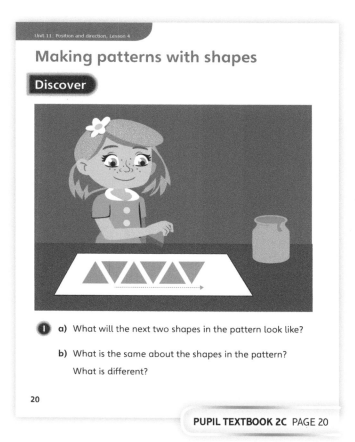

WAYS OF WORKING   Pair work

ASK

- Question **1** a): *What will the next two shapes look like from the girl's point of view? Is it different from your point of view?*
- Question **1** b): *Is there more than one way to describe the differences between the two shapes?*

IN FOCUS   Question **1** b) requires children to apply their learning about rotation to describe the differences between the two shapes in the pattern core. Children may revert to using words and phrases such as 'upside down' or 'other way round.' Having the vocabulary related to rotation available for children to refer to can help prompt a more mathematical description.

ANSWERS

Question **1** a): The next two shapes will be

Question **1** b): All the shapes are triangles. They all have three sides. They are all the same size and colour. The triangles make a half turn after each shape in the pattern (clockwise or anticlockwise).

Making patterns with shapes

Discover

1 a) What will the next two shapes in the pattern look like?

b) What is the same about the shapes in the pattern? What is different?

20

PUPIL TEXTBOOK 2C PAGE 20

Share

WAYS OF WORKING   Whole class teacher led

ASK

- Question **1** a): *Do your triangles look different?*
- Question **1** b): *Does the direction of the turn matter?*
- *What would the pattern look like if the triangle turned a quarter turn clockwise each time?*

IN FOCUS   Question **1** b) illustrates how children can use their understanding of rotation to describe how the orientation of the triangle changes in the pattern. Ash's comment reinforces the concept that direction of rotation does not change the end position when the shape goes through a half turn.

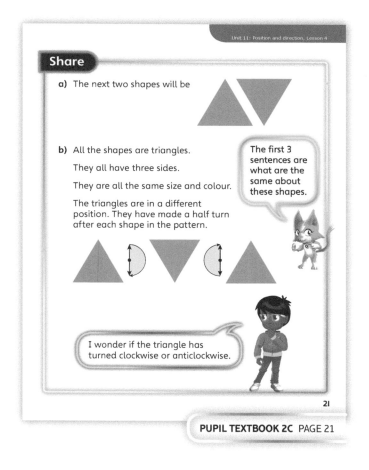

Share

a) The next two shapes will be

b) All the shapes are triangles.

They all have three sides.

They are all the same size and colour.

The triangles are in a different position. They have made a half turn after each shape in the pattern.

The first 3 sentences are what are the same about these shapes.

I wonder if the triangle has turned clockwise or anticlockwise.

21

PUPIL TEXTBOOK 2C PAGE 21

Think together

WAYS OF WORKING Whole class teacher led (I do, We do, You do)

ASK

- *What is the repeating part of the pattern?*
- *How do you know which shape comes next?*
- *Can you describe how the shapes change in the patterns?*

IN FOCUS Question ❸ has two different shapes and each shape has a different type of rotation. Children may be tempted to repeat the first three shapes as they look like a unit due to their orientation. Encourage them to look carefully so that they realise that the pattern's core has four terms. This problem requires children to apply their understanding of rotation in order to describe the pattern.

STRENGTHEN Have corresponding shapes for children to arrange or draw around in order to replicate the patterns. Discuss when the shapes start to repeat and how the shapes turn and in which direction.

DEEPEN Challenge children to make a new pattern similar to the one in question ❸. Can children use the same shapes in the same order but change how they turn in order to create a different pattern?

ASSESSMENT CHECKPOINT Use question ❷ to assess whether children can identify the pattern's core. Question ❸ will determine not only whether children can identify the pattern's core but also whether they can use the correct vocabulary of rotation in order to describe the pattern.

ANSWERS

Question ❶ a): The ▮ comes next in the pattern.

Question ❶ b): The ▮ makes a quarter turn each time.

Question ❷ : A small △ is missing.

Question ❸ : ▭◖▯

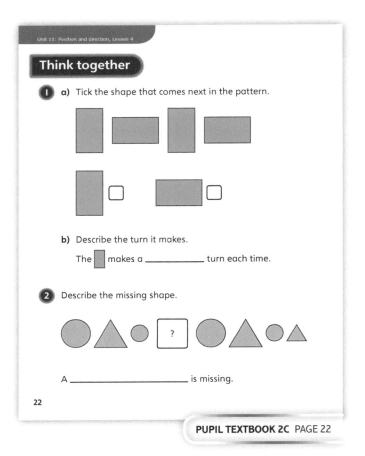

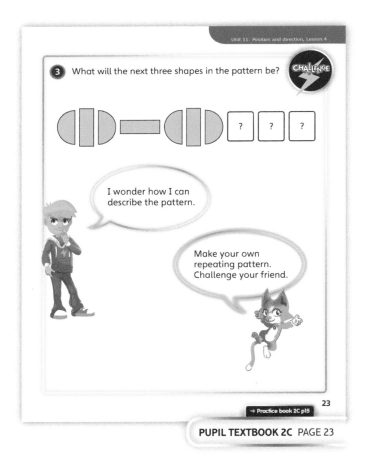

PUPIL TEXTBOOK 2C PAGE 22

PUPIL TEXTBOOK 2C PAGE 23

Practice

WAYS OF WORKING Pair work

IN FOCUS Question **5** requires children to identify the shape that does not fit the pattern. In order to do this, children need to recognise how each shape has been rotated. They then need to justify their decision by describing how the rotation of their chosen shape does not fit the pattern. Have a copy of the shapes for children to physically rotate to support their understanding.

STRENGTHEN Where possible, provide children with 2D shapes so that they can replicate the patterns in the problems. As children are physically rotating the shapes, talk to them about what they are doing. Have the key vocabulary available for children to refer to so as to support their descriptions of the patterns. Ask them to create their own simple patterns by drawing around or printing with 2D shapes, carrying out a rotation for each term.

DEEPEN Ask children to create a pattern with two or more lines. The shapes should rotate as they go from left to right and from top to bottom. Can children write a description of their pattern? Can they describe their partner's pattern?

ASSESSMENT CHECKPOINT Use questions **1** to **3** to check whether children can identify the pattern's core and how the shapes have been rotated, and question **4** to assess their confidence in using the vocabulary of rotation to describe a pattern.

Question **5** will determine whether children can identify a shape that does not fit the rule of the pattern and if they can reason and justify by applying their understanding of rotation.

ANSWERS Answers for the **Practice** part of the lesson appear in the separate **Practice and Reflect answer guide**.

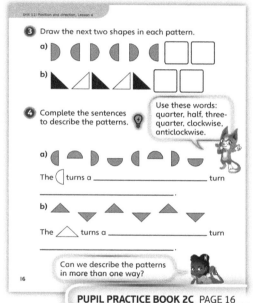

PUPIL PRACTICE BOOK 2C PAGE 15

PUPIL PRACTICE BOOK 2C PAGE 16

Reflect

WAYS OF WORKING Pair work

IN FOCUS In this part of the lesson, children need to think carefully about what they have learned in order to create their own pattern. The complexity of their pattern will indicate how secure children are in understanding and describing rotation.

ASSESSMENT CHECKPOINT This problem will determine whether children are able to apply their knowledge to create their own pattern.

ANSWERS Answers for the **Reflect** part of the lesson appear in the separate **Practice and Reflect answer guide**.

PUPIL PRACTICE BOOK 2C PAGE 17

After the lesson ⏸

- Were children consistent in their use of correct mathematical language to describe rotation?
- Did children make links between this lesson and previous lessons?

End of unit check

Don't forget the *Power Maths* unit assessment grid on p26.

WAYS OF WORKING Group work – adult led

IN FOCUS This section asks children to correctly use key language associated with position and movement. The questions require children to understand amount (in quarters) and direction of turn and to be able to identify repeating cores within a pattern.

Think!

WAYS OF WORKING Pair work

IN FOCUS This question requires children to be able to describe the position of an object in relation to other objects. It assesses whether children can apply the correct vocabulary while giving enough information to avoid ambiguity.

Key vocabulary in this question includes: above, below, beside, next to, top, bottom, left, right, between.

Encourage children to think through or discuss the questions they would like to ask before writing in **My journal**.

ANSWERS AND COMMENTARY Children who have mastered this unit will be able to use correct mathematical language to describe position and lateral and rotational movement. Children will be able to follow a series of instructions related to movement and they will be able to plan a series of instructions to arrive at a desired goal.

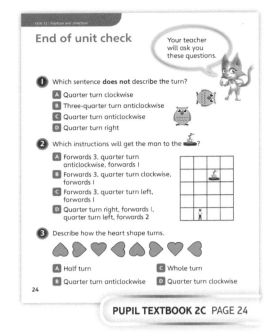

PUPIL TEXTBOOK 2C PAGE 24

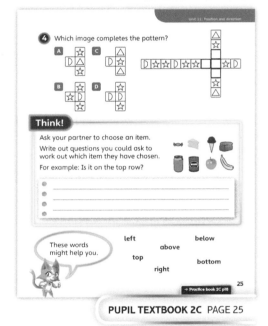

PUPIL TEXTBOOK 2C PAGE 25

Q	A	WRONG ANSWERS AND MISCONCEPTIONS	STRENGTHENING UNDERSTANDING
1	C	Incorrect answers may indicate that children do not understand the terms clockwise and anticlockwise or have confused left and right.	Provide practical opportunities to practise, such as moving around a grid drawn on the playground, so that children can practise giving and following instructions. Provide children with a circular piece of card or paper with clockwise/right and anticlockwise/left drawn on it, which they can refer to in the playground.
2	B	A and C suggest children do not know the difference between clockwise and anticlockwise or left and right. D suggests miscounting.	
3	D	Wrong answers may indicate that children's ability to describe rotation is not secure.	
4	C	Choosing A suggests that children have concentrated solely on the vertical pattern, whereas choosing B or D suggests that children have not identified the repeating core.	Throughout the **End of unit check**, encourage children to describe each movement that is made so that they become secure in using the key language correctly.

My journal

WAYS OF WORKING Independent thinking

ANSWERS AND COMMENTARY

Encourage children to eliminate as many objects as possible with their first question. For example, asking *Is it in the top row?* allows children to rule out four objects straight away. Asking *Is it between two other objects?* will tell children whether the object is at the end of a row. Children then only need to ask one final question to solve the problem.

Provide children with a laminated copy of the objects and a dry-wipe pen so that they can cross out objects as they are eliminated. Ask: *How can you rule out as many objects as possible? How many objects did your question rule out? Could you ask a different question to rule out even more?* To ensure that children are using and applying the key language, ask them to include at least one of the words presented by Sparks in each of their questions. Challenge children to use a different word for each question that they ask.

PUPIL PRACTICE BOOK 2C PAGE 18

Power check

WAYS OF WORKING Independent thinking

ASK

- *How confident do you feel when you describe the position of an object?*
- *Do you now find it easier to follow a set of instructions related to movement?*
- *Do you still feel unsure about any of the key language?*
- *Has your ability to identify and describe repeating patterns improved?*

Power play

WAYS OF WORKING Pair work

IN FOCUS Use this game to see whether children can follow instructions relating to movement and to check that they are secure in their understanding of the direction and extent of a turn. Use counters and demonstrate the game first by playing against the whole class. To keep track of which direction the player is facing, draw an arrow on each counter to indicate the front of the counter.

If children are confident playing the game, they could roll two or three dice at a time to give them a series of instructions to follow. Ensure that children check that they can carry out all the instructions before moving their counter for the first time.

ANSWERS AND COMMENTARY If children struggle to make turns correctly, provide them with a paper circle divided into quarters with a quarter turn clockwise and a quarter turn anticlockwise drawn on it.

PUPIL PRACTICE BOOK 2C PAGE 19

After the unit ⏸

- Are there opportunities in other curriculum areas where children can apply their learning from this unit?
- Were all children confident using the key language in this unit?

Strengthen and **Deepen** activities for this unit can be found in the *Power Maths* online subscription.

Unit 12
Problem solving and efficient methods

Mastery Expert tip! "This unit brings together many of the key ideas that have been taught in previous units. It provides further opportunities for children to become confident at using the bar model to represent problems of different types."

Don't forget to watch the Unit 12 video!

WHY THIS UNIT IS IMPORTANT

This unit brings together the key ideas of number that have been addressed in previous units and provides an opportunity for children to practise all four operations.

The use of the bar model is consistent throughout as this method allows children to clearly see which operation is needed to complete parts of a question at any given time.

A focus throughout the unit is to ensure that the methods that children use are as efficient as possible. Children must justify their choice of methods, rather than simply using the column method for all questions.

WHERE THIS UNIT FITS

→ Unit 11: Position and direction

→ **Unit 12: Problem solving and efficient methods**

→ Unit 13: Time

This unit mainly builds on work from Units 1, 2 and 3, focussing in particular on addition and subtraction, but also using the context of money (Unit 4) and touching on multiplication and division (Units 5 and 6) towards the end of the unit.

Before they start this unit, it is expected that children:

- know how to use the bar model to represent information given in a word problem
- understand how to distinguish between the four operations
- know key number facts to use within mental calculations.

ASSESSING MASTERY

Children who have mastered this unit will be able to fluently select the appropriate operation that is needed to complete a given step of a problem and will be able to use the bar model to represent these problems. They will also be able to select an efficient method to solve the calculation, rather than simply using the column method by default.

COMMON MISCONCEPTIONS	STRENGTHENING UNDERSTANDING	GOING DEEPER
Children may focus on the numbers in a question rather than the context and select the wrong operation to complete the question.	Encourage children to use the bar model to represent calculations using the four operations.	Ask children to find all possible solutions that satisfy a problem and work in a way that ensures all solutions are found.
Children may use inefficient methods rather than carefully considering the numbers in the question.	Use resources to help children work in more efficient ways, such as Base 10 equipment, to count in 10s rather than 1s.	Create maths stories for all four operations, ensuring they contain more than one step using different operations.

Unit 12: Problem solving and efficient methods

Use these pages to introduce the problem-solving unit, ensuring that children understand what this is and what being efficient means.

STRUCTURES AND REPRESENTATIONS

Bar model: This model is crucial for this unit as it represents the questions and problems that children are presented with and enables them to identify what operation is required to solve different stages of the problem.

40	
17	?

Number line: This model helps children work in an efficient way, such as counting in steps of 10 rather than 1.

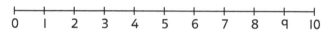

```
0   1   2   3   4   5   6   7   8   9   10
```

100 square: This model helps children see the links between numbers and again helps children work in a more efficient way.

1	2	3	4	5	6	7	8	9	10
11	12	13	14	15	16	17	18	19	20
21	22	23	24	25	26	27	28	29	30
31	32	33	34	35	36	37	38	39	40
41	42	43	44	45	46	47	48	49	50
51	52	53	54	55	56	57	58	59	60
61	62	63	64	65	66	67	68	69	70
71	72	73	74	75	76	77	78	79	80
81	82	83	84	85	86	87	88	89	90
91	92	93	94	95	96	97	98	99	100

KEY LANGUAGE

There is some key language that children will need to know as part of the learning in this unit:

→ part, whole, part-whole

→ add, addition, more than, +

→ subtract, subtraction, difference, change, take away, less than, −

→ divide, division, share, ÷

→ multiply, multiplication, lots of, ×

→ altogether, groups of, total, sum, total cost

→ representation, bar model, efficient

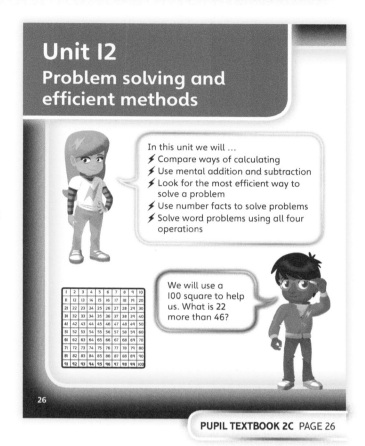

Unit 12
Problem solving and efficient methods

In this unit we will …
⚡ Compare ways of calculating
⚡ Use mental addition and subtraction
⚡ Look for the most efficient way to solve a problem
⚡ Use number facts to solve problems
⚡ Solve word problems using all four operations

We will use a 100 square to help us. What is 22 more than 46?

26

PUPIL TEXTBOOK 2C PAGE 26

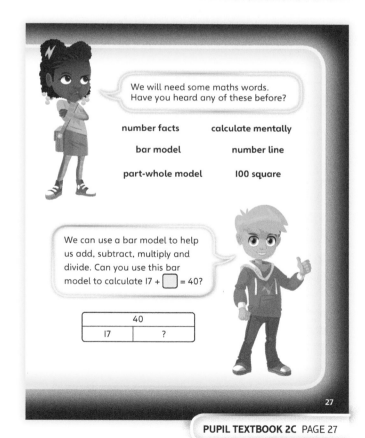

We will need some maths words. Have you heard any of these before?

number facts	calculate mentally
bar model	number line
part-whole model	100 square

We can use a bar model to help us add, subtract, multiply and divide. Can you use this bar model to calculate 17 + ⬜ = 40?

40	
17	?

27

PUPIL TEXTBOOK 2C PAGE 27

My way, your way!

Learning focus

In this lesson, children will solve money problems using a variety of addition and subtraction strategies.

Small steps

→ Previous step: Making patterns with shapes
→ **This step: My way, your way!**
→ Next step: Using number facts

NATIONAL CURRICULUM LINKS

Year 2 Number – Number and Place Value

Use place value and number facts to solve problems.

Year 2 Number – Addition and Subtraction

Recognise and use the inverse relationship between addition and subtraction and use this to check calculations and solve missing number problems.

ASSESSING MASTERY

Children can identify different ways to solve the same problem and identify the efficiency of different methods, counting forwards or backwards during calculations, and switching between counting on in 10s and 1s as appropriate. Children can use the bar model to represent word problems and use this to identify the correct operations to solve each step.

COMMON MISCONCEPTIONS

Children may focus on the numbers within questions, ignoring the words, and therefore choose the incorrect operation or the wrong calculation to solve the problem. Ask:
• *Can the bar model be used to identify the operation to be used?*

STRENGTHENING UNDERSTANDING

If children are finding it difficult to interpret the calculation needed to solve each problem, provide a completed bar model to help with this process. Alternatively, provide opportunities for children to create their own bar models from word problems using strips of paper or coloured rods of different lengths.

GOING DEEPER

Challenge children to identify different methods to solve the same problem and identify strengths and weaknesses of each method. Can children identify the most efficient method and explain why? Children should record all steps of their working and use mathematical signs to increase the complexity of their answers.

KEY LANGUAGE

In lesson: bar model, strategy, method, operation, addition, +, subtraction, −, change

Other language to be used by the teacher: efficient

STRUCTURES AND REPRESENTATIONS

Bar model, number line, column method

RESOURCES

Mandatory: coins, completed number line, blank number line

Optional: completed bar model, coloured rods

 In the eTextbook of this lesson, you will find interactive links to a selection of teaching tools.

Before you teach

• Are children confident interpreting word problems?
• How will you support children during the lesson?

Discover

WAYS OF WORKING Pair work

ASK

- *Do you know the price to post the letter? Do you know the price to post the parcel?*
- *Can a bar model be used to model this question?*

IN FOCUS In question ❶ a), children are required to interpret the picture shown and identify how to solve the problem. Children may see the numbers 35 and 15 and the words 'more than' and assume they must complete 35 + 15 to solve the problem.

In question ❶ b), children are required to understand the concept of change. Some children may require support for this since they need to know that £1 is the same as 100p in order to calculate the change to be given from a £1 coin. If this concept is not understood, children may simply subtract 1 from the price calculated in part a).

ANSWERS

Question ❶ a): It will cost 85p to post the letter and the parcel.

Question ❶ b): There will be 15p change from a £1 coin.

My way, your way!

Discover

It is 35p for the letter.

The parcel will cost 15p more than the letter.

❶ **a)** How much will it cost in total to post the letter and the parcel?

b) How much change will there be from a £1 coin?

28

PUPIL TEXTBOOK 2C PAGE 28

Share

WAYS OF WORKING Whole class teacher led

ASK

- Question ❶ a): *How can you calculate the total price to post the parcel?*
- Question ❶ a): *Which part of the bar model shows that the parcel costs 15p more to post than the letter?*
- Question ❶ b): *Why can addition and subtraction be used to calculate the answer to the same problem?*

IN FOCUS In this part of the lesson it is important for children to understand the different ways to answer the same question, and the different representations that highlight these different methods. Children may use different mental strategies to calculate the answer to the problem. Children should be able to count in 10s and 5s as an efficient way to solve the problem and should understand the benefits of working in this way, as opposed to counting in 1s. It is also important for children to understand how addition or subtraction can both be used to solve the same problem.

STRENGTHEN Encourage children to role play being a shopkeeper and a customer to further strengthen their understanding of change. This should strengthen the real-life context that the problem presents and increase the likelihood of the correct change being calculated as the customer wants the correct change and the shopkeeper does not want to give money away.

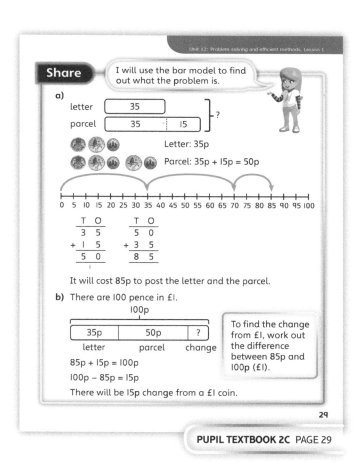

Share

I will use the bar model to find out what the problem is.

a)

letter | 35
parcel | 35 | 15

Letter: 35p

Parcel: 35p + 15p = 50p

$$\begin{array}{r} T\ O \\ 3\ 5 \\ +\ 1\ 5 \\ \hline 5\ 0 \\ {}_1 \end{array} \qquad \begin{array}{r} T\ O \\ 5\ 0 \\ +\ 3\ 5 \\ \hline 8\ 5 \end{array}$$

It will cost 85p to post the letter and the parcel.

b) There are 100 pence in £1.

100p

| 35p | 50p | ? |
| letter | parcel | change |

To find the change from £1, work out the difference between 85p and 100p (£1).

85p + 15p = 100p

100p − 85p = 15p

There will be 15p change from a £1 coin.

29

PUPIL TEXTBOOK 2C PAGE 29

Think together

WAYS OF WORKING Whole class teacher led (I do, We do, You do)

ASK
- *What is the unknown in each question?*
- *Which operation is needed at each stage of the problem?*

IN FOCUS Challenge children to think if the same method is appropriate for all questions. Each different method should be celebrated as 'my way is not better than your way, it's just different'. Encourage children to record all steps of their working, rather than completing multiple steps mentally which will increase the likelihood of calculation errors. Children may need support in understanding how this does not reduce the efficiency of calculation, but increases the reliability of their calculations.

STRENGTHEN Provide children with physical resources to create the bar models represented in each question. Manipulating the bars and creating the bar model will strengthen their understanding of which operation is required at different stages of the problem.

DEEPEN Challenge children to record the answers to questions ❶ and ❸ using the signs < and > to mathematically show if Sam has enough money in both situations.

ASSESSMENT CHECKPOINT Check to see that children can explain what the different parts of the bar model represent and how these help to determine the correct operation to solve the problem.

ANSWERS

Question ❶ : 45 + 45 = 90

The total cost is 90p.

Sam does have enough money because 90p < £1.

Question ❷ : 35 + 35 = 70

100p − 70p = 30p

Sam will get 30p change.

Question ❸ : £1 is enough money.

card 1 [45p ┊ 20p] ⎫
                        ⎬ 100p
card 2 [35p]   ⎭

Sam does have enough money.

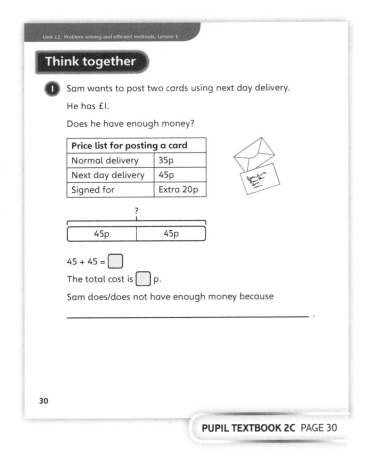

Think together

❶ Sam wants to post two cards using next day delivery.

He has £1.

Does he have enough money?

Price list for posting a card	
Normal delivery	35p
Next day delivery	45p
Signed for	Extra 20p

?
| 45p | 45p |

45 + 45 = ☐
The total cost is ☐ p.
Sam does/does not have enough money because
_____ .

30

PUPIL TEXTBOOK 2C PAGE 30

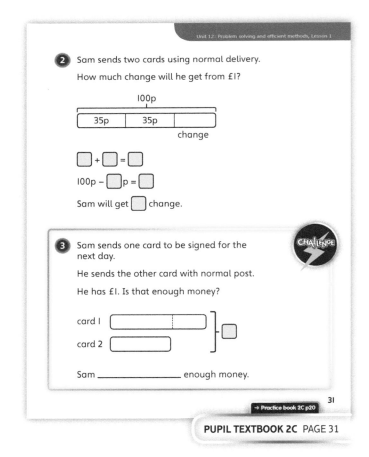

❷ Sam sends two cards using normal delivery.

How much change will he get from £1?

100p
| 35p | 35p | |
                change

☐ + ☐ = ☐
100p − ☐ p = ☐
Sam will get ☐ change.

❸ Sam sends one card to be signed for the next day.

He sends the other card with normal post.

He has £1. Is that enough money?

CHALLENGE

card 1 [┊] ⎫ ☐
card 2 [ ]   ⎭

Sam _____ enough money.

→ Practice book 2C p20

31

PUPIL TEXTBOOK 2C PAGE 31

Practice

WAYS OF WORKING Independent thinking

IN FOCUS In this part of the lesson, some problems have not been broken down into steps and therefore children are required to work out the two steps themselves and draw their own bar models. Although a bar model has been provided to help children understand the structure of the problem, allow them to use whatever calculation method they want to solve the problems.

STRENGTHEN Continue to provide any children who find it difficult to interpret each problem with bar models that have been made to represent each problem. These will increase the likelihood that children will identify the two steps within the question and the appropriate operation required to solve the problem.

DEEPEN Challenge children to create their own two-step word problems using the context of money.

ASSESSMENT CHECKPOINT Check what mental strategies children are using in calculations. Encourage children to not count forward and backwards in 1s as this is an inefficient method and is more likely to lead to calculation errors.

ANSWERS Answers for the **Practice** part of the lesson appear in the separate **Practice and Reflect answer guide**.

Reflect

WAYS OF WORKING Independent thinking

IN FOCUS In this section of the lesson, children are presented with a money context using amounts in pounds. Some children may think that this increases the difficulty of the problem and this should be discussed as a class. Children should solve the problem independently and then discuss the different methods that have been used. It is important for children to understand that the column method does not always need to be used. Other methods, such as a number line, a mental strategy or counting in 10s, may be more efficient.

ASSESSMENT CHECKPOINT Check if children can verbalise the method they used to solve the problem. Further assessments can be made to see if children can identify the efficiency of their method compared to others' following class discussions.

ANSWERS Answers for the **Reflect** part of the lesson appear in the separate **Practice and Reflect answer guide**.

After the lesson ⏸

- Are children able to use more than one method to solve different styles of questions?
- Is there a strategy that the whole class finds more difficult to use, that may require additional practice?

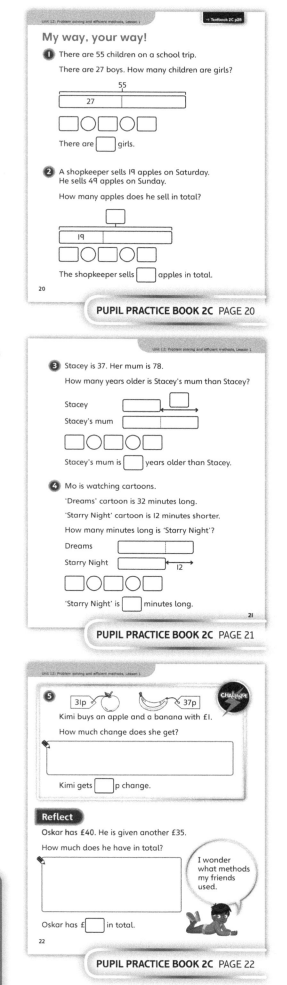

PUPIL PRACTICE BOOK 2C PAGE 20

PUPIL PRACTICE BOOK 2C PAGE 21

PUPIL PRACTICE BOOK 2C PAGE 22

Using number facts

Learning focus

In this lesson, children will make links between calculations to calculate unknown quantities, based on similarities and differences between the parts and the wholes.

Small steps

→ Previous step: My way, your way!
→ **This step: Using number facts**
→ Next step: Using number facts and equivalence

NATIONAL CURRICULUM LINKS

Year 2 Number – Number and Place Value

Use place value and number facts to solve problems.

Year 2 Number – Addition and Subtraction

Recognise and use the inverse relationship between addition and subtraction and use this to check calculations and solve missing number problems.

ASSESSING MASTERY

Children can use known or given number facts as an efficient way to solve additional unknowns.

COMMON MISCONCEPTIONS

Children may see each calculation as a new question and therefore use an inefficient strategy to find the solution rather than build on what they already know. Similarly, children may only refer back to the initial fact that they have been given, rather than make links to their subsequent findings. Ask:
• *What is the same and what is different to what you already know?*

STRENGTHENING UNDERSTANDING

Using concrete manipulatives to model the different facts that are known and what needs to be calculated will increase the likelihood of children being able to identify what is the same and what can be used to solve the subsequent problem. Alternatively, allowing children to highlight or colour the different parts of the calculations that are the same will help them make stronger links.

GOING DEEPER

Children should be able to spot patterns within questions and, as a result, continue the pattern by creating subsequent calculations of their own, or create their own series of calculations that link in a similar way.

KEY LANGUAGE

In lesson: addition, part, whole, pattern

Other language to be used by the teacher: related, similar, different, link

STRUCTURES AND REPRESENTATIONS

Part-whole model

RESOURCES

Mandatory: Base 10 equipment, blank part-whole models

Optional: coloured pencils

 In the eTextbook of this lesson, you will find interactive links to a selection of teaching tools.

Before you teach

• How will you encourage children to use the most efficient calculation strategy?
• How will you ensure that children are exposed to the methods and approaches used by others?

Discover

WAYS OF WORKING Pair work

ASK

- *How do the different questions link to each other?*
- *What is the same and what is different in each question?*

IN FOCUS In this part of the lesson, children can use a given fact, 5 + 8 = 13, to work out unknown quantities. Encourage children to use this fact in the subsequent calculations, rather than calculating each answer separately.

ANSWERS

Question **1** a): 15 is 10 more than 5. If 5 + 8 = 13, then 15 + 8 will be 10 more than this answer.

Therefore, 15 + 8 = 23.

Question **1** b): 25 + 8 = 33

35 + 8 = 43

8 + 45 = 53

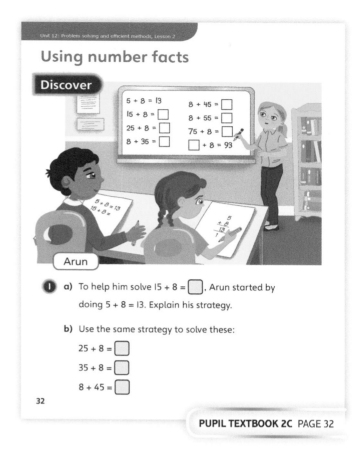

PUPIL TEXTBOOK 2C PAGE 32

Share

WAYS OF WORKING Whole class teacher led

ASK

- *What is changing? What is staying the same?*
- *Where can you see 5 + 8 in each calculation?*

IN FOCUS In this part of the lesson, it is important for children to see the links between the different calculations presented. The use of Base 10 equipment helps to show that only the number of tens changes in each calculation, as opposed to the number of ones. Therefore, the number of ones in the whole will not change.

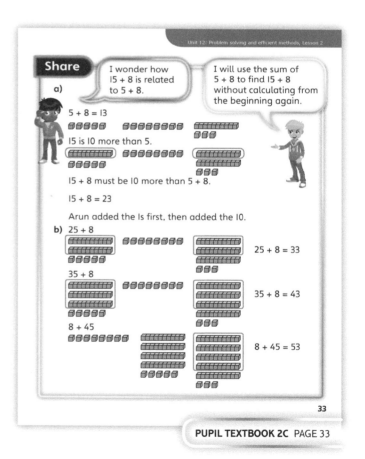

PUPIL TEXTBOOK 2C PAGE 33

Think together

Whole class teacher led (I do, We do, You do)

ASK

- *What is changing? What is staying the same?*
- *Is there a pattern in the calculations that are shown? Could this be continued?*

IN FOCUS In this part of the lesson, children look at how they can use the answer to one calculation to work out another. They must look at what has stayed the same and what has changed in order to relate the calculations to each other. These questions differ to previous ones as one of the parts, and therefore the whole, does not simply increase by 10 each time, but instead the parts may be 10, 20, or 30 more or less than those in the original calculation.

STRENGTHEN Allowing children to continue to use Base 10 equipment will help them see links between the different parts in the calculations. Alternatively, encourage children to highlight or colour the parts of the calculations that are the same to help them make stronger links.

DEEPEN Ask children to identify the pattern that links the different calculations within a question. Children can continue this pattern by making their own calculations, or create their own series of calculations that link together in a particular way.

ASSESSMENT CHECKPOINT Assess whether children can verbalise the connections between the calculations within a question. Are children using known facts to calculate new unknowns or are they treating each calculation separately?

If children are spotting, continuing and creating patterns, check to see if they are comfortable at reordering the parts of the addition calculations and if they are using more complex patterns, such as increasing both or alternate numbers by 10.

ANSWERS

Question ❶ a): 79 is 20 more than 59. Therefore 79 + 6 = 85.

Question ❶ b): 29 is 30 less than 59. Therefore 29 + 6 = 35.

Question ❷ : 67 is 30 more than 37. Therefore 24 + 67° = 91.

Question ❸ : 28 + 36 = 64

　　　　　76 is 40 more than 36. Therefore 76 + 28 = 104.

　　　　　38 is 10 more than 28. 26 is 10 less than 36. Therefore 28 + 36 = 38 + 26 = 64.

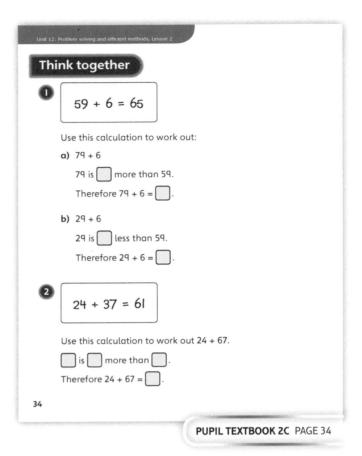

Think together

❶ $59 + 6 = 65$

Use this calculation to work out:

a) $79 + 6$

79 is ☐ more than 59.

Therefore $79 + 6 = ☐$.

b) $29 + 6$

29 is ☐ less than 59.

Therefore $29 + 6 = ☐$.

❷ $24 + 37 = 61$

Use this calculation to work out $24 + 67$.

☐ is ☐ more than ☐.

Therefore $24 + 67 = ☐$.

34

PUPIL TEXTBOOK 2C PAGE 34

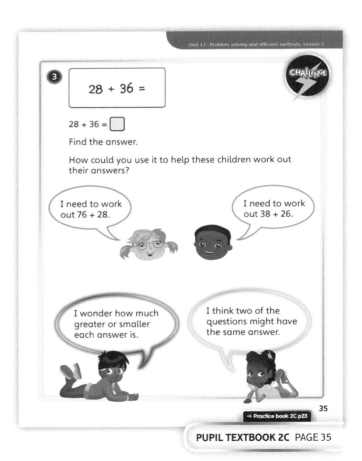

❸ $28 + 36 =$

$28 + 36 = ☐$

Find the answer.

How could you use it to help these children work out their answers?

I need to work out 76 + 28.

I need to work out 38 + 26.

I wonder how much greater or smaller each answer is.

I think two of the questions might have the same answer.

35

→ Practice book 2C p23

PUPIL TEXTBOOK 2C PAGE 35

Practice

WAYS OF WORKING Independent thinking

IN FOCUS In this part of the lesson, children are required to make links between calculations to find unknown quantities. In question **2**, children's understanding of place value is tested. The focus should not be on finding the total of each calculation, but again on what is the same and different between the calculations. Question **4** is different as one of the parts increases or decreases by 1 for the first time as opposed to by a multiple of 10. Question **5** shows children they can work out an answer without actually doing any calculation; they just need to be able to compare numbers. It is important that children can reason this verbally and communicate it on paper too.

STRENGTHEN Allow children to continue to work with concrete manipulatives to make the initial calculation. They must then adapt this calculation to reflect the new calculation and describe the changes they are making to one of the parts and how this will affect the whole.

DEEPEN How many different ways can ?5 + ?? = 65 be completed? Ask children to make a prediction of the number of different ways and then work systematically to find all the possible solutions.

ASSESSMENT CHECKPOINT Check children's understanding by asking them to explain the links between the different calculations that they are presented with in each question. Children should be able to verbalise these similarities and differences and how they can be used to calculate subsequent unknowns.

ANSWERS Answers for the **Practice** part of the lesson appear in the separate **Practice and Reflect answer guide**.

Reflect

WAYS OF WORKING Independent thinking

IN FOCUS In this part of the lesson, for the first time children are presented with one of the parts and the whole for both calculations. To answer the written question, children do not need to solve each calculation and work out each missing number. They should instead be able to verbalise how knowing that the whole of the second calculation is 20 more than in the first calculation will affect the missing parts in both calculations.

ASSESSMENT CHECKPOINT Check to see which children solve each calculation to answer the question as opposed to using their understanding of the links between the numbers within the calculations.

ANSWERS Answers for the **Reflect** part of the lesson appear in the separate **Practice and Reflect answer guide**.

After the lesson ⏸

- Did children use efficient methods to solve questions and make links between calculations?
- How will you encourage children to work efficiently?

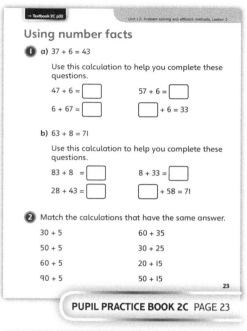

→ Textbook 2C p32   Unit 12: Problem solving and efficient methods, Lesson 2

Using number facts

1 a) 37 + 6 = 43

Use this calculation to help you complete these questions.

47 + 6 = ☐   57 + 6 = ☐

6 + 67 = ☐   ☐ + 6 = 33

b) 63 + 8 = 71

Use this calculation to help you complete these questions.

83 + 8 = ☐   8 + 33 = ☐

28 + 43 = ☐   ☐ + 58 = 71

2 Match the calculations that have the same answer.

30 + 5   60 + 35
50 + 5   30 + 25
60 + 5   20 + 15
90 + 5   50 + 15

23

PUPIL PRACTICE BOOK 2C PAGE 23

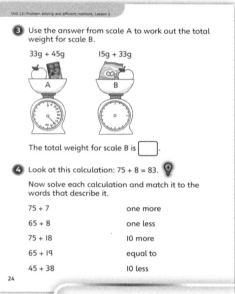

Unit 12: Problem solving and efficient methods, Lesson 2

3 Use the answer from scale A to work out the total weight for scale B.

33g + 45g   15g + 33g

The total weight for scale B is ☐.

4 Look at this calculation: 75 + 8 = 83. 💡

Now solve each calculation and match it to the words that describe it.

75 + 7   one more
65 + 8   one less
75 + 18   10 more
65 + 19   equal to
45 + 38   10 less

24

PUPIL PRACTICE BOOK 2C PAGE 24

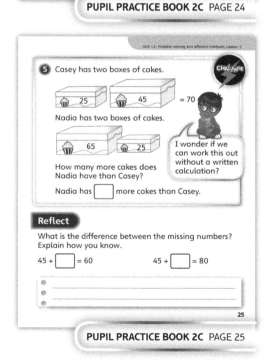

Unit 12: Problem solving and efficient methods, Lesson 2

5 Casey has two boxes of cakes.

25   45   = 70

Nadia has two boxes of cakes.

65   25

I wonder if we can work this out without a written calculation?

How many more cakes does Nadia have than Casey?

Nadia has ☐ more cakes than Casey.

Reflect

What is the difference between the missing numbers? Explain how you know.

45 + ☐ = 60   45 + ☐ = 80

25

PUPIL PRACTICE BOOK 2C PAGE 25

Using number facts and equivalence

Learning focus

In this lesson, children will use known number facts to determine whether the total calculated is feasible, without completing the whole calculation.

Small steps

→ Previous step: Using number facts
→ **This step: Using number facts and equivalence**
→ Next step: Using a 100 square

NATIONAL CURRICULUM LINKS

Year 2 Number – Number and Place Value

Use place value and number facts to solve problems.

Year 2 Number – Addition and Subtraction

Recognise and use the inverse relationship between addition and subtraction and use this to check calculations and solve missing number problems.

ASSESSING MASTERY

Children can use known number facts to reason if a calculation is possible. Children can recognise that it is not necessary to complete a calculation to check if it is correct, and can recalculate if it is identified as incorrect.

COMMON MISCONCEPTIONS

Children will be required to move between questions that require addition and subtraction. As a result, some children may complete the wrong operation. Ask:
• *What operation do you need to complete or check this calculation?*

STRENGTHENING UNDERSTANDING

If children find recall of number facts difficult, provide number bonds within 20 and related multiples of 10 facts and encourage children to refer to these, identifying which facts relate to each question.

GOING DEEPER

Challenge children to 'be the teacher' to help explain mistakes that have been made and provide advice to help prevent the same mistakes happening again. Display these in the classroom as addition and subtraction top tips.

KEY LANGUAGE

In lesson: error, incorrect, addition, +, subtraction, –, total, exchange, column

Other language to be used by the teacher: sensible, feasible, possible

STRUCTURES AND REPRESENTATIONS

Column method, part-whole model

RESOURCES

Mandatory: place value chart

Optional: Base 10 equipment, key number facts

 In the eTextbook of this lesson, you will find interactive links to a selection of teaching tools.

Before you teach

• Can children recall key number facts to check calculations?
• Would children benefit from having key number facts to refer to throughout the lesson?

Discover

WAYS OF WORKING Pair work

ASK

- *Do you have to complete the whole calculation to see if it is correct?*
- *What known facts can you use to prove each calculation is incorrect?*

IN FOCUS In this part of the lesson, children identify errors in calculations and determine whether answers are possible or not. Children must be able to identify how they know a calculation is incorrect and if there is more than one way that this can be identified.

ANSWERS

Question **1** a): 3 tens + 3 tens = 6 tens, not 5 tens.

Question **1** b): 36 + 20 is 56. This is already greater than 53 without adding the extra 7 ones.

81 – 20 is 61, which is less than 66. There is also another 5 to subtract, so 66 must be incorrect.

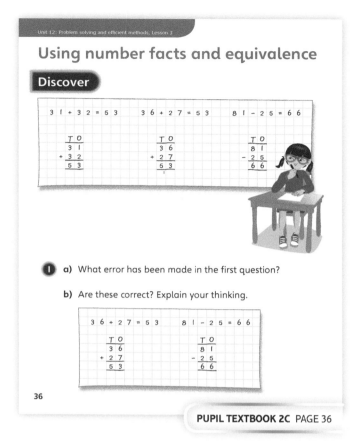

Using number facts and equivalence

Discover

1 a) What error has been made in the first question?

b) Are these correct? Explain your thinking.

36

PUPIL TEXTBOOK 2C PAGE 36

Share

WAYS OF WORKING Whole class teacher led

ASK

- *Are Astrid and Flo's ways of finding that the calculations are incorrect the same as yours, or different?*
- *Can you explain the mistake the children made during their calculations?*

IN FOCUS Encourage children to use a fact that they do know, 30 + 30, to identify that the calculation must be incorrect. As soon as they have identified this, they should recalculate the problem to find the correct answer. Encourage the use of other methods as well and challenge children to explain their reasoning using resources.

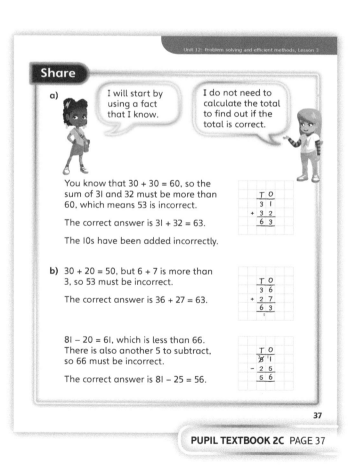

Share

a) I will start by using a fact that I know.

I do not need to calculate the total to find out if the total is correct.

You know that 30 + 30 = 60, so the sum of 31 and 32 must be more than 60, which means 53 is incorrect.

The correct answer is 31 + 32 = 63.

The 10s have been added incorrectly.

b) 30 + 20 = 50, but 6 + 7 is more than 3, so 53 must be incorrect.

The correct answer is 36 + 27 = 63.

81 – 20 = 61, which is less than 66. There is also another 5 to subtract, so 66 must be incorrect.

The correct answer is 81 – 25 = 56.

37

PUPIL TEXTBOOK 2C PAGE 37

Think together

WAYS OF WORKING Whole class teacher led (I do, We do, You do)

ASK

- *What fact can you use to prove question ① is incorrect?*
- *What mistake do you think has been made in each question?*

IN FOCUS Children must now efficiently identify if a question is correct or incorrect and then calculate the correct answer. Encourage children to use known facts within this process, rather than follow a procedural method to find the mistake.

STRENGTHEN Children who find this difficult can use concrete manipulatives, such as Base 10 equipment, to model each problem. Ask children to complete the calculations in different orders so they can identify which facts they can use to disprove each one.

DEEPEN Deepen understanding by asking children to provide more than one way to prove that each calculation is incorrect. Challenge children further by asking them to find different ways that the incorrect answer could be made by changing the whole and/or one of the parts.

ASSESSMENT CHECKPOINT Check to see if children can provide a fact and explain how it can be used to disprove each solution, rather than working procedurally through the calculations to find a mistake.

ANSWERS

Question ① : 54 + 10 is 64 which is already greater than 62 before the ones have been added.

Also, 4 ones + 8 ones is greater than 10 so the answer cannot be sixty-something.

Adding 4 to 8 makes 12. You need to carry the 1 into the tens column. Adding together the 5, 1 and 1 tens makes 7 tens. The answer is 72.

Question ② : The calculation is set out incorrectly – the 3 should represent ones, not tens, so it is in the wrong column.

Adding 3 ones and 6 ones makes 9 ones.

Add on the 5 tens, and you get 59.

Question ③ : 43 – 2 is 41, so subtracting 4 must give a smaller answer.

To do this calculation correctly will require an exchange as 4 is greater than 3. Take 1 ten from the tens column and put it next to the 3 to make 13. Subtracting 4 from this gives 9 ones.

You have 3 tens left so the answer is 39.

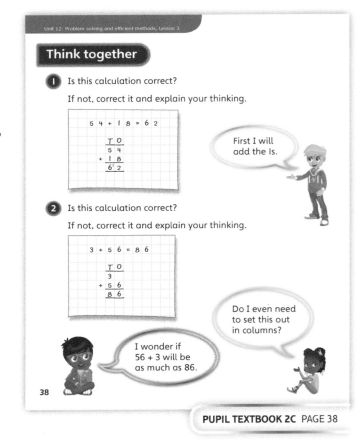

PUPIL TEXTBOOK 2C PAGE 38

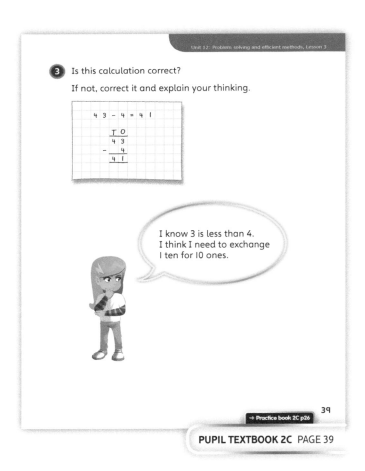

PUPIL TEXTBOOK 2C PAGE 39

Practice

WAYS OF WORKING Independent thinking

IN FOCUS This section requires children to use different facts to identify whether calculations are correct or incorrect. Different strategies are presented that can be used to calculate the answer to addition and subtraction problems.

STRENGTHEN Provide children with number facts that could be used to prove calculations are right or wrong for these questions and ask them to match the number fact to each question and explain how it helps.

DEEPEN Children can again be challenged to 'be the teacher' and work out where each calculation has gone wrong and give advice to prevent the same mistakes from happening again.

ASSESSMENT CHECKPOINT Assess whether children are using known facts to determine whether calculations are incorrect, rather than working procedurally to spot when a mistake has been made. Children should again be encouraged to explain the fact that they have used and how it helps to prove that the calculation is incorrect.

ANSWERS Answers for the **Practice** part of the lesson appear in the separate **Practice and Reflect answer guide**.

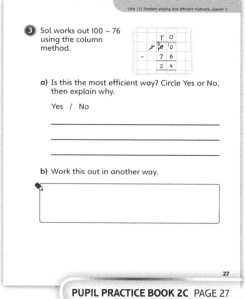

PUPIL PRACTICE BOOK 2C PAGE 26

PUPIL PRACTICE BOOK 2C PAGE 27

Reflect

WAYS OF WORKING Independent thinking

IN FOCUS This is a diagnostic question. Discuss the incorrect answers with children and talk about common misconceptions that have been made.

ASSESSMENT CHECKPOINT Check to see that children can explain why the two incorrect answers are not possible and what known facts can be used to establish this.

ANSWERS Answers for the **Reflect** part of the lesson appear in the separate **Practice and Reflect answer guide**.

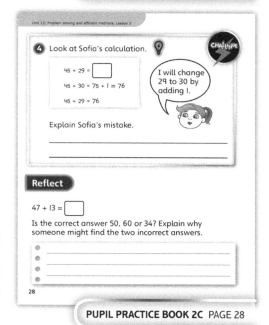

PUPIL PRACTICE BOOK 2C PAGE 28

After the lesson ⏸

- Did children understand the importance of using known number facts to check calculations?
- Will they be able to use a similar strategy to calculate if their own calculations are correct in future?

Using a 100 square

Learning focus

In this lesson, children will become more familiar with the 100 square and use it to confidently count forward and backwards in steps of ten and one in addition and subtraction problems.

Small steps

→ Previous step: Using number facts and equivalence
→ **This step: Using a 100 square**
→ Next step: Getting started

NATIONAL CURRICULUM LINKS

Year 2 Number – Number and Place Value

Use place value and number facts to solve problems.

Year 2 Number – Addition and Subtraction

Solve problems with addition and subtraction, using concrete objects and pictorial representations, including those involving numbers, quantities and measures.

ASSESSING MASTERY

Children can add and subtract in steps of ten and one and represent these visually on a 100 square. They can link moving on a 100 square to addition and subtraction and make steps within a calculation in different orders.

COMMON MISCONCEPTIONS

Children often do not know where to go at the end of a row. Sometimes they go back on the same row and get 45 + 8 = 43. They think of each row as a number line, not about the numbers themselves. Children may have seen a 100 square with 1 in the bottom left corner, and so move up a row to find 10 more. Ask:
• *What is one more than 50? Is 10 more than 45, 35?*

STRENGTHENING UNDERSTANDING

To increase familiarity with the 100 square, practise counting from 1 to 100 and 100 to 1 using the 100 square. To aid understanding of adding and subtracting 10 with the 100 square, Base 10 equipment can also be used.

GOING DEEPER

Ask children to describe journeys from one number to another in different ways using the 100 square. For example, describe moving from 13 to 36: 13 + 10 = 23 (down one row), 23 + 10 = 33 (down one row), 33 + 3 = 36 (along 3 square to the right), or 13 + 3 = 16 (3 squares to the right), 16 + 20 = 36 (down 2 rows).

KEY LANGUAGE

In lesson: square, row, column, more than, less than, across, down, right, left

Other language to be used by the teacher: support

STRUCTURES AND REPRESENTATIONS

100 square, number line

RESOURCES

Mandatory: laminated 100 square, 1–100 number line

Optional: Base 10 equipment, part-whole model

 In the eTextbook of this lesson, you will find interactive links to a selection of teaching tools.

Before you teach

• Have children used the 100 square before?
• Do they find it easiest for calculating within 100?
• Can other resources supplement the 100 square?

Discover

WAYS OF WORKING Pair work

ASK

- *How many numbers are there in each row? How many rows are there?*
- *What is 10 more than 45?*
- *What is 20 more than 45?*
- *How can the 100 square be used to show this?*

IN FOCUS In this part of the lesson, children re-familiarise themselves with the 100 square. Remind children that there are 10 numbers on each row and that there are 10 rows. Recap how to use the 100 square when children reach the end of a row. Question ❶ a) helps with this process. Remind children that when they count on from 50, they then need to move to 51 on the next row down.

ANSWERS

Question ❶ a): 8 more than 45 is 53. Count along 5 to 50, then count on 3 more to 53.

Question ❶ b): 32 more than 45 is 77. 30 more than 45 is 75 (move down 3 spaces from 45 on the 100 square), 2 more than 45 is 47 (move 2 spaces to the right on the 100 square).

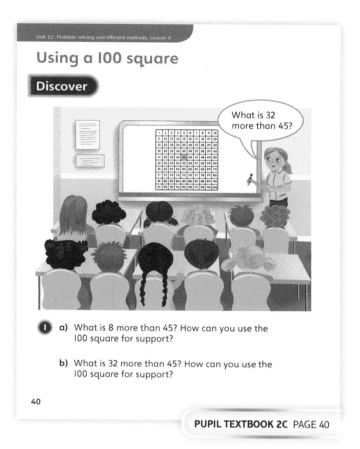

Using a 100 square

Discover

What is 32 more than 45?

❶ a) What is 8 more than 45? How can you use the 100 square for support?

b) What is 32 more than 45? How can you use the 100 square for support?

40

PUPIL TEXTBOOK 2C PAGE 40

Share

WAYS OF WORKING Whole class teacher led

ASK

- *Is there more than one way to calculate 45 + 8?*
- *In which direction do you move when counting backwards?*
- *How does moving along the rows and columns link to addition and subtraction?*

IN FOCUS In this part of the lesson, children are exposed to different ways that the 100 square could be used to calculate the same question. For example, in question ❶ a), you could count on 8 jumps of 1, or you could add 10 by moving down one row and then count back 2.

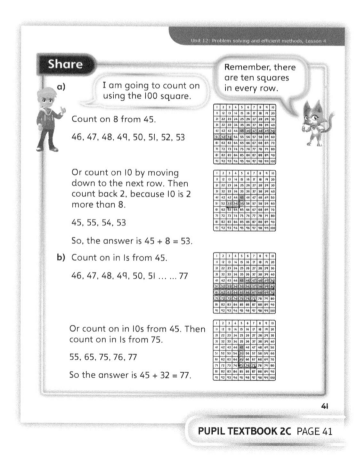

Share

Remember, there are ten squares in every row.

a) I am going to count on using the 100 square.

Count on 8 from 45.

46, 47, 48, 49, 50, 51, 52, 53

Or count on 10 by moving down to the next row. Then count back 2, because 10 is 2 more than 8.

45, 55, 54, 53

So, the answer is 45 + 8 = 53.

b) Count on in 1s from 45.

46, 47, 48, 49, 50, 51 … … 77

Or count on in 10s from 45. Then count on in 1s from 75.

55, 65, 75, 76, 77

So the answer is 45 + 32 = 77.

41

PUPIL TEXTBOOK 2C PAGE 41

Think together

WAYS OF WORKING Whole class teacher led (I do, We do, You do)

ASK

- *Does the order that you add or subtract in matter?*
- *Why is having ten numbers in a row useful?*
- *How does the 100 square help with adding and subtracting in 10s and 1s?*

IN FOCUS This part of the lesson provides an opportunity for children to count on and backwards, completing addition and subtraction problems using the 100 square. It also requires the number line to be used to strengthen links between how these jumps are shown in different ways when using different resources.

In question **3**, children could record the jumps on the number line in different ways. To follow Millie's working, children could jump backwards in 2 steps of 10 or 1 jump of 20 then 1 jump of 6 or 6 jumps of 1. Highlighting the different ways that children record this on their number line will highlight the different mental calculation strategies they are using.

STRENGTHEN Provide children with part-whole models to help them record the partitioned number in tens and ones. This could be partitioned further to show how many jumps of 10 are required.

Children can record the steps that they take on a laminated 100 square, once they have established the number of jumps of 10 and 1 they need to take. This allows children to check that the number of jumps they have made matches the question.

DEEPEN How many different journeys can you take with the same starting and finishing number? How are these different journeys shown differently on a number line?

ASSESSMENT CHECKPOINT Check that children can link the jumps they are making on the 100 square to the question they are solving. See which children are using inefficient methods such as only counting in 1s, rather than counting in 10s and 1s.

ANSWERS

Question **1** : 36 more than 52 is 88.

Question **2** : 45 less than 76 is 31.

Question **3** : 2 jumps of 10 from 68 to 58, and 58 to 48, and then 6 jumps of 1 to 42 (or one jump of 6).

Or, 1 jump of 6 and then 2 jumps of 10.

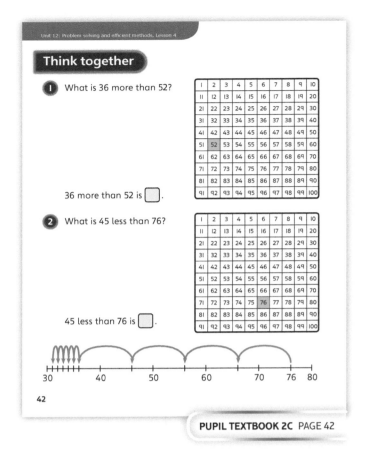

Think together

1 What is 36 more than 52?

36 more than 52 is ☐.

2 What is 45 less than 76?

45 less than 76 is ☐.

42

PUPIL TEXTBOOK 2C PAGE 42

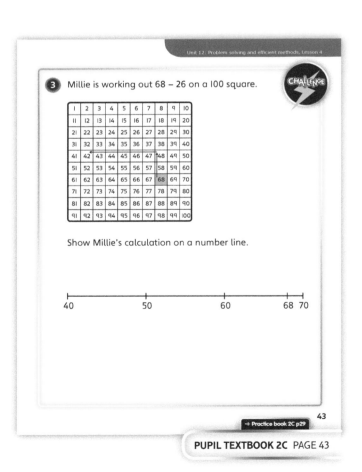

3 Millie is working out 68 − 26 on a 100 square.

CHALLENGE

Show Millie's calculation on a number line.

43

→ Practice book 2C p29

PUPIL TEXTBOOK 2C PAGE 43

Practice

WAYS OF WORKING Independent thinking

IN FOCUS These questions give children the opportunity to work independently using the 100 square and a number line to support and visually show addition and subtraction calculations. Throughout the questions, children are required to move forwards and backwards in 10s and 1s and relate these jumps to addition and subtraction. Children may work in different ways and these differences should be highlighted and celebrated to expose children to different methods that can be used to answer the same questions.

STRENGTHEN Allowing children to work with Base 10 equipment alongside the 100 square will help them understand how to move around and link movements to addition, subtraction, counting on and counting backwards in jumps of 10.

DEEPEN Ask children to represent 42 – 24 in as many different ways as they can on a number line and on the 100 square, ensuring that the representations on each resource match each other for each possible way.

ASSESSMENT CHECKPOINT Check to see that children can explain how the jumps that they have recorded on the 100 square and the number line link to each other and to addition and subtraction. Children should be expected to work in jumps of 10s and 1s, rather than only in 1s.

ANSWERS Answers for the **Practice** part of the lesson appear in the separate **Practice and Reflect answer guide**.

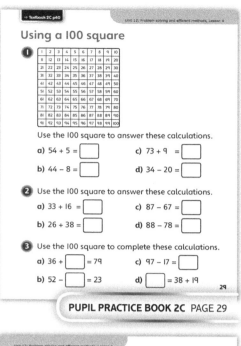

Using a 100 square

1. Use the 100 square to answer these calculations.

   a) 54 + 5 = ☐   c) 73 + 9 = ☐

   b) 44 – 8 = ☐   d) 34 – 20 = ☐

2. Use the 100 square to answer these calculations.

   a) 33 + 16 = ☐   c) 87 – 67 = ☐

   b) 26 + 38 = ☐   d) 88 – 78 = ☐

3. Use the 100 square to complete these calculations.

   a) 36 + ☐ = 79   c) 97 – 17 = ☐

   b) 52 – ☐ = 23   d) ☐ = 38 + 19

PUPIL PRACTICE BOOK 2C PAGE 29

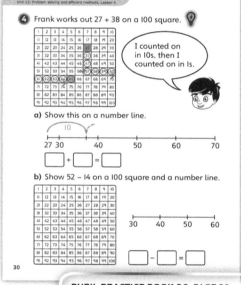

4. Frank works out 27 + 38 on a 100 square.

   I counted on in 10s, then I counted on in 1s.

   a) Show this on a number line.

   27 30   40   50   60   70

   ☐ + ☐ = ☐

   b) Show 52 – 14 on a 100 square and a number line.

   30   40   50   60

   ☐ – ☐ = ☐

PUPIL PRACTICE BOOK 2C PAGE 30

Reflect

WAYS OF WORKING Independent thinking

IN FOCUS This **Reflect** improves children's understanding of commutativity. Encourage children to explain how the jumps they have shown on the 100 square show what has been added and why both methods result in the same total.

ASSESSMENT CHECKPOINT Check to see if children can explain what is the same and what is different about the two different calculations that they have shown on the same 100 square. Check if children can use the correct mathematical vocabulary during these explanations. Reflect also on whether it is easier or more efficient to start with the bigger number.

ANSWERS Answers for the **Reflect** part of the lesson appear in the separate **Practice and Reflect answer guide**.

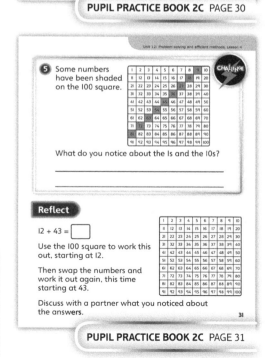

5. Some numbers have been shaded on the 100 square.

   What do you notice about the 1s and the 10s?

   _____

   _____

Reflect

12 + 43 = ☐

Use the 100 square to work this out, starting at 12.

Then swap the numbers and work it out again, this time starting at 43.

Discuss with a partner what you noticed about the answers.

PUPIL PRACTICE BOOK 2C PAGE 31

After the lesson ⏸

- Are children comfortable counting in 10s and 1s rather than only in 1s?
- Did children who began by counting in 1s recognise how this was an inefficient method of calculation?

Getting started

Learning focus

In this lesson, children will find multiple answers to the same questions and increase in confidence at choosing a starting point and using trial and improvement to work from it.

Small steps

→ Previous step: Using a 100 square
→ **This step: Getting started**
→ Next step: Missing numbers

NATIONAL CURRICULUM LINKS

Year 2 Number – Addition and Subtraction

Recognise and use the inverse relationship between addition and subtraction to check calculations and solve missing number problems.

ASSESSING MASTERY

Children can find multiple answers to the same problem and are confident at choosing a starting point and using trial and improvement to work from it.

COMMON MISCONCEPTIONS

In the questions provided, it is likely that children will consider all of the different ways to make the target number and forget that there is a limitation in place where each number can only be used once. Ask:
• *Is each solution possible using the number cards?*

Children may also repeat solutions or work in a way where they miss possible solutions if they are trying to find all the ways to satisfy the problem. Ask:
• *Have you worked in a systematic way to find all the solutions?*

STRENGTHENING UNDERSTANDING

Some children may find the addition and subtraction in the problems a barrier to accessing the problems. Provide children with numbers bonds within 20 to increase the ease of access to the problem.

GOING DEEPER

Encourage children to find multiple solutions to the same problem and develop the way they work to find all possible solutions. Challenge children to find all the possible ways to solve each question. Encourage children to work in a systematic way to prove they have found all possible solutions.

KEY LANGUAGE

In lesson: partition, trial and improvement, solutions, possible, impossible, sum, total, digit

Other language to be used by the teacher: strategy

STRUCTURES AND REPRESENTATIONS

Part-whole model

RESOURCES

Mandatory: number cards 1–9, number sentence scaffolds

Optional: number bonds within 20, starting point prompts

 In the eTextbook of this lesson, you will find interactive links to a selection of teaching tools.

 Before you teach
• Are children confident problem solving?
• Can children find more than one answer?

Discover

WAYS OF WORKING Pair work

ASK

- *What does sum mean?*
- *How many different ways can you make 14?*

IN FOCUS This part of the lesson introduces the problem that will remain the focus for the lesson. It is important that children understand the essence of the problem: that there is only one of each digit card and as a result the same number cannot be used more than once.

ANSWERS

Question ① a): 5 + 9 = 14 or 6 + 8 = 14

Question ① b): 1 + 9 + 4 = 14

           1 + 8 + 5 = 14

           1 + 7 + 6 = 14

           2 + 9 + 3 = 14

           2 + 8 + 4 = 14

           2 + 7 + 5 = 14

           3 + 6 + 5 = 14

PUPIL TEXTBOOK 2C PAGE 44

Share

WAYS OF WORKING Whole class teacher led

ASK

- *If you choose 3 as the first card, what do you then need to think about?*
- *Would all the numbers greater than 2 work?*

IN FOCUS This section of the lesson emphasises the trial and improvement thinking process. Ensure children understand that if 2 did not work, 1 would not work either. Similarly, both 3 and 4 would need to be paired with a number larger than 9. Starting with 9 and working down, you can have 9 and 5, or 8 and 6.

In question ① b), using the 9 + 5 solution given for ① a), children can find most possible solutions by partitioning 5 or 9. A similar process could be gone through to partition 6 and 8, giving the additional solutions 2 + 4 + 8 and 6 + 1 + 7.

One further combination, 3 + 7 + 4, is not valid because it doesn't include a digit that Filip could have. Encourage children to think about which cards they have already used and which cards they have not to help them find more solutions.

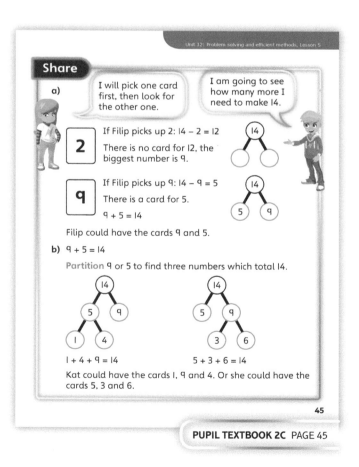

PUPIL TEXTBOOK 2C PAGE 45

Think together

Whole class teacher led (I do, We do, You do)

ASK

- *Why has a table been used to record the different possible ways to make 14?*
- *Why have 13 and 12 been crossed out? Will you need to cross out any other numbers?*

IN FOCUS This part of the lesson helps children understand that, instead of working randomly and choosing any starting card, they can work in a more systematic way, starting with the largest or smallest card and working through all possibilities. This is demonstrated in the table in question ❶.

STRENGTHEN Provide children with a set of number cards so they can play the game or explore for themselves. This will help children to see that they cannot use 7 + 7 = 14 because they only have one of each card.

DEEPEN Challenge children to find all of the possible ways to make 14 using 2 and 3 cards. This will provide an opportunity for children to realise that trial and improvement is a good strategy to get you started, but you need to move to working systematically to find all the possible solutions.

ASSESSMENT CHECKPOINT Assess whether children are working systematically or randomly choosing a starting point.

ANSWERS

Question ❶ : ~~3 + 11~~, ~~4 + 10~~, 5 + 9, 6 + 8, ~~7 + 7~~, 8 + 6, 9 + 5

Question ❷ : 1 + 4 + 9

2 + 3 + 9

5 + 1 + 8

5 + 2 + 7

5 + 3 + 6

Question ❸ : 5 + 9, 3 + 7 + 4

5 + 9, 2 + 8 + 4

5 + 9, 1 + 7 + 6

6 + 8, 1 + 4 + 9

6 + 8, 3 + 2 + 9

6 + 8, 5 + 2 + 7

6 + 8, 3 + 7 + 4

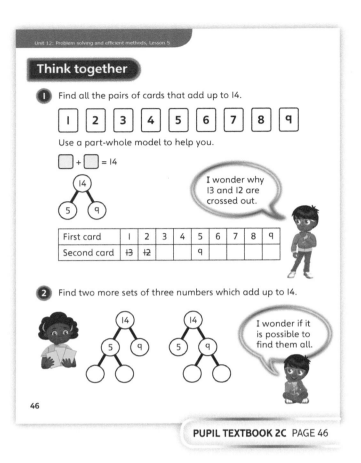

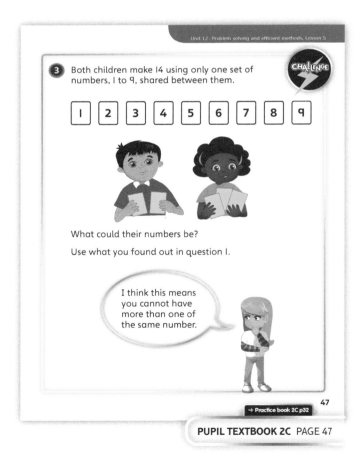

PUPIL TEXTBOOK 2C PAGE 46

PUPIL TEXTBOOK 2C PAGE 47

Practice

WAYS OF WORKING Independent thinking

IN FOCUS In this part of the lesson, children apply what they have learned about working systematically to questions with new totals. Question **3** requires children to think slightly differently as their place value understanding is tested.

STRENGTHEN Children who find these questions or the concept of only using a digit once difficult should continue to be provided with number cards to 'act out' the problem. If children find choosing a number to start from difficult, provide them with a starting point to work from.

DEEPEN Children who can complete the questions should be encouraged to find all the possible answers systematically. Questions **2** and **5** can be completed in many different ways. Question **2** is similar to the example from earlier in the lesson and the same restriction could be applied where each digit can only be used once. Question **5** also builds on work from the previous lesson.

ASSESSMENT CHECKPOINT For all questions, children should be able to explain how they have chosen to start the question, what they have learned from this starting point and how they can justify that their answer meets the criteria in the question. This will allow their understanding of addition, commutativity, place value and problem solving to be assessed.

ANSWERS Answers for the **Practice** part of the lesson appear in the separate **Practice and Reflect answer guide**.

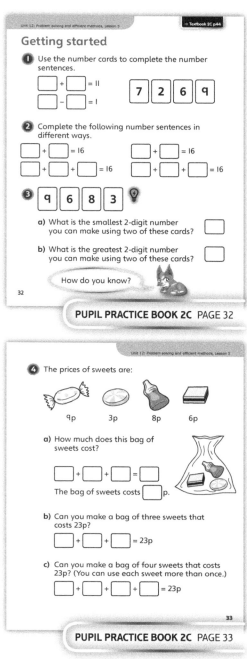

PUPIL PRACTICE BOOK 2C PAGE 32

PUPIL PRACTICE BOOK 2C PAGE 33

Reflect

WAYS OF WORKING Independent thinking

IN FOCUS This question again requires children to choose their own starting point. From this point they can use trial and improvement to try and complete the problem. Encourage children to find as many different ways to complete the problem as possible.

ASSESSMENT CHECKPOINT Children should be able to explain where they chose to start, why they chose this point and what they learned from this choice.

ANSWERS Answers for the **Reflect** part of the lesson appear in the separate **Practice and Reflect answer guide**.

After the lesson ⏸

- Were children comfortable with choosing their own starting point and making mistakes?
- What was a successful way to encourage children to take risks during the lesson?

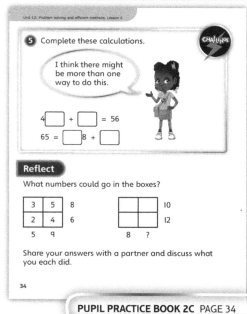

PUPIL PRACTICE BOOK 2C PAGE 34

Missing numbers

Learning focus

In this lesson, children will identify what they know from a question and use it to work out unknowns, rearranging number sentences as appropriate.

Small steps

→ Previous step: Getting started
→ **This step: Missing numbers**
→ Next step: Mental addition and subtraction (1)

NATIONAL CURRICULUM LINKS

Year 2 Number – Number and Place Value

Use place value and number facts to solve problems.

Year 2 Number – Addition and Subtraction

Recognise and use the inverse relationship between addition and subtraction and use this to check calculations and solve missing number problems.

ASSESSING MASTERY

Children can identify what is known and not known from a given problem and use their understanding of the inverse to rearrange a calculation to confirm what they need to calculate and which operation will be needed to achieve this. Children can use the bar model to visually represent this process.

COMMON MISCONCEPTIONS

Children are likely to see the numbers, but may ignore the context and so use the wrong operation. Ask:
• *Does using a bar model help work out which operation you need to find the answer?*

Children who use inefficient methods to calculate, such as counting in 1s, are likely to make errors. Ask:
• *What resources would help you to use a more efficient calculation method?*

STRENGTHENING UNDERSTANDING

Allowing children to work with resources to support mental calculations will increase efficiency and reduce errors from inefficient methods. Encourage children who find interpreting the question difficult to use the bar model to represent it. If they find this difficult, provide resources to manipulate the bars, such as coloured rods. If this is still too difficult, provide completed bar models to help children identify the necessary operation.

GOING DEEPER

Challenge children to explore how a whole that has been split into three parts can be represented in different ways, completing the fact family for these calculations.

KEY LANGUAGE

In lesson: missing number, unknown, altogether

Other language to be used by the teacher: represent, donate

STRUCTURES AND REPRESENTATIONS

Part-whole model, bar model, number line

RESOURCES

Mandatory: Base 10 equipment

Optional: coloured rods to create bar models, completed bar models, number line, blank part-whole models, bead string, place value counters, money

 In the eTextbook of this lesson, you will find interactive links to a selection of teaching tools.

Before you teach

• Will children find interpreting questions difficult?
• How will you support children during the lesson?

Discover

Unit 12: Problem solving and efficient methods, Lesson 6

WAYS OF WORKING Pair work

ASK

- *Can you rearrange the number sentences to show what you are trying to find out?*
- *Would using a bar model help with this process?*

IN FOCUS In this part of the lesson, children need to interpret what the question is asking them to calculate. They are provided with a number sentence as support, but encourage them to manipulate the sentence to show what they are trying to find out. For example, in question ① a), £55 = £20 + ? could be rearranged as £55 – £20 = ?. Support children with this by encouraging their use of the bar model to represent the amounts Marta has.

ANSWERS

Question ① a): £55 = £20 + £35

Marta had £35 before her birthday.

Question ① b): £55 + £45 = £100

Marta needs to save £45.

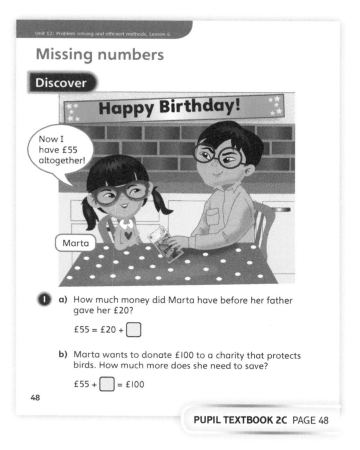

Missing numbers

Discover

Happy Birthday!

Now I have £55 altogether!

Marta

① a) How much money did Marta have before her father gave her £20?

£55 = £20 + ☐

b) Marta wants to donate £100 to a charity that protects birds. How much more does she need to save?

£55 + ☐ = £100

48

PUPIL TEXTBOOK 2C PAGE 48

Share

WAYS OF WORKING Whole class teacher led

ASK

- *How are the pictures similar? How are the pictures different?*
- *How do the number sentences relate to the models?*

IN FOCUS In this part of the lesson, children are exposed to different representations that show the problem and help to calculate the answer in an efficient way. The use of Base 10 equipment, for example, is an effective way to move children on to counting more efficiently than in 1s.

STRENGTHEN Some children may find other resources more useful to interpret the problem. Providing children with a choice of resources to use may increase effectiveness of the resource. Other resources that might be useful include bead strings, place value counters and real money.

Share

a)

I know one part is 20 and the whole is 55. I need to work out the missing part.

To find a part I can do a subtraction: 55 – 20 = ?

I can draw or use ▦ ▦ to help me.

55 = 20 + 35

Marta had £35 before her father gave her £20.

49

PUPIL TEXTBOOK 2C PAGE 49

Think together

WAYS OF WORKING Whole class teacher led (I do, We do, You do)

ASK

- *Can the bar model help to represent the problem?*
- *What method do you find the easiest to calculate each answer?*

IN FOCUS This section of the lesson allows children to use different methods to complete the same question. Some children may find some methods suggested difficult to use and as a result may use methods of their own.

In question ❸, it may not be obvious that the value represented by the star ❸ is the same for all calculations.

STRENGTHEN If children are unsure of what is known and unknown and, as a result, of what operation is needed to complete the question, allow them to use the bar model for support. The use of coloured rods or strips of paper will help with this process as children are able to move the bars around to understand the problem.

DEEPEN Children can continue the sequence of calculations found in question ❸ by either adding more calculations before or after the first and final calculations. Alternatively, they could create their own sequence of calculations that follows a similar pattern.

ASSESSMENT CHECKPOINT Check to see whether children can identify what is known and what is unknown. Can they then use what is known to calculate the unknown? Check to see if children can explain the different parts of the bar model and how this helps to identify the operation needed to complete the problem.

ANSWERS

Question ❶: $18 + 22 = 40$

$40 - 18 = 22$

22 more cups are needed to fill the box.

Question ❷: $38 + 30 = 68$

Joe needs 30p more.

Question ❸: ☆ = 34

$22 + 34 = 56$

$23 + 34 = 57$

$24 + 34 = 58$

$25 + 34 = 59$

$26 + 34 = 60$

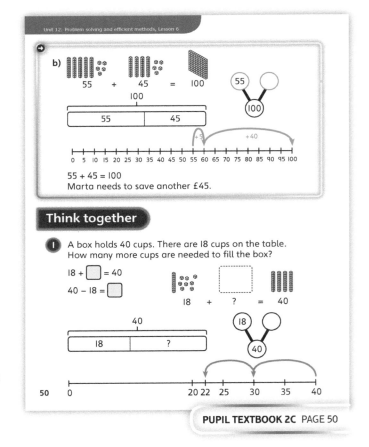

PUPIL TEXTBOOK 2C PAGE 50

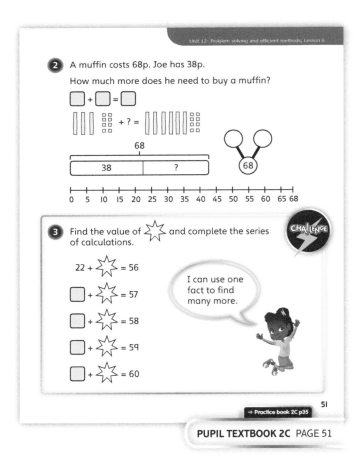

PUPIL TEXTBOOK 2C PAGE 51

Practice

WAYS OF WORKING Independent thinking

IN FOCUS These questions test children's understanding of the part-whole model, and how the parts and whole relate to each other and can be used to calculate unknowns. This is scaffolded in question ❶ as there are no unknowns and children can use number bonds to 20 to help recognise if a calculation would not make sense. Children's answers to question ❶ and how the parts and the whole relate can be used to support other questions. Question ❹ is open-ended and children can use their strategy from the lesson to work out different ways that it can be completed.

STRENGTHEN Children who find the part-whole model too abstract should continue to create bar models. Alternatively, provide a completed bar model for each question, although physically making the model will allow children to manipulate and move the parts to model the calculations they are recording.

DEEPEN Provide children with a part-whole model where the whole has been split into three parts. Challenge children to record all possible addition and subtraction calculations for this fact family.

ASSESSMENT CHECKPOINT Children should be able to verbalise what the parts and the whole are in each question and how knowledge of this helped them to solve each question.

ANSWERS Answers for the **Practice** part of the lesson appear in the separate **Practice and Reflect answer guide**.

Reflect

WAYS OF WORKING Independent thinking

IN FOCUS In this part of the lesson, all support has been removed and children must apply what they have learned throughout the lesson to the abstract calculations containing a missing number. At this stage, children may have different methods to solve the same problem and these should be shared with the class.

ASSESSMENT CHECKPOINT Check children's explanations of how they solved each question to assess their understanding of the relationship between the parts and wholes in additions and subtractions.

ANSWERS Answers for the **Reflect** part of the lesson appear in the separate **Practice and Reflect answer guide**.

After the lesson

- Have children mastered how the parts and the whole relate to each other in additions and subtractions?
- Did children learn different ways to solve the same questions from class discussions?

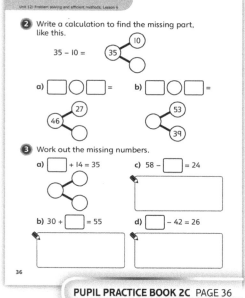

PUPIL PRACTICE BOOK 2C PAGE 35

PUPIL PRACTICE BOOK 2C PAGE 36

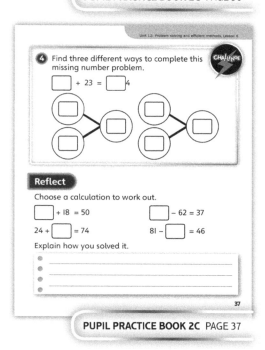

PUPIL PRACTICE BOOK 2C PAGE 37

Mental addition and subtraction

Learning focus

In this lesson, children will use what they know to calculate unknown quantities. Children will apply methods and strategies that they have learned in previous lessons.

Small steps

→ Previous step: Missing Numbers
→ **This step: Mental addition and subtraction (1)**
→ Next step: Mental addition and subtraction (2)

NATIONAL CURRICULUM LINKS

Year 2 Number – Addition and Subtraction

Solve problems with addition and subtraction using concrete objects and pictorial representations, including those involving numbers, quantities and measures.

ASSESSING MASTERY

Children can make links between questions and use these links in order to work in a more efficient manner. Children can apply calculation strategies learned from previous lessons and are flexible with the method that they use, based on the question they are presented with.

COMMON MISCONCEPTIONS

Children may not spot relationships between facts so they calculate from the beginning each time. Ask:
• *Can you use any known facts to help with the calculation?*

STRENGTHENING UNDERSTANDING

The use of manipulatives such as Base 10 equipment will help children be more efficient in their mental calculations.

GOING DEEPER

Encourage children to visualise the steps that they are completing during mental calculations. Being able to visualise numbers in this way and describe what they can see pictorially or in writing will help them work more effectively in this way.

KEY LANGUAGE

In lesson: calculate mentally, efficient, incorrect, addition, +, subtraction, –

Other language to be used by the teacher: method

STRUCTURES AND REPRESENTATIONS

Part-whole model, number line

RESOURCES

Mandatory: Base 10 equipment

Optional: bead string, number line

 In the eTextbook of this lesson, you will find interactive links to a selection of teaching tools.

Before you teach

- How will you support children who found it difficult to identify the unknown values in the previous lesson?
- How can we refine the methods used by children to be more efficient?

Discover

Pair work

ASK

- *What do you know?*
- *What do you need to find out?*
- *Can you represent the information as a bar model?*

IN FOCUS Children must look at the information given about Tim and his family and work out what they know and what they don't know. A bar model could help to determine this and how the known and unknown quantities relate to each other.

ANSWERS

Question ❶ a): Tim's brother is 17 years old.

Question ❶ b): Tim's mum is 37 years old.

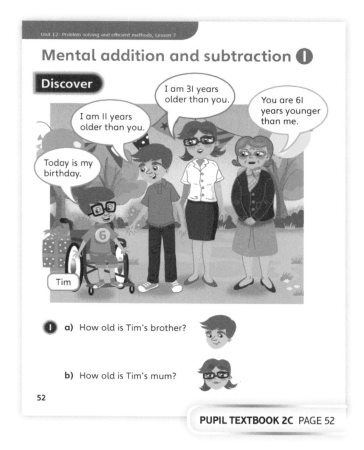

PUPIL TEXTBOOK 2C PAGE 52

Share

WAYS OF WORKING Whole class teacher led

ASK

- *What is the most efficient method that you can use?*
- *Can you use what you have already calculated to help you with the second calculation?*

IN FOCUS In this part of the lesson, it is important to discuss the different methods that children use to calculate the answers to the same question. Children may have become reliant on the column method and may resort to using that as suggested by Astrid. Discuss that this is not necessary and it is more efficient to mentally add the 1s as the mental calculation will not require regrouping.

Question ❶ b) could be answered by returning to Tim's age and calculating 31 years more than this, or by considering how many more years older Tim's mum is than Tim's brother, and working from the previous answer. It is likely that this will need to be modelled for children to understand.

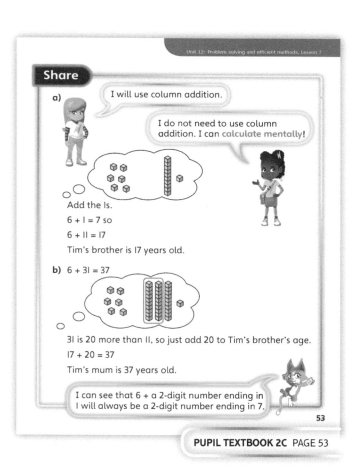

PUPIL TEXTBOOK 2C PAGE 53

Think together

WAYS OF WORKING Whole class teacher led (I do, We do, You do)

ASK

- *How can Base 10 equipment be used to help you work efficiently?*
- *Do you have to return to Tim's age to solve question* ❷ *? Why not?*

IN FOCUS This section of the lesson again allows children to discuss the different methods that can be used to solve the same problem. Question ❷ highlights that it is not always the most efficient method to return to the original information. If children were to do this they would then have to recalculate what they have already worked out, rather than simply working from a previous answer.

STRENGTHEN Using Base 10 equipment will help children discover different mental methods that they can use to calculate the age of the different family members. It will also make it easier for children to count on in 10s and 1s, rather than just 1s.

DEEPEN Encourage children to visualise the calculations that they complete mentally. Ask them to draw pictorially what they can see, or write down what they can see at different stages of their mental calculation.

ASSESSMENT CHECKPOINT Check to see if children are working in an efficient way, or if they are still counting on in 1s. Also, check to see that children are building on what they have already calculated, rather than returning to the original information each time. Question ❸ provides an opportunity to assess the different mental calculation strategies that children are comfortable using.

ANSWERS

Question ❶ : 6 + 61 = 67

Tim's grandma is 67 years old.

Question ❷ : 37 + 40 = 77 or 6 + 31 + 40 = 77

Tim's grandpa is 77 years old.

Question ❸ : Responses will vary. It is likely that children will be able to do most in their head but will find 36 + 7 and 36 − 7 most difficult as these questions cross the 10 boundary.

25 + 4 = 29	25 − 4 = 21
42 + 30 = 72	42 − 30 = 12
36 + 7 = 43	36 − 7 = 29
28 + 12 = 40	38 − 18 = 20

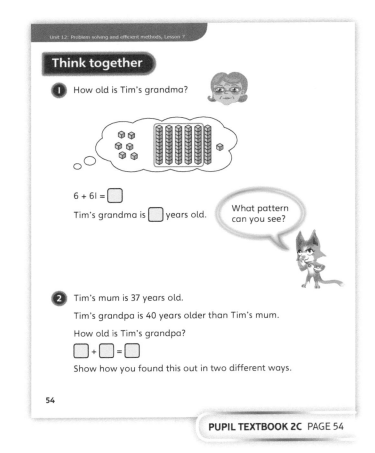

Unit 12: Problem solving and efficient methods, Lesson 7

Think together

❶ How old is Tim's grandma?

6 + 61 = ☐

Tim's grandma is ☐ years old.

What pattern can you see?

❷ Tim's mum is 37 years old.

Tim's grandpa is 40 years older than Tim's mum.

How old is Tim's grandpa?

☐ + ☐ = ☐

Show how you found this out in two different ways.

54

PUPIL TEXTBOOK 2C PAGE 54

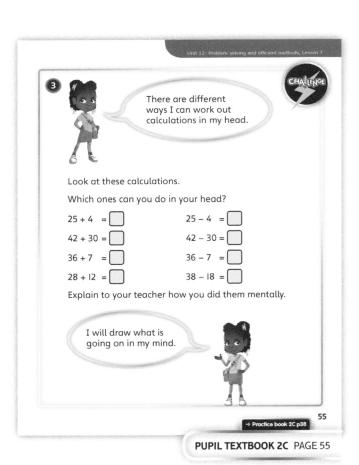

❸ There are different ways I can work out calculations in my head.

Look at these calculations.

Which ones can you do in your head?

25 + 4 = ☐	25 − 4 = ☐
42 + 30 = ☐	42 − 30 = ☐
36 + 7 = ☐	36 − 7 = ☐
28 + 12 = ☐	38 − 18 = ☐

Explain to your teacher how you did them mentally.

I will draw what is going on in my mind.

55

→ Practice book 2C p38

PUPIL TEXTBOOK 2C PAGE 55

Practice

WAYS OF WORKING Independent thinking

IN FOCUS The **Practice** questions allow children to apply what they have learned in this and previous lessons. Children should be making links between numbers in different calculations and using known facts to efficiently calculate unknowns. They are also required to identify errors within calculations and should explain how they know calculations are incorrect. Encourage their use of mental methods as they work through the problems.

STRENGTHEN Using resources, as modelled in question ❶ with the bead string, will help children make links between questions. If, in this example, two different bead strings are used, children will be more likely to be able to comment on what is the same and what is different in the different calculations.

DEEPEN Encourage children to continue to visualise the mental calculations they complete. Explaining these to each other or drawing a pictorial representation will again strengthen this process and expose children to different mental strategies.

ASSESSMENT CHECKPOINT Children should be able to explain how they know that calculations are incorrect or how they have used information effectively in order to be efficient. Check to see which children are treating each question as a new calculation and as a result are not being efficient.

ANSWERS Answers for the **Practice** part of the lesson appear in the separate **Practice and Reflect answer guide**.

Reflect

WAYS OF WORKING Pair work

IN FOCUS In this part of the lesson, the different methods that children have used throughout the lesson should be discussed. These can then be applied to the different questions presented. Children may have different methods to complete the same question and these again should be celebrated.

ASSESSMENT CHECKPOINT Check to see if children can apply an appropriate mental calculation for each calculation given. The method that they use should be an efficient way to solve the calculation, rather than used blindly.

ANSWERS Answers for the **Reflect** part of the lesson appear in the separate **Practice and Reflect answer guide**.

After the lesson

- Do children have a range of strategies that they can use appropriately according to the question type?
- Are children working in an efficient way for the majority of calculations?
- Can children visualise the maths that they are completing and explain what they see to their peers?

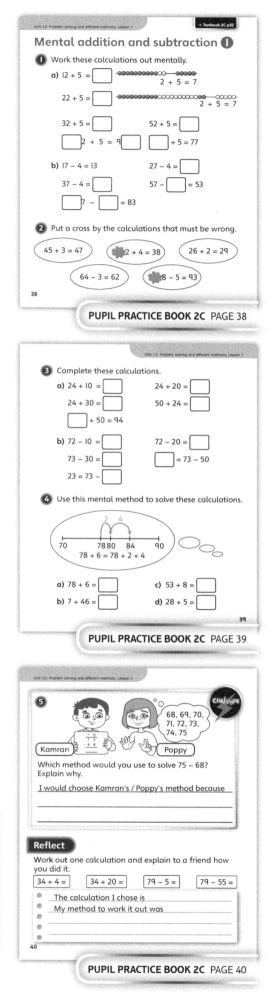

PUPIL PRACTICE BOOK 2C PAGE 38

PUPIL PRACTICE BOOK 2C PAGE 39

PUPIL PRACTICE BOOK 2C PAGE 40

Mental addition and subtraction ②

Learning focus

In this lesson, children will learn how to add or subtract a multiple of 10 to or from a number and then adjust to reflect the amount that should have been added or subtracted.

Small steps

→ Previous step: Mental addition and subtraction (1)
→ **This step: Mental addition and subtraction (2)**
→ Next step: Efficient subtraction

NATIONAL CURRICULUM LINKS

Year 2 Number – Addition and Subtraction

Solve problems with addition and subtraction using concrete objects and pictorial representations, including those involving numbers, quantities and measures.

ASSESSING MASTERY

Children can add or subtract a multiple of 10 to or from a number to represent a near multiple of 10 and then adjust the total appropriately to reflect the actual calculation.

COMMON MISCONCEPTIONS

Children are likely to confuse whether they should add or subtract 1 or 2 in the final stage of a mental calculation. For example, they may add 20 rather than 19 but then add another 1 to the total, rather than subtracting. Ask:
• *Can you show your calculation on a number line to show what needs to be added or subtracted?*

STRENGTHENING UNDERSTANDING

Using a number line will help children see the total amount that has been added or subtracted to or from a number and whether the final stage of the mental calculation requires addition or subtraction.

GOING DEEPER

Children should have the opportunity to work forwards and backwards through problems to gain a deeper understanding of the method. Working in pairs and explaining stages that they complete and then asking their partner to tell them the starting number, final number or whole calculation will also deepen their understanding.

KEY LANGUAGE

In lesson: adjust, addition, +, subtraction, –, difference, change

Other language to be used by the teacher: extra, count on

STRUCTURES AND REPRESENTATIONS

Number line, 100 square

RESOURCES

Mandatory: 1–100 number line, laminated 100 square

Optional: Base 10 equipment

 In the eTextbook of this lesson, you will find interactive links to a selection of teaching tools.

Before you teach

• Are children confident using a number line to show addition and subtraction?
• What are the barriers children may have to accessing the strategy taught in this lesson?

Discover

WAYS OF WORKING Pair work

ASK

- *Is it easier to add (or subtract) multiples of 10, or to use numbers like 19, 28 or 37?*
- *How could you use multiples of 10 to help with these calculations?*

IN FOCUS Use this part of the lesson to introduce children to the strategy of adding or subtracting a multiple of 10 to or from a number. Explain that this is an easier mental step and they can then adjust the answer by an appropriate amount to reflect the calculation that they are completing.

ANSWERS

Question ❶ a): A skateboard and a pair of knee-pads cost £45.

Question ❶ b): Gary's skateboard cost £37.

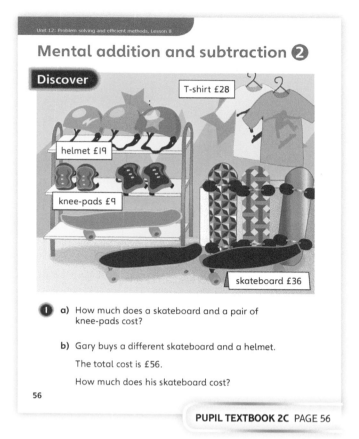

PUPIL TEXTBOOK 2C PAGE 56

Share

WAYS OF WORKING Whole class teacher led

ASK

- *What is the same and what is different for the methods used in parts a) and b)?*
- *Why don't you subtract as the final stage for both questions?*

IN FOCUS This section of the lesson visually demonstrates to children the process of making the next 10 and adjusting, using a 100 square and a number line. It will be useful for children to model the stages of the calculations on these representations in order to understand the process of adjusting and the differences between addition and subtraction.

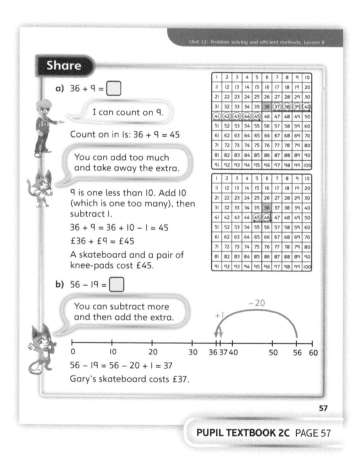

PUPIL TEXTBOOK 2C PAGE 57

Think together

Whole class teacher led (I do, We do, You do)

ASK

• *Why do you sometimes add and sometimes take away during the final step in the calculation?*
• *Can this only be used for numbers that are 1 away from 10?*

IN FOCUS These questions model adding and subtracting near multiples of 10 again using the 100 square and a number line. Questions **1** and **2** do not show the final adjusting stage and children must work out whether it is necessary to adjust by adding or subtracting 1 at the final stage.

STRENGTHEN Drawing the stages of the calculation on a number line will help to show what has been added or subtracted at different stages in the process. Using actual money alongside this will also help children to understand how much has been added or subtracted at different points.

DEEPEN Deepen understanding by challenging children to answer questions such as: *I start from a number, I add 20 to this number and then add another 1. The number that I finish on is 37. What calculation did I do?*

ASSESSMENT CHECKPOINT Check that children can verbalise why they either add or subtract within the final stage of the calculation process. If they can explain which operation is necessary then they understand the method.

ANSWERS

Question **1** : 54 + 19 = 73

54 + 20 − 1 = 73

The total cost is £73.

Question **2** : 50 − 29 = 21

50 − 29 = 50 − 30 + 1 = 21

Lois will get £21 change.

Question **3** : 56 − 29 = 27

37 + 18 = 55

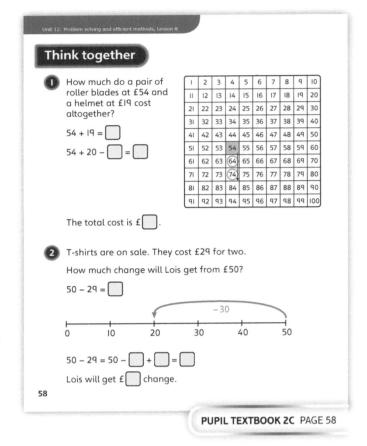

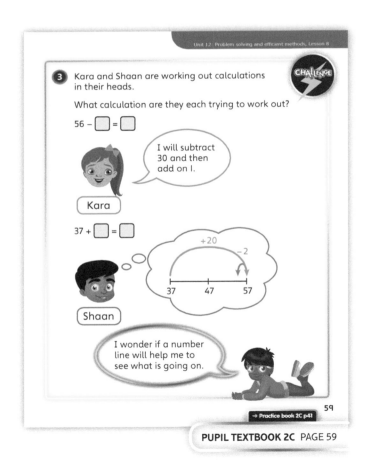

PUPIL TEXTBOOK 2C PAGE 58

PUPIL TEXTBOOK 2C PAGE 59

Practice

WAYS OF WORKING Independent thinking

IN FOCUS Questions ❶ and ❷ practise the method that has been introduced in the earlier parts of the lesson. Questions ❸ and ❹ practise a slight variation of the method as both numbers have been changed by the same amount to make the mental calculation easier. Children may need additional guidance for this method as they will need to be clear on what makes a calculation easier to complete mentally.

STRENGTHEN Allow children to continue to work with a 100 square or number line to enforce the use of this method, rather than an alternative method that children are more familiar and confident with.

DEEPEN Children can work in pairs to create questions for their partner to solve that are similar to question ❺ using either of the methods practised within this lesson.

ASSESSMENT CHECKPOINT Check to see if children can explain the mental calculations that they are completing and if they are using a particular method, such as partitioning or counting on or back.

ANSWERS Answers for the **Practice** part of the lesson appear in the separate **Practice and Reflect answer guide**.

Reflect

WAYS OF WORKING Independent thinking

IN FOCUS This section of the lesson allows children to demonstrate their understanding of the strategy that they have learned during the lesson. Allow children to complete this independently and then share and critique the accuracy of each other's explanations.

ASSESSMENT CHECKPOINT Check children's explanation to assess their understanding of the method learned in this lesson.

ANSWERS Answers for the **Reflect** part of the lesson appear in the separate **Practice and Reflect answer guide**.

After the lesson ⏸

- Are children able to effectively use the strategy of adding or subtracting near multiples of 10 to and from numbers?
- Would children benefit from additional practice to strengthen their understanding?

→ Textbook 2C p56   Unit 12: Problem solving and efficient methods, Lesson 8

Mental addition and subtraction ❷

❶ Complete these calculations.

26 + 9 = ☐   34 − 9 = ☐

43 + 8 = ☐   26 − 8 = ☐

27 + 29 = ☐   45 − 28 = ☐

68 + 28 = ☐   32 − 19 = ☐

Remember to do these in your head.

❷ Complete these calculations.

a) 78 + 18

To work this out, I can add ☐ and then subtract ☐.

78 + 20 − ☐ = ☐

b) 26 + 59

To work this out, I can add ☐ and then subtract ☐.

26 + 60 − ☐ = ☐

41

PUPIL PRACTICE BOOK 2C PAGE 41

❸ Samira draws this to help her answer 80 − 45.

80 − 45
(−1) (−1)
79 − 44 = 35

Use it to help you work out these calculations.

a) 70 − 38 = ☐   c) 90 − 49 = ☐

b) 30 − 17 = ☐   d) 100 − 26 = ☐

Explain how you got your answers.

_____

_____

❹ Draw lines to match the calculations that give the same answers.

35 + 19   39 − 26

90 − 55   45 + 20

40 − 27   34 + 20

47 + 18   89 − 54

42

PUPIL PRACTICE BOOK 2C PAGE 42

❺ ☐ − ☐ = 26   CHALLENGE

To work out this calculation, Dylan subtracted 40 and then added one. The answer was 26.

What calculation did he do?

Reflect

Write a top tip for adding 18.

• _____

Write a top tip for subtracting 19.

• _____

43

PUPIL PRACTICE BOOK 2C PAGE 43

Efficient subtraction

Learning focus

In this lesson, children will look at efficient methods for subtracting. They will be challenged to not always use the column method, but to choose an appropriate method based on the question they are presented with.

Small steps

→ Previous step: Mental addition and subtraction (2)
→ **This step: Efficient subtraction**
→ Next step: Solving problems – addition and subtraction

NATIONAL CURRICULUM LINKS

Year 2 Number – Number and Place Value

Use place value and number facts to solve problems.

ASSESSING MASTERY

Children can identify an appropriate and efficient subtraction method based on the question that they are presented with. Children start to spot patterns to help them with subtraction.

COMMON MISCONCEPTIONS

Children may feel that they have to use the column method for subtraction. Ask:
• *Is there a more efficient method you can use?*

STRENGTHENING UNDERSTANDING

Using a number line will help children to see alternative methods that could be used for some questions, such as 97 – 89. If children identify where 89 and 97 are on the number line they can see that counting on is an easier and more efficient strategy than using the column method.

GOING DEEPER

Ask children to create a list of their own calculations that best suit taking away, finding the difference, counting on and making 10. Children should be able to justify why each calculation best suits each method.

KEY LANGUAGE

In lesson: efficient, near, count on, take away, subtract, difference

Other language to be used by the teacher: break apart

STRUCTURES AND REPRESENTATIONS

Number line

RESOURCES

Mandatory: blank number line

Optional: counters, 100 square

 In the eTextbook of this lesson, you will find interactive links to a selection of teaching tools.

Before you teach

• Do children over-rely on the column method as the only way to calculate subtraction problems?
• How will you offer extra support to make them confident in an additional method?

Discover

Efficient subtraction

WAYS OF WORKING Pair work

ASK

- *Is the column method always the most efficient method to use for subtraction?*
- *When does using the column method make mistakes more likely?*

IN FOCUS In this part of the lesson, it is important to discuss the different methods that children in the class feel comfortable using for subtraction. It is also important to establish that at different times, different methods are more efficient.

ANSWERS

Question ❶ a): 61 − 18 = 43

Question ❶ b): 61 − 56 = 5

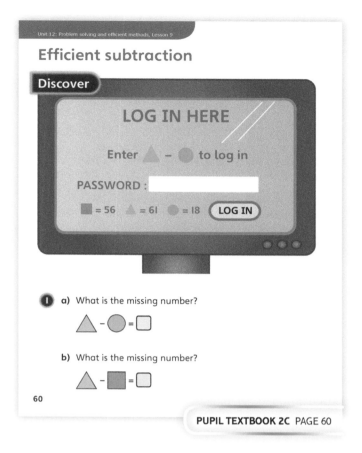

PUPIL TEXTBOOK 2C PAGE 60

Share

WAYS OF WORKING Whole class teacher led

ASK

- *Why is Astrid's method not efficient?*
- *What method would be more efficient to use?*

IN FOCUS Question ❶ a) models drawing 61 circles and crossing out 18 of them (a strategy that some children may suggest to use). Discuss whether this is an efficient method to calculate 61 − 18. Discuss how this calculation could be completed more efficiently mentally.

Question ❶ b) can be approached in two ways. Children could first subtract the correct multiple of 10 (50), and then the correct number of ones (6). Alternatively, they could find the difference by counting up from 56 to 61.

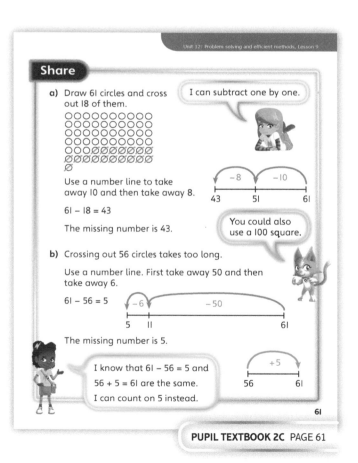

PUPIL TEXTBOOK 2C PAGE 61

Think together

WAYS OF WORKING Whole class teacher led (I do, We do, You do)

ASK

• *Is taking away the most efficient method to solve these problems?*

• *What resource could you use to show a more efficient strategy?*

IN FOCUS This part of the lesson requires children to consider what the most efficient method for subtraction is, rather than resorting to the column method.

STRENGTHEN Provide children with a number line that they can identify both numbers on, and a visual of the starting number as circles, as in question ❶, to clearly show if taking away is the most efficient way to solve the problem.

DEEPEN Challenge children to create their own questions that best suit taking away, counting on and rounding and adjusting (from the previous lesson).

ASSESSMENT CHECKPOINT Check to see which method children are choosing to use and if they can justify why this is the best method to use for each question.

ANSWERS

Question ❶ : 56 – 18 = 38

Question ❷ : 56 – 49 = 7   56 – 47 = 9

56 – 48 = 8   56 – 46 = 10

Question ❸ : 81 – 72 = 9 (count on)

48 – 8 = 40 (take away)

81 – 8 = 73 (round and adjust, 80 – 8 + 1)

72 – 24 = 48 (change to 72 – 48 = ? and use rounding and adjusting, for example 72 – 50 + 2)

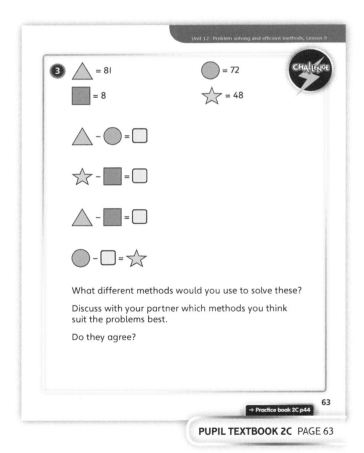

PUPIL TEXTBOOK 2C PAGE 62

PUPIL TEXTBOOK 2C PAGE 63

Practice

WAYS OF WORKING Independent thinking

IN FOCUS This part of the lesson provides an opportunity for children to work independently to choose the most efficient calculation method for each question.

STRENGTHEN Recording the information that they are given as a bar model may help children identify the most efficient method to use if they can see the relative size of the bars and relate this to the most appropriate strategy.

DEEPEN Ask children to draw a pictorial representation to demonstrate how the method they have used to solve each question is the most efficient.

ASSESSMENT CHECKPOINT Check to see if children can justify the method that they have chosen for each question and why they think this is the most efficient choice.

ANSWERS Answers for the **Practice** part of the lesson appear in the separate **Practice and Reflect answer guide**.

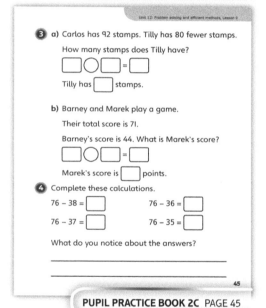

PUPIL PRACTICE BOOK 2C PAGE 44

Reflect

WAYS OF WORKING Independent thinking

IN FOCUS Allow children to work independently to choose the method that they believe is the most efficient to solve each calculation. Once the class have done this, allow them to share, critique and build on each other's opinions.

ASSESSMENT CHECKPOINT The quality of children's verbal or written explanations will allow you to make assessments of the clarity of their understanding of the different methods.

ANSWERS Answers for the **Reflect** part of the lesson appear in the separate **Practice and Reflect answer guide**.

After the lesson ⏸

- How did children respond to the methods presented in the lesson?
- Which method were children least comfortable using?
- How could children become more confident at using this method?

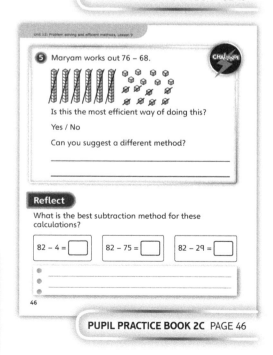

PUPIL PRACTICE BOOK 2C PAGE 46

Solving problems – addition and subtraction

Learning focus

In this lesson, children will solve a variety of different 1- and 2-step problems that will require appropriate calculation strategies.

Small steps

→ Previous step: Efficient subtraction
→ **This step: Solving problems – addition and subtraction**
→ Next step: Solving problems – multiplication and division

NATIONAL CURRICULUM LINKS

Year 2 Number – Addition and Subtraction

- Recognise and use the inverse relationship between addition and subtraction and use this to check calculations and solve missing number problems.
- Solve problems with addition and subtraction using concrete objects and pictorial representations, including those involving numbers, quantities and measures.

ASSESSING MASTERY

Children can decide fluently whether a problem involves addition, subtraction, or both operations. As a result of this understanding, they can choose appropriate strategies to solve the problem in an efficient manner.

COMMON MISCONCEPTIONS

Children may not use an appropriate method to solve the problem. Ask:
- *What method is the most efficient to solve the problem? What other methods have you considered?*

STRENGTHENING UNDERSTANDING

Support children to build bar models and manipulate the parts and the whole to increase their understanding of the problem and the likelihood that they choose the correct operation to solve the problem.

GOING DEEPER

Children should find the most efficient method for each problem. Ask children to explain why they think each method is the most efficient. Alternatively, challenge children to draw what they are visualising with their mental calculations.

KEY LANGUAGE

In lesson: bar model, total cost, change, left over, addition, +, subtraction, –, whole, part

Other language to be used by the teacher: represent, method

STRUCTURES AND REPRESENTATIONS

Bar model, part-whole model

RESOURCES

Mandatory: blank bar models

Optional: coloured rods or strips of paper to create the bar model, laminated part-whole diagrams

 In the eTextbook of this lesson, you will find interactive links to a selection of teaching tools.

Before you teach ⏸

- Will children find it difficult to interpret the problems?
- How will you provide additional support?

Discover

Pair work

ASK

- *What does total mean?*
- *Do you need to add or subtract for each question?*
- *How could the bar model be used to represent each question?*

IN FOCUS This part of the lesson begins with a simple addition problem. Children should be able to complete this question as a result of their place value knowledge, or by counting on from 58 in 4 jumps of 10.

The second part of the question is more complex and it is likely that children will need to draw the bar model in order to understand how to solve it. To solve the question, children will also have to remember that £1 = 100p.

ANSWERS

Question ① a): A cup of tea and a teacake costs 98p.

Question ① b): One piece of toast costs 48p.

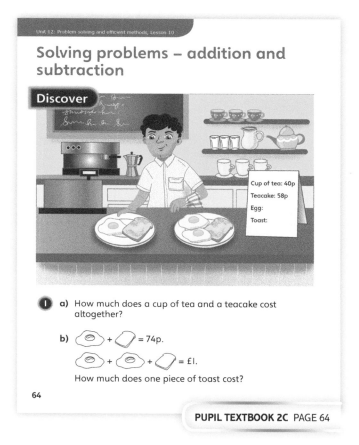

PUPIL TEXTBOOK 2C PAGE 64

Share

WAYS OF WORKING Whole class teacher led

ASK

- *Why has addition been used for the first question?*
- *How can you calculate the price of one egg in the second question?*
- *Can you represent all the information that you know as a bar model?*

IN FOCUS This part of the lesson highlights how the bar model can be used to represent all of the information that is known and what is required to be calculated. The part-whole model can then additionally be used to highlight that subtraction should be used to calculate the information that the question requires you to find: the price of the toast.

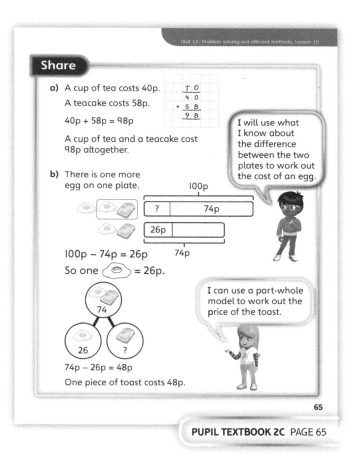

PUPIL TEXTBOOK 2C PAGE 65

Think together

WAYS OF WORKING Whole class teacher led (I do, We do, You do)

ASK

- *Where on each bar model shows the number that you need to find?*
- *What is the most efficient calculation strategy for each question?*

IN FOCUS In these questions, the bar model is provided to support children with the decision to use addition or subtraction. Children should be able to link the numbers shown on the bars to numbers found in the question and use this representation to establish whether addition or subtraction is needed to find the solution.

STRENGTHEN Making the bar model using rods of different lengths will allow children to move the rods around and gain a greater understanding of whether addition or subtraction is necessary.

DEEPEN Challenge children to create their own story that involves a combination of addition and subtraction. To deepen understanding further, ask them to draw a bar model including a ? to show what must be calculated.

ASSESSMENT CHECKPOINT Check to see if children can recognise whether a problem requires addition or subtraction. Assess whether children can explain how they know, with the use of a bar model to help, as opposed to guessing.

ANSWERS

Question **1** : 58p – 26p = 32p.

A teacake costs 32p more than an egg.

Question **2** : 70p – 40p – 26p = 4p

Filip gets 4p change.

Question **3** : = 30 cm

= 25 cm

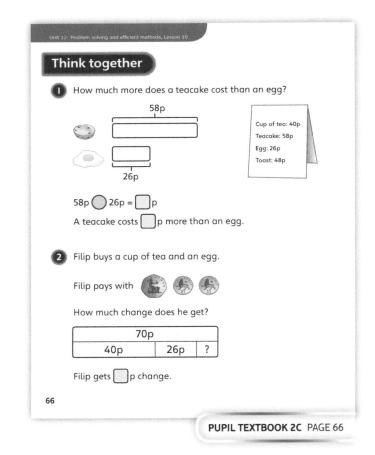

PUPIL TEXTBOOK 2C PAGE 66

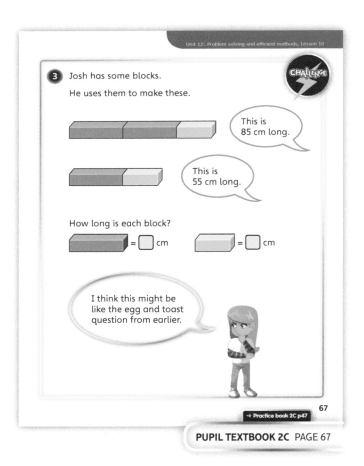

PUPIL TEXTBOOK 2C PAGE 67

Practice

WAYS OF WORKING Independent thinking

IN FOCUS In this part of the lesson, children are no longer provided with the bar model to assist them in making the decision about the appropriate operation to use. Encourage children to draw their own model to help them with this decision. Some questions are 2-step problems. Encourage children to keep a record of the information that they calculate as they go, rather than completing too many steps mentally, which may lead to errors.

STRENGTHEN Provide children with blank bar models with parts of appropriate sizes to match the questions. Children can then position values given to them in the question in appropriate parts to help them identify the operation they must use to solve the problem.

DEEPEN Challenge children to rank the difficulty of each question and justify why they think questions are easier or harder than each other. This will make children carefully consider the steps that they took to complete the question and the efficiency of these steps.

ASSESSMENT CHECKPOINT Check to see that children have chosen the correct operation for each question, that their bar models match the information provided in the question, and that the bars are in the appropriate orientation to each other.

ANSWERS Answers for the **Practice** part of the lesson appear in the separate **Practice and Reflect answer guide**.

Reflect

WAYS OF WORKING Independent thinking

IN FOCUS In this part of the lesson, children are required to work backwards from the abstract calculation and create a maths story to match. Allow children to do this independently and then share the different stories with the class.

ASSESSMENT CHECKPOINT Check to see whether children use appropriate mathematical language within their maths story. Children can be assessed to see if they can identify which calculation matches the maths story of others in their class.

ANSWERS Answers for the **Reflect** part of the lesson appear in the separate **Practice and Reflect answer guide**.

After the lesson ⏸

- Did children use the bar model effectively to model the problems that they were presented with?
- What was the most common misconception that the use of the bar model elicited?

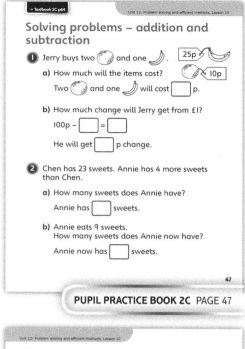

PUPIL PRACTICE BOOK 2C PAGE 47

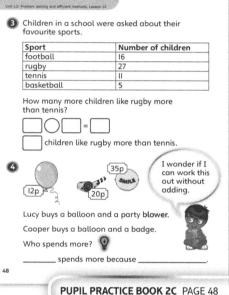

PUPIL PRACTICE BOOK 2C PAGE 48

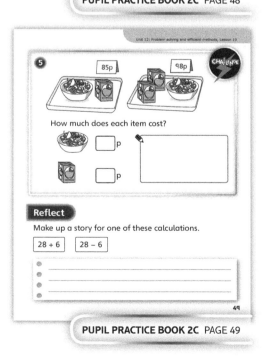

PUPIL PRACTICE BOOK 2C PAGE 49

Solving problems – multiplication and division

Learning focus

In this lesson, children will solve multiplication and division problems. They will decide if a problem requires multiplication or division to solve it, using the bar model to help make their choice.

Small steps

→ Previous step: Solving problems – addition and subtraction

→ **This step: Solving problems – multiplication and division**

→ Next step: Solving problems using the four operations

NATIONAL CURRICULUM LINKS

Year 2 Number – Multiplication and Division

- Solve problems involving multiplication and division, using materials, arrays, repeated addition, mental methods, and multiplication and division facts, including problems in contexts.
- Show that multiplication of two numbers can be done in any order (commutative) and division of one number by another cannot.

ASSESSING MASTERY

Children can decide fluently whether a problem requires multiplication or division. Children can choose appropriate strategies to solve the problem in an efficient manner.

COMMON MISCONCEPTIONS

Children may struggle to know which operation they need. They may simply look at the numbers and guess the operation, ignoring the context. Ask:

- *Can you use a bar model to show the operation you used to find the unknown?*

STRENGTHENING UNDERSTANDING

Give bar models to children who find it difficult to represent the problems, so they have a better chance of choosing the correct operation. Provide multiplication and division facts for children to select the appropriate fact from.

GOING DEEPER

Ask children to create their own maths story for multiplication or division, or both, in a multi-step problem, and draw their own bar model to represent the story. Children can then solve each other's problems in pairs.

KEY LANGUAGE

In lesson: multiply, ×, divide, ÷, bar model, total cost, share, equally

Other language to be used by the teacher: operation, equal parts

STRUCTURES AND REPRESENTATIONS

Bar model

RESOURCES

Mandatory: coloured rods to make the bar model (or pre-cut strips of card)

Optional: times-table facts

 In the eTextbook of this lesson, you will find interactive links to a selection of teaching tools.

Before you teach

- Do children need to recap key multiplication and division learning points before this lesson?

Discover

ASK

• *Can you draw a bar model to represent these problems?*
• *What needs to be the same for all of the bars?*

IN FOCUS In this part of the lesson, children are expected to apply what they have been practising during recent lessons, using the bar model for addition, subtraction, multiplication and division word problems. It is important for children to remember that for these questions it is vital that the bars are equal in length to accurately represent the question. Using repeated addition may help some children effectively make this jump.

ANSWERS

Question ❶ a): $5 + 5 + 5 + 5$ or $5 \times 4 = £20$

Question ❶ b): One ball costs £2.
Three balls cost £6.

Or, 3 is half of 6, so half of £12 = £6.

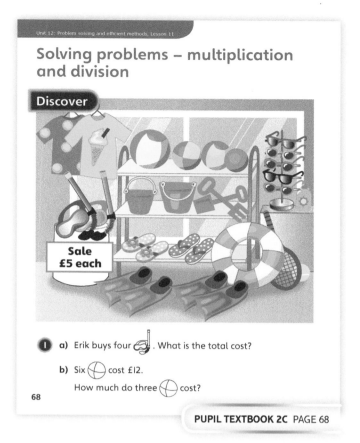

Solving problems – multiplication and division

Discover

❶ a) Erik buys four 🤿. What is the total cost?

b) Six ⊕ cost £12.
How much do three ⊕ cost?

68

PUPIL TEXTBOOK 2C PAGE 68

Share

WAYS OF WORKING Whole class teacher led

ASK

• *Do you always have to find the price of one item?*
• *Is there a more efficient way to calculate the answer?*
• *Who calculated the answer to part b) in the same way as Flo?*

IN FOCUS In this part of the lesson, children are shown each question using the bar model. This should help children to see how the bar model can be used for multiplication and division questions. Again, it is important to highlight to children that the bars in each question are equal in length.

Question ❶ b) also discusses halving as an alternative way to calculate the answer. This is more efficient than calculating the price of one ball and then multiplying by 3.

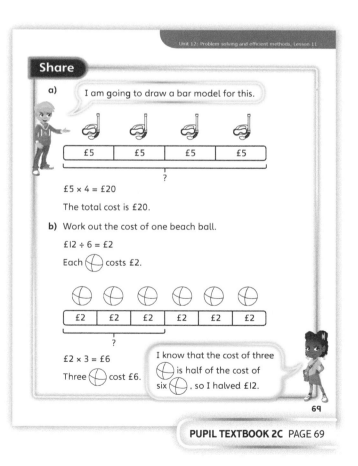

Share

a) I am going to draw a bar model for this.

| £5 | £5 | £5 | £5 |

$£5 \times 4 = £20$

The total cost is £20.

b) Work out the cost of one beach ball.

$£12 \div 6 = £2$

Each ⊕ costs £2.

| £2 | £2 | £2 | £2 | £2 | £2 |

$£2 \times 3 = £6$

Three ⊕ cost £6.

I know that the cost of three ⊕ is half of the cost of six ⊕, so I halved £12.

69

PUPIL TEXTBOOK 2C PAGE 69

Think together

WAYS OF WORKING Whole class teacher led (I do, We do, You do)

ASK
• *How does the bar model help you to work out if the question needs multiplication or division?*
• *What is the most efficient way to calculate each answer?*

IN FOCUS In this section of the lesson, children are provided with bar models to help with their decision of whether each question requires multiplication or division.
Question **3** shows a number of the same items grouped in different ways, for example, one box of 20 is the same as two boxes of 10. Some children may simply want to work out how many lollies there are altogether and then half this number. Alternatively, some may want to half each group, which they will find difficult for the boxes of 5 lollies, rather than create groups of the same number of objects.

STRENGTHEN Provide children who find skip counting or remembering division and multiplication facts difficult with times-table facts that they can refer to, to help with calculations.

DEEPEN Children can create their own story that involves either multiplication or division. To deepen understanding further, they can draw a bar model including a ? to show what must be calculated.

ASSESSMENT CHECKPOINT Check to see which children are able to correctly identify which questions require multiplication or division. They should be able to justify how they know, rather than just guessing.

ANSWERS

Question **1** : 10 × 2 = 20

There are 20 👟 altogether.

Question **2** : 30 ÷ 5 = 6

One pair of sunglasses costs £6.

Question **3** : Each child gets 30 lollies.

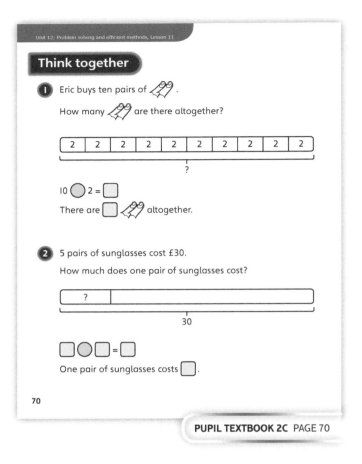

PUPIL TEXTBOOK 2C PAGE 70

PUPIL TEXTBOOK 2C PAGE 71

Practice

WAYS OF WORKING Independent thinking

IN FOCUS In the questions in this part of the lesson, children are no longer given bar models to help them. Encourage children to draw bar models in the space provided and record the calculation that they are completing.

STRENGTHEN Children who find drawing the bar model difficult should have the opportunity to make it with resources first, in order for mistakes to be made in a way that can easily be changed.

DEEPEN In question ④, challenge children to find how many different ways the packs of balloons can be shared between the two children. Although the end result will be the same, it will tackle the misconception that items must be shared in 1s.

ASSESSMENT CHECKPOINT Check to see that children have identified the operation correctly and that the bar model reflects the information given in the question accurately.

ANSWERS Answers for the **Practice** part of the lesson appear in the separate **Practice and Reflect answer guide**.

Reflect

WAYS OF WORKING Independent thinking

IN FOCUS In this section of the lesson, children are required to work backwards from the abstract calculation and create a word problem to match. Allow children to do this independently and then share the different stories with the class.

ASSESSMENT CHECKPOINT Check to see whether children use appropriate mathematical language within their maths story. Assess whether children can identify which calculation matches the maths story of other children in the class.

ANSWERS Answers for the **Reflect** part of the lesson appear in the separate **Practice and Reflect answer guide**.

After the lesson ⏸

- Which operation did children find most difficult?
- Would children benefit from additional practice of this operation before moving on?

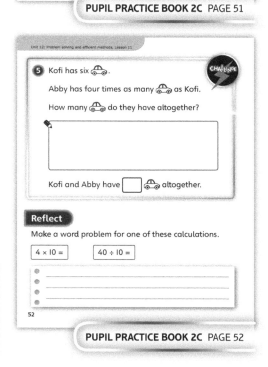

PUPIL PRACTICE BOOK 2C PAGE 50

PUPIL PRACTICE BOOK 2C PAGE 51

PUPIL PRACTICE BOOK 2C PAGE 52

Solving problems using the four operations

Learning focus

In this lesson, children will practise the four operations. They will solve problems with multiple steps and use the bar model to represent these steps.

Small steps

→ Previous step: Solving problems – multiplication and division
→ **This step: Solving problems using the four operations**
→ Next step: Telling and writing time to the hour and the half hour

NATIONAL CURRICULUM LINKS

Year 2 Number – Addition and Subtraction

Solve problems with addition and subtraction using concrete objects and pictorial representations, including those involving numbers, quantities and measures.

Year 2 Number – Multiplication and Division

Solve problems involving multiplication and division, using materials, arrays, repeated addition, mental methods, and multiplication and division facts, including problems in contexts.

ASSESSING MASTERY

Children can represent problems using the bar model and select the appropriate operation to solve the problem. Children carefully choose the most efficient method to solve the problem.

COMMON MISCONCEPTIONS

Children may mix up the operations needed to solve different problems. This is especially likely as this is the first time all four operations have been used in the same lesson. Ask:
• *Can you represent the problem using the bar model? How does this show which operation to use?*

STRENGTHENING UNDERSTANDING

Show examples of the four operations displayed in different ways using bar models. Children can make their bar model look the same by knowing the operation, or make a bar model based on information in the question and work out the operation from the examples. Making the bar model with rods before drawing it is easier.

GOING DEEPER

Ask children to identify where questions with more than one operation can be completed in different ways. Children should record the different ways of completing them and explain why others cannot be completed in this way.

KEY LANGUAGE

In lesson: bar model, representation, addition, +, subtraction, −, multiplication, ×, division, ÷, altogether, left over, difference, change

Other language to be used by the teacher: operation

STRUCTURES AND REPRESENTATIONS

Bar model, part-whole model, number line

RESOURCES

Mandatory: coloured rods

Optional: bar models showing the four operations, Base 10 equipment

 In the eTextbook of this lesson, you will find interactive links to a selection of teaching tools.

Before you teach

• What misconceptions have previously been seen that are likely to occur again?
• How will these misconceptions be addressed?

Discover

Unit 12: Problem solving and efficient methods, Lesson 12

WAYS OF WORKING Pair work

ASK

- *How many apples are in the bags? How many apples are in the boxes?*
- *Can you draw a bar model to represent this information?*

IN FOCUS In this part of the lesson, children are required, for the first time, to choose one of the four operations to solve the problem. Encourage children to work efficiently, and not to use repeated addition to calculate the answer.

ANSWERS

Question ① a): 6 × 2 = 12 apples in bags, 2 × 5 = 10 apples in boxes.

The total number of apples is 12 + 10 = 22 apples.

There are 22 apples altogether.

Question ① b): 3 × 5 = 15 apples. 25 − 15 = 10.

There are 10 apples left.

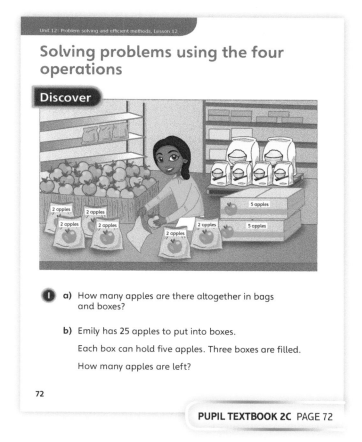

Solving problems using the four operations

Discover

① **a)** How many apples are there altogether in bags and boxes?

b) Emily has 25 apples to put into boxes.

Each box can hold five apples. Three boxes are filled.

How many apples are left?

72

PUPIL TEXTBOOK 2C PAGE 72

Share

WAYS OF WORKING Whole class teacher led

ASK

- *Why have the bars been arranged like this?*
- *Why are some of the bars the same length?*

IN FOCUS In this part of the lesson, children are presented with the information as a bar model. Discussions about these representations will help children to correctly make similar representations for later questions.

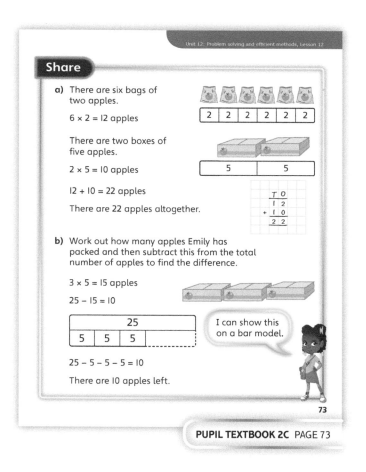

Share

a) There are six bags of two apples.

6 × 2 = 12 apples

There are two boxes of five apples.

2 × 5 = 10 apples

12 + 10 = 22 apples

There are 22 apples altogether.

b) Work out how many apples Emily has packed and then subtract this from the total number of apples to find the difference.

3 × 5 = 15 apples

25 − 15 = 10

25 − 5 − 5 − 5 = 10

There are 10 apples left.

I can show this on a bar model.

73

PUPIL TEXTBOOK 2C PAGE 73

Think together

WAYS OF WORKING Whole class teacher led (I do, We do, You do)

ASK

- *Why do some questions need more than one operation?*
- *Should all steps of the problem be done at the same time? Why not?*

IN FOCUS In this section of the lesson, children are initially provided with bar models and calculation scaffolds to help them interpret the question. These are then removed for question ❸ where children are required to apply what they have learned from previous questions.

In question ❸, children are required to recognise three different stages within one calculation. It may support children to think: 'First I will…', 'Then I will…', and 'Finally I will …'.

STRENGTHEN Provide resources, such as Base 10 equipment, to help children with their calculations. These are more favourable than leaving children to count in 1s to find the answer. Alternatively, provide key number facts that children could choose from to solve the questions.

DEEPEN Challenge children to make their own maths stories that use three operations at a time. Working in this open way will challenge children to find a context where this is possible and use numbers that will work for the three operations.

ASSESSMENT CHECKPOINT Check to see whether children can explain why, at different stages of each question, different operations are needed. Children should relate the answers that they give to both the information in the question and the bar model. Children should also be using known facts to calculate the answers rather than counting forward or backwards in 1s. Check to see how children are calculating each answer.

ANSWERS

Question ❶ : 3 × 10 = 30

2 × 4 = 8

30 + 8 = 38

The total cost of the rice is £38.

Question ❷ : 2 × 2 = 4

20 − 4 = 16

Mantas has £16 left.

Question ❸ : Liam can buy 5 small bags of rice.

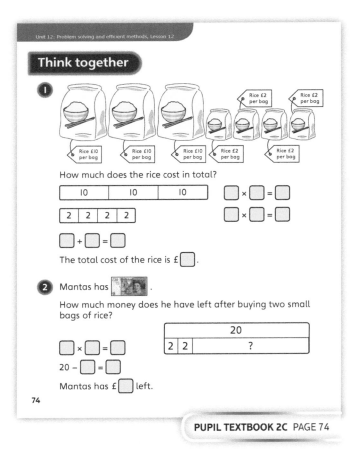

PUPIL TEXTBOOK 2C PAGE 74

PUPIL TEXTBOOK 2C PAGE 75

Practice

WAYS OF WORKING Independent thinking

IN FOCUS Questions in this section of the lesson allow children to practise using the four operations in similar situations and will challenge children's number sense. The questions begin with the operations being treated separately and then combine the operations within different steps of the problem in an increasingly difficult way.

Children have not been provided with a bar model for questions in this part of the lesson. Encourage children to draw a bar model to help them understand the necessary operation at different stages of the calculation.

STRENGTHEN Children may need support to correctly draw or make bar models for the more complex, multi-step questions. If this is a step too far, provide bar models, highlighting the different steps of the question.

DEEPEN It is possible to answer some questions in different ways or orders. Challenge children to explore the possibilities, using different strategies, and record these as written calculations.

ASSESSMENT CHECKPOINT Ask children to explain why they have chosen to complete the different steps of a question in a particular order. These explanations will allow you to assess their understanding.

ANSWERS Answers for the **Practice** part of the lesson appear in the separate **Practice and Reflect answer guide**.

Reflect

WAYS OF WORKING Independent thinking

IN FOCUS Give children the opportunity to work independently to write their own maths story problems based on the calculations given. Children should then have the opportunity to share their stories with others in the class.

ASSESSMENT CHECKPOINT Check to see whether the language that children use for the different stages of the story matches the operation that they are required to use.

ANSWERS Answers for the **Reflect** part of the lesson appear in the separate **Practice and Reflect answer guide**.

After the lesson ⏸

- Do children recognise the effectiveness of the bar model?
- Are children using the bar model of their own accord?

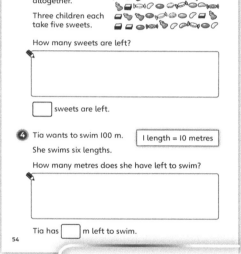

PUPIL PRACTICE BOOK 2C PAGE 53

PUPIL PRACTICE BOOK 2C PAGE 54

PUPIL PRACTICE BOOK 2C PAGE 55

End of unit check

Don't forget the *Power Maths* unit assessment grid on p26.

WAYS OF WORKING Group work – adult led

IN FOCUS The focus of these questions is whether children can select the appropriate operation as a result of the problems they are presented with, and solve these using an efficient strategy.

Think!

WAYS OF WORKING Pair work or small groups

IN FOCUS This question requires children to select an appropriate operation as a result of the information that they are provided with.

Children must work with multiplication and division at different stages of the question and self-identify where these stages occur.

Children should aim to work in an efficient way as a result of their mental calculations.

ANSWERS AND COMMENTARY Children who have mastered this unit will be able to fluently select the appropriate operation that is needed to complete a given step of a problem, and will be able to use the bar model to represent these problems. They will also be able to select an efficient method to solve the calculation, rather than simply using the column method by default.

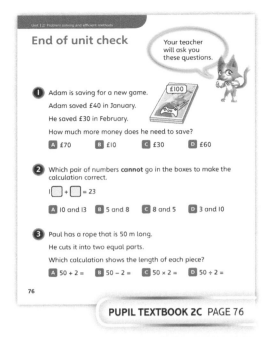

PUPIL TEXTBOOK 2C PAGE 76

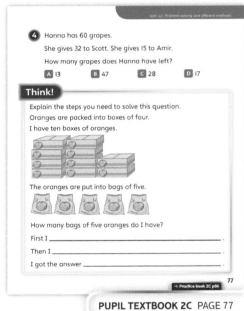

PUPIL TEXTBOOK 2C PAGE 77

Q	A	WRONG ANSWERS AND MISCONCEPTIONS	STRENGTHENING UNDERSTANDING
1	C	A suggests children have simply added the 2 numbers. B suggests children have simply subtracted one number from the other. D suggests children have calculated how much more money Adam needs just based on what he has saved in January.	Children who are still finding it difficult to interpret the word problems that they are given, and as a result are choosing the incorrect operation or guessing an operation based on the numbers that they see, should have additional exposure to the bar model.

Children should have the opportunity to build bar models as a result of reading or hearing word problems. They should also have the opportunity to create word problems of their own from completed bar models. Alternatively, they could match bar models to word problems and/or calculations. |
2	A	If children have answered B, C or D they are likely to have ignored the 1 before the first blank box indicating one ten.	
3	D	A, B or C suggest that children do not fully understand 'equal parts' or do not fully understand the context of the problem.	
4	A	B suggests children have simply added the number of grapes that Hanna has given away. C suggests children have only taken away the number of grapes that Hanna gave to Scott. D suggests they have calculated the difference between the number of grapes that Scott and Amir have been given.	

My journal

WAYS OF WORKING Independent thinking

ANSWERS AND COMMENTARY

First I multiply 4 by 10. $4 \times 10 = 40$. There are 40 oranges altogether.

Then I divide 40 by 5. $40 \div 5 = 8$.

I got the answer 8. There are 8 bags of 5 oranges.

If children are finding it hard to identify the correct operation to complete the different stages of the task, ask: *What does each number represent? Could you use resources to represent the oranges, the boxes and the bags? Could you draw a bar model to represent the information that you are given?*

Power check

WAYS OF WORKING Independent thinking

ASK

- *What mental calculation strategies did you use for addition problems at the beginning of this unit?*
- *What mental calculation strategies do you now have for addition problems?*

Power play

WAYS OF WORKING Pair work or small groups

IN FOCUS Use this **Power play** to assess whether children are confident at identifying when to use addition, subtraction and division. Children should be able to use mental strategies to calculate all the answers. There may be different methods used for the second part as some children may relate what each character drops to the original amount they had, rather than considering the amount as a whole. Discussions about efficiency of their methods could be had at this point.

ANSWERS AND COMMENTARY $26 + 24 = 50$ (6 ones and 4 ones = 10 ones = 1 ten, 2 tens + 2 tens + 1 ten = 5 tens). There are 50 pieces of bread in total.

There are 30 pieces of bread left. Children should be able to recognise that this can be calculated by combining the 13 pieces Hansel dropped and the 7 pieces Gretel dropped. They should use the known number fact $13 + 7 = 20$ and mentally subtract this from 50, either by counting backwards in jumps of 10 or using the known number fact of 5 tens – 2 tens is 3 tens.

Each bird gets 6 pieces of bread. 3 of the birds get 18 pieces altogether. Children should recognise that the problem requires division from the language 'share equally'. The most efficient method is to use the known fact $5 \times 6 = 30$ to calculate $30 \div 5 = 6$. Then use the number fact $3 \times 6 = 18$ to calculate 18 pieces for 3 birds together.

After the unit ⏸

- Are children now confident at selecting the correct operation needed to solve a problem?
- Do children understand how to be efficient in their calculations, and do they have a variety of different strategies to use?

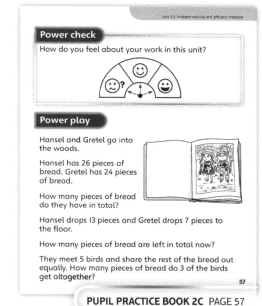

Unit 12: Problem solving and efficient methods → Textbook 2C p76

End of unit check

My journal

Explain the steps you need to solve this question.

Oranges are packed into boxes of four.

I have ten boxes of oranges.

The oranges are put into bags of five.

How many bags of five oranges do I have?

First I _____

Then I _____

I got the answer _____

56

PUPIL PRACTICE BOOK 2C PAGE 56

Power check

How do you feel about your work in this unit?

Power play

Hansel and Gretel go into the woods.

Hansel has 26 pieces of bread. Gretel has 24 pieces of bread.

How many pieces of bread do they have in total?

Hansel drops 13 pieces and Gretel drops 7 pieces to the floor.

How many pieces of bread are left in total now?

They meet 5 birds and share the rest of the bread out equally. How many pieces of bread do 3 of the birds get altogether?

57

PUPIL PRACTICE BOOK 2C PAGE 57

Strengthen and **Deepen** activities for this unit can be found in the *Power Maths* online subscription.

Unit 13
Time

Don't forget to watch the Unit 13 video!

Mastery Expert tip! "When I taught this unit, I used as many opportunities as possible outside of each lesson to practise the skills the children were learning. For example, I gave some children the responsibility to keep a check on five-minute reading activities and to let us know when five minutes had passed. They really enjoyed the practice!"

WHY THIS UNIT IS IMPORTANT

This unit will develop children's ability to tell and write the time to five minutes, including quarter past and to the hour. Children will link intervals of time to the number line, and know the number of minutes in an hour, and hours in a day.

Children will also use the number line to understand start and end times, and the interval of time between the two. Children will solve problems using these new concepts and previous learning, including word problems, and comparing and sequencing questions.

WHERE THIS UNIT FITS

→ Unit 12: Problem solving and efficient methods

→ **Unit 13: Time**

→ Unit 14: Weight, volume and temperature

This unit builds on the concepts of time learned in Year 1 and will draw on comparing and ordering skills, whilst linking to knowledge of the number line and part-whole model.

Before they start this unit, it is expected that children:
- can find o'clock and half-past times on an analogue clock
- can count forwards and backwards reliably in 5s up to 60
- recognise and understand the word 'quarter'.

ASSESSING MASTERY

Children who have mastered this unit will be able to read, write and show the time on a clock to five minutes. They will confidently use the vocabulary 'past', 'to', 'o'clock', 'half past', 'quarter past' and 'quarter to'. They will be able to use start times and end times to identify durations of time, and be able to use these elements to confidently solve mathematical problems. Children will recognise that there are 24 hours in a day and be able to explain how these 24 hours are represented and shown on an analogue clock.

COMMON MISCONCEPTIONS	STRENGTHENING UNDERSTANDING	GOING DEEPER
Children may confuse the two clock hands, either reading them incorrectly or drawing them incorrectly.	It may be beneficial to provide children with a colour-coded clock to manipulate (to help further, the hands could be labelled). If the colour-coding matched that in the **Pupil Textbook** then this would help secure the link between the concrete and pictorial representation.	Children could be challenged regularly to improve their fluency and recognition of key vocabulary by quizzing them on the words and coloured segments labelled on the clock.
Children may find the concept of recognising a quarter of the analogue clock, or which quarter is 'past' and which is 'to', difficult. For children who are struggling with this concept, you could provide a colour-coded clock face with the quarters labelled clearly on it.	The clock could also be labelled and colour-coded, where appropriate, with key vocabulary such as 'quarter', 'half', 'past', 'to'.	To do this you could take away one or two of the labels. Ask: *What is missing from the clock's labels? How do you know? What does that label mean?*

WAYS OF WORKING

Use these pages to introduce the unit focus to children. You can use the characters to explore different ways of working too.

STRUCTURES AND REPRESENTATIONS

Clock tool: Pictures of clock faces are used regularly to represent times. They are used for demonstration purposes and also as the basis of problems to solve. When presented with a clock face with no hands, children will be encouraged to complete these representations to demonstrate their understanding.

Number line: This model helps children visualise the order of numbers. It can help them count on and back from a given starting point and help them identify patterns within the count. In this unit the number line will be used to represent minutes within an hour and so will go from 0 to 60.

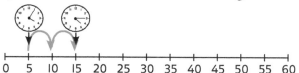

KEY LANGUAGE

There is some key language that children will need to know as part of the learning in this unit:

→ hands, face, hour, minute, analogue

→ o'clock, past, to, half past, quarter past, quarter to, quarter of an hour

→ almost, same, units, last, convert, how long, left, passed, shorter, longer, fastest, slowest

→ five, ten, fifteen, twenty, twenty-five, thirty, thirty-five, forty, forty-five, fifty, fifty-five, sixty

→ 5, 10, 15, 20, 25, 30, 35, 40, 45, 50, 55, 60

→ time, start time, end time, duration, time taken, finish, forwards, backwards, twice

→ 24 hours, day, daytime, night time, around the clock, am, pm

→ midday, midnight, morning, afternoon

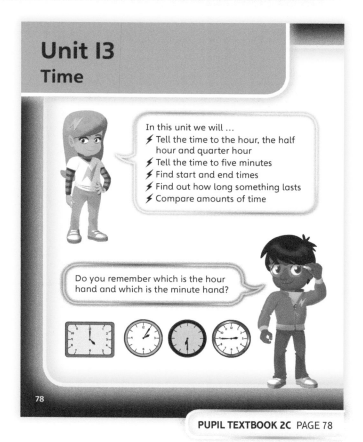

PUPIL TEXTBOOK 2C PAGE 78

PUPIL TEXTBOOK 2C PAGE 79

Telling and writing time to the hour and the half hour

Learning focus

In this lesson, children will recap their learning about measuring time. They will read and describe times to the hour and the half hour.

Small steps

→ Previous step: Solving problems using the four operations

→ **This step: Telling and writing time to the hour and the half hour**

→ Next step: Telling time to the quarter hour

NATIONAL CURRICULUM LINKS

Year 2 Measurement – Time

Tell the time to the hour and half past the hour and draw the hands on a clock face to show these times (year 1).

ASSESSING MASTERY

Children can confidently read analogue clocks showing times to the hour and the half hour. Children can identify and explain the meanings of the hour and minute hands, and can draw hands showing 'o'clock' and 'half-past' times on blank clock faces.

COMMON MISCONCEPTIONS

Children may confuse the two clock hands. Provide a colour-coded clock to manipulate, showing, for example, 2 o'clock. Ask:
• *What tells you that it is 2 o'clock? Which hand is showing that it is exactly to the hour and no minutes?*

Children may incorrectly assume that the hour hand 'jumps' from one hour to the next, without travelling gradually through the hour. This may lead children to draw 'half-past' times with the hour hand pointing directly at the hour. Show children a real clock, pointing at an 'o'clock' time. Ask:
• *What happens to the hour hand as we move to half past 2? Does the hour hand jump from one hour directly to the next?*

STRENGTHENING UNDERSTANDING

To strengthen understanding, give children pictures of different activities linked to a time of day, such as brushing teeth or going to bed, and get them to order these events on a storyboard with the clock times shown. Alternatively, ask children to draw their own pictures to create their own storyboard.

GOING DEEPER

Give children an investigation to find out what is happening around the school at different times of the day. Provide a time table with 'o'clock' and 'half-past' times listed against a blank space for them to record each activity. Children should be given the responsibility of checking the clock to know when to complete their investigations. While this will develop their ability to recognise the times, it will also have the added benefit of developing their awareness of how long an hour or half an hour 'feels'.

KEY LANGUAGE

In lesson: minute hand, o'clock, half past, hour hand

Other language to be used by the teacher: time, hour, minute, analogue

STRUCTURES AND REPRESENTATIONS

Colour-coded clock tool

RESOURCES

Optional: analogue clock manipulatives, vocabulary flash cards, analogue clock and written time flash cards

 In the eTextbook of this lesson, you will find interactive links to a selection of teaching tools.

Before you teach

• Is your classroom environment set up to allow for children to read the time easily and regularly?
• Could you provide children with experience of different types of analogue clock to develop their fluency?

Discover

Unit 13: Time, Lesson 1

Telling and writing time to the hour and the half hour

WAYS OF WORKING Pair work

ASK

- *What times do you recognise in this picture?*
- *Can you recognise and describe any patterns you can see in the clock times?*
- *What do you notice about where the hour hands are pointing in the half-past times?*
- *Which time is hidden?*

IN FOCUS Use the picture to recap and briefly assess children's current understanding. Begin by reinforcing the idea that the hour hand does not jump from hour to hour, but travels between each number gradually.

ANSWERS

Question **1** a): The trips leave at half past 11, 12 o'clock, half past 12, 1 o'clock, half-past 1 and 2 o'clock.

Question **1** b): The last clock will show half past 2.

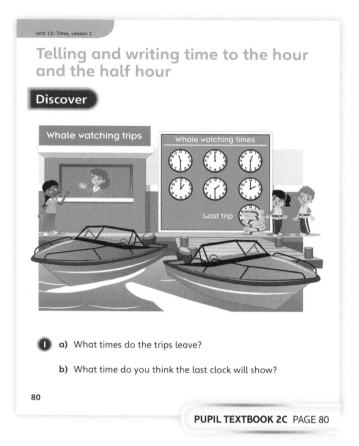

Discover

1 a) What times do the trips leave?

b) What time do you think the last clock will show?

80

PUPIL TEXTBOOK 2C PAGE 80

Share

WAYS OF WORKING Whole class teacher led

ASK

- *What would the clock look like if the boat left at X o'clock / half past X?*
- *Can you draw / make X o'clock / half past X?*
- *Why does the minute hand point to the 6 when it is a half-past time?*
- *What is the next half-past time after X o'clock?*

IN FOCUS Use this opportunity to recap the two potential misconceptions listed in the **Common misconceptions** section. Allow children the opportunity to show their understanding of times by showing times on clock manipulatives, drawing times onto blank clock faces or calling out times when shown different clocks.

PUPIL TEXTBOOK 2C PAGE 81

Think together

ASK

Question **1** :
- *Which hand is Dexter talking about? How do you know?*
- *How can you tell which hour it is? What hand should you look at?*
- *What might you be doing at that time of day?*

Question **2** :
- *What is different about this clock to the last one?*
- *What would you be doing at this time in the afternoon? What about in the morning?*
- *What do you recognise about the hour hand on this clock?*

IN FOCUS Questions **1** and **2** give children the opportunity to practise their recognition of 'o'clock' and 'half-past' times. Discuss with children the clues they can use to easily identify an 'o'clock' time and a 'half-past' time.

STRENGTHEN For all questions in this section of the lesson, encourage children to make the times shown. Additionally, have flash cards available with 'o'clock' and 'half-past' times on them, shown both on an analogue clock and as a time written in words. Ask: *Can you find the matching time and explain how you know it is the same? Is it an o'clock or half-past time?*

DEEPEN If children are successful in sorting all the clock faces shown in question **3** , ask if they are all the possible times that could be sorted into those categories. Ask: *Can you draw any missing times and put them in the correct circle? Can you explain how you know you have organised them correctly?*

ASSESSMENT CHECKPOINT At this point in the lesson, children should be able to confidently identify both the hour hand and minute hand on an analogue clock. They should be able to read 'o'clock' times and 'half-past' times. Assess whether children can recognise that, and explain how, the hour hand changes as the time moves from being on the hour to half past the hour.

ANSWERS

Question **1** : The time is 3 o'clock.

Question **2** : The time is half past 3.

Question **3** a): o'clock times: A, D, F

half-past times: B, C, E, G

Question **3** b): The minute hand points to the 12 for o'clock times.

Question **3** c): The minute hand points to the 6 for half-past times.

PUPIL TEXTBOOK 2C PAGE 82

PUPIL TEXTBOOK 2C PAGE 83

Practice

WAYS OF WORKING Independent thinking

IN FOCUS Question **1** offers the opportunity for children to recognise the differences between 'o'clock' and 'half-past' times. Ask: *What is different between 'o'clock' and 'half-past' times? How are the hands different?*

STRENGTHEN Question **2** requires children to practise recording the vocabulary of the times they have been studying in the lesson. Provide flash cards with the vocabulary written on them to assist children with this.

For children struggling with question **3**, offer them either plastic clock manipulatives to make the time shown or flash cards with different times shown as a picture of an analogue clock and in words.

DEEPEN For children who have recognised the mistake that Sam has made in question **4**, ask if they can write some advice for Sam. What will they say to help her understand her mistake? Encourage the use of pictures or resources to show her where she has gone wrong.

Question **5** could be deepened by requiring children to prove their ideas using evidence. Ask children to prove their ideas are correct using pictures or resources.

ASSESSMENT CHECKPOINT Children should be showing confident understanding of the minute and hour hands on an analogue clock. They should be able to clearly explain how the two hands look during an 'o'clock' time and a 'half-past' time and should be able to describe the similarities and differences they can see. Children should be able to confidently and accurately draw these times on to blank clock faces or make them using manipulatives.

ANSWERS Answers for the **Practice** part of the lesson appear in the separate **Practice and Reflect answer guide**.

Reflect

WAYS OF WORKING Pair work

IN FOCUS Give children time to come up with their own ideas about what is the same about the two types of times. Once they have done so and recorded their thinking, provide children with the opportunity to share their ideas with their partner. If they have different ideas, can they convince their partner that they are correct?

ASSESSMENT CHECKPOINT At this point in the lesson, children should be able to recognise the similarities between the two types of time. Listen to children's discussions and reasoning as, through discussing the similarities, they are also likely to discuss the differences too.

ANSWERS Answers for the **Reflect** part of the lesson appear in the separate **Practice and Reflect answer guide**.

After the lesson ⏸

- Are children able to confidently explain the differences between how the minute and hour hands work?
- How will you build in more opportunities to practise these skills throughout the school day?

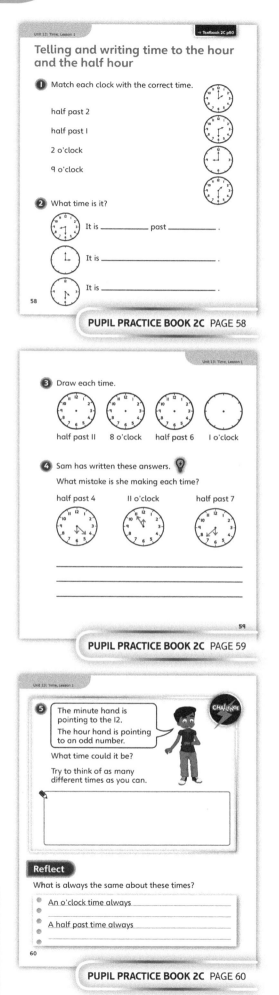

PUPIL PRACTICE BOOK 2C PAGE 58

PUPIL PRACTICE BOOK 2C PAGE 59

PUPIL PRACTICE BOOK 2C PAGE 60

Telling time to the quarter hour

Learning focus

In this lesson, children will describe times using the vocabulary of 'quarter past' and 'quarter to'. They will confidently read and record times on an analogue clock.

Small steps

→ Previous step: Telling and writing time to the hour and the half hour
→ **This step: Telling time to the quarter hour**
→ Next step: Telling time to 5 minutes

NATIONAL CURRICULUM LINKS

Year 2 Measurement – Time

Tell and write the time to five minutes, including quarter past/to the hour, and draw the hands on a clock face to show these times.

ASSESSING MASTERY

Children can identify 'quarter past' and 'quarter to', using the hour and minute hands, and match this vocabulary against pictures of appropriate clock faces. Children can recognise that the word 'past' refers to the previous hour and 'to' refers to the following hour, as well as being able to use their understanding to accurately record the hands on a blank analogue clock.

COMMON MISCONCEPTIONS

Children may find it difficult to recognise a quarter of the analogue clock or which quarter is 'past' and which is 'to'. Provide a colour-coded clock face with the quarters labelled clearly on it. Ask:
• *What hour is this quarter just past? What hour is this quarter leading to?*

STRENGTHENING UNDERSTANDING

To help children develop their fluency with half past, o'clock, quarter past and quarter to, draw a large chalk circle on the playground with those points of the clock labelled. Children should run to the correct point on the clock face when the vocabulary is called out by the teacher.

GOING DEEPER

Deepen understanding by asking children questions such as:
• *How many quarters of an hour are there in one hour?*
• *If the time was half past 2, how many 'quarters of an hour' would there be until half past 3?*
• *How about from 3 o'clock to quarter past 4?*

KEY LANGUAGE

In lesson: quarter past, quarter to

Other language to be used by the teacher: hour, minute, hand, time, o'clock, half past, almost

STRUCTURES AND REPRESENTATIONS

Colour-coded clock tool

RESOURCES

Optional: analogue clock manipulatives, vocabulary flash cards, analogue clock and written time flash cards, rope

 In the eTextbook of this lesson, you will find interactive links to a selection of teaching tools.

Before you teach ⏸

• Have the children made the link between their learning in this unit and the learning in the unit on fractions?
• How could you make this link explicit in your teaching?

Discover

Unit 13: Time, Lesson 2

WAYS OF WORKING Pair work

ASK

- *What times do you recognise?*
- *What do the two hands mean on the clock?*
- *Are there any times you cannot read? What is the same and different about those ones and the ones you do know?*
- *What time will the monkeys be fed?*
- *What does the hour hand look like on each clock face? Does it always point directly at an hour?*

IN FOCUS Use this picture as an opportunity to begin discussing the similarities and differences between the times the children have already learned and those that are new. Recap the potential misconception of not recognising how the hour hand moves during the hour to ensure children avoid the misconception later in the lesson.

ANSWERS

Question **1** a): The 🐅 will be fed at quarter past 5.

Question **1** b): The 🐧 will be fed at quarter to 6.

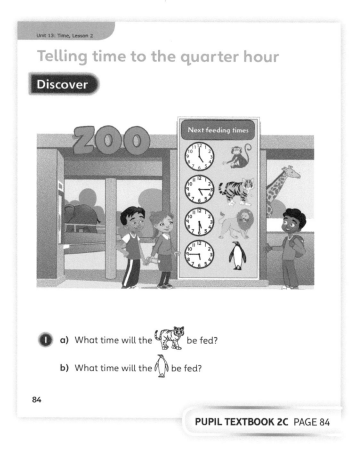

PUPIL TEXTBOOK 2C PAGE 84

Share

WAYS OF WORKING Whole class teacher led

ASK

- *What does a quarter of an hour look like?*
- *How is the minute hand changing for each clock time?*
- *What do you notice about where the hour hand is at quarter-past and quarter-to times?*
- *What time will the next quarter of an hour be? What would it look like?*
- *What does quarter 'past' mean? Past what?*
- *What does quarter 'to' mean? To what?*
- *If the time is quarter to the next o'clock time, how many quarters of an hour have gone by since the last o'clock time?*

IN FOCUS During this stage of the lesson, give children different times of when zoo exhibits open and close. When given the times, children could be asked to show the time using either a picture or an analogue clock they can manipulate. Be sure to reinforce the fact that the hour hand travels through the hours and does not jump from one to the next. To make this section more practical, 12 children could be arranged in a circle to mark the divisions on an analogue clock. Using two pieces of rope, one longer than the other, four other children could create the hands.

PUPIL TEXTBOOK 2C PAGE 85

Think together

WAYS OF WORKING Whole class teacher led (I do, We do, You do)

ASK

Question **1** :
• *How will you read the analogue clock?*
• *What clues can you look for to know if the time reads quarter to or quarter past?*

Question **2** :
• *Where is the minute hand pointing in the first clock? What about in the second clock?*

IN FOCUS The image in question **1** reinforces the idea of quarter to and quarter past. Use the shaded part of the picture to reinforce the concept.

STRENGTHEN In question **2** , if children are struggling to read the times, encourage them to use an analogue clock to help show the times. Ask them to start at 8 o'clock and move the minute hand through to quarter past. Does their clock match one of the clocks in the picture?

DEEPEN In question **3** , ask children to investigate how many different solutions they can find. Can they organise and explain their answer?

ASSESSMENT CHECKPOINT At this point children should be more confident when reading 'quarter-past' and 'quarter-to' times. They should be able to explain what is meant by this vocabulary and be able to record these times on both analogue clocks and pictures of blank analogue clocks. Look for their confident and fluent understanding and use of the minute and hour hands.

ANSWERS

Question **1** a): The reptile house opens at quarter past 10.

Question **1** b): The reptile house closes at quarter to 4.

Question **2** : You can meet the macaws at quarter past 8 and quarter to 3.

Question **3** : Children should make accurate times using pictures or concrete resources.

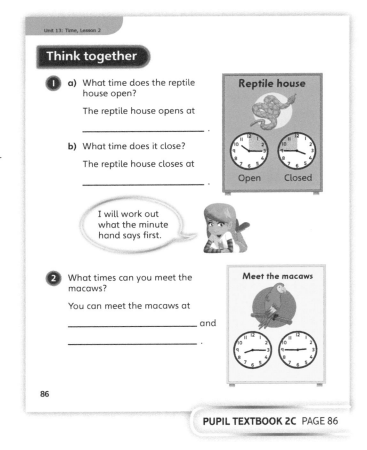

PUPIL TEXTBOOK 2C PAGE 86

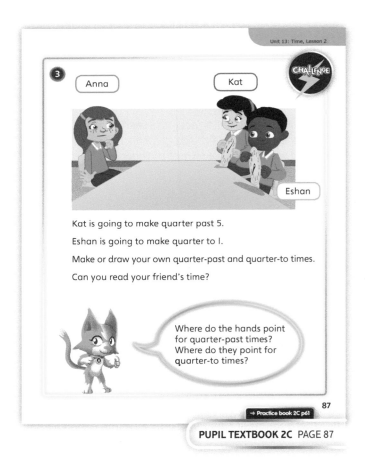

PUPIL TEXTBOOK 2C PAGE 87

Practice

WAYS OF WORKING Independent thinking

IN FOCUS Questions **1** and **2** scaffold children's understanding of 'quarter to' and 'quarter past' by providing them with shaded representations of the times. They also allow children the opportunity to work with clocks of different shapes and sizes to help develop their fluency.

STRENGTHEN For children struggling to match the clocks with the right times in questions **1**, **2** and **3**, it may be beneficial, as in the previous lesson, to offer children flash cards with the pictures and written names of times on them. Can children find the matching times? Ask children what clues they will look for in the pictures and in the written names. How could they use the clues to help them find the matching time more quickly?

DEEPEN Use question **5** to deepen children's reasoning and explanation skills. Ask children what part of the lesson they think Malik did not understand. Ask: *What would you say to Malik to help him understand?* Can children use a resource or picture to help Malik understand his mistake?

ASSESSMENT CHECKPOINT At this point in the lesson, the children should be able to confidently recognise and record 'quarter-to' and 'quarter-past' times on an analogue clock. They should be able to describe what is meant by 'to' and 'past' and how these relate to the preceding and following hours.

ANSWERS Answers for the **Practice** part of the lesson appear in the separate **Practice and Reflect answer guide**.

Reflect

WAYS OF WORKING Pair work

IN FOCUS This question offers a good opportunity to observe children's reasoning. Pay particular attention to children's reasoning when it comes to quarter to six and quarter past six. Ask children to explain why a clock, showing quarter past six, is not showing quarter to six. Can they explain how they are different?

ASSESSMENT CHECKPOINT Look for children to be able to explain the similarities and differences between the clock faces shown in the question. Children should be able to clearly explain why only one of the clocks shows the correct time.

ANSWERS Answers for the **Reflect** part of the lesson appear in the separate **Practice and Reflect answer guide**.

After the lesson ⏸

- How confident are children with the concept of 'to' and 'past'?
- How many opportunities were there to problem solve in this lesson?

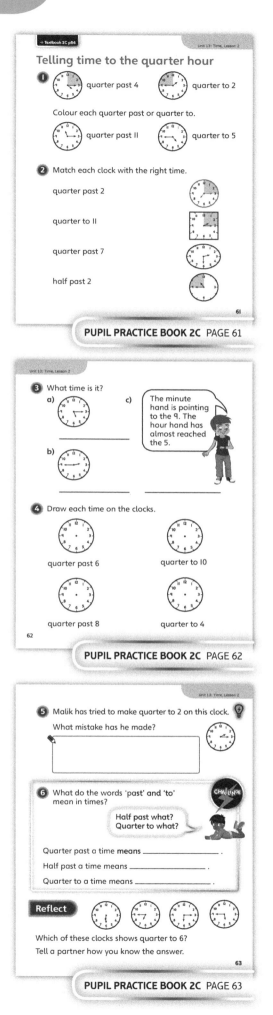

PUPIL PRACTICE BOOK 2C PAGE 61

PUPIL PRACTICE BOOK 2C PAGE 62

PUPIL PRACTICE BOOK 2C PAGE 63

Telling time to 5 minutes

Learning focus

In this lesson, children continue to develop their ability to read an analogue clock by learning to read the five-minute intervals. They will link this to their prior learning about half past, quarter to and quarter past.

Small steps

→ Previous step: Telling time to the quarter hour
→ **This step: Telling time to 5 minutes**
→ Next step: Minutes in an hour

NATIONAL CURRICULUM LINKS

Year 2 Measurement - Time

Tell and write the time to five minutes, including quarter past/to the hour, and draw the hands on a clock face to show these times.

ASSESSING MASTERY

Children can recognise any time where the minute hand is pointing directly to a number on the clock face. Children can read and record times on an analogue clock and link their understanding to the vocabulary they have already learned in the unit so far.

COMMON MISCONCEPTIONS

Children may confuse the numbers around the edge of the clock, showing the hours, with a representation of the minutes. For example, they may read 'five minutes past 10' as 'one minute past 10'. Ensure children are able to access a clock that has each individual minute marked around the clock face. Ask:
- *What do these small marks around the edge show? How many minutes have you counted when you get to the first number? How about the second number? How many minutes are in between each number?*

STRENGTHENING UNDERSTANDING

Children could be given opportunities to count in 5s through activities like counting games, counting songs and specially prepared dot-to-dots.

GOING DEEPER

Encourage children to look for times that they recognise around them. This could include investigating a specially prepared television scheduling magazine that shows the times either as written names or on analogue clocks. Can children create a timetable of programmes they would watch?

KEY LANGUAGE

In lesson: past, to, five

Other language to be used by the teacher: half, quarter, minutes, hour, o'clock, ten, twenty, twenty-five, thirty-five, fifty-five

STRUCTURES AND REPRESENTATIONS

Clock tool

RESOURCES

Optional: analogue clock manipulatives, vocabulary flash cards, analogue clock and written time flash cards

 In the eTextbook of this lesson, you will find interactive links to a selection of teaching tools.

Before you teach ⏸

- Are children confident counting in 5s?
- How will you make this lesson as hands-on as possible? What resources could you provide beyond the clocks?

Discover

WAYS OF WORKING Pair work

ASK

- *What time does the watch say?*
- *What time is five minutes from the time shown?*
- *What time would the bus have arrived if it had got there five minutes early?*

IN FOCUS When looking at this picture with children, present an analogue clock with minute divisions around the outside. Ensure that children recognise how the numbers around the outside do not match the minutes that the minute hand shows.

ANSWERS

Question ❶ a): The bus will arrive at twenty-five past 1.

Question ❶ b): The bus will arrive at twenty to 2.

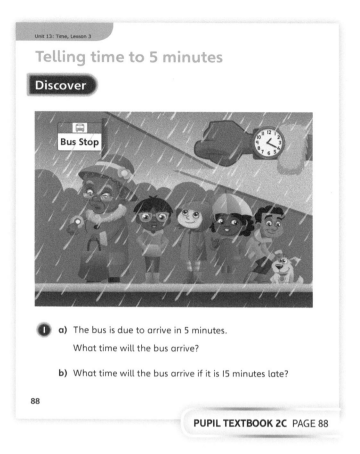

Telling time to 5 minutes

Discover

❶ **a)** The bus is due to arrive in 5 minutes.
What time will the bus arrive?

b) What time will the bus arrive if it is 15 minutes late?

88

PUPIL TEXTBOOK 2C PAGE 88

Share

WAYS OF WORKING Whole class teacher led

ASK

- *What are the numbers on the clock for? Do they show the number of minutes? How can you use them to help?*
- *What does X minutes past Y look like on a clock?*
- *What does it mean when the minute hand points to the number X?*
- *Why is it useful to know how to skip count in 5s when you are telling the time?*
- *What time is five minutes more than X past Y?*
- *How many minutes past the hour is half past X / quarter past X / quarter to X?*

IN FOCUS Be sure to make this part of the lesson as hands-on as possible. Ask children to match flash cards to the correct part of a clock. For example, a flash card saying 'ten to' should be matched to the number 10 on the analogue clock. Children could also move around a large clock drawn out on the playground, counting the five-minute intervals as they move.

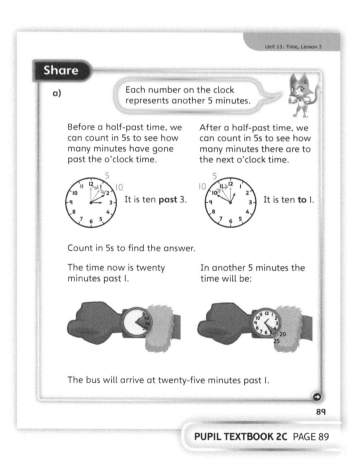

Share

a) Each number on the clock represents another 5 minutes.

Before a half-past time, we can count in 5s to see how many minutes have gone past the o'clock time.

It is ten **past** 3.

After a half-past time, we can count in 5s to see how many minutes there are to the next o'clock time.

It is ten **to** 1.

Count in 5s to find the answer.

The time now is twenty minutes past 1.

In another 5 minutes the time will be:

The bus will arrive at twenty-five minutes past 1.

89

PUPIL TEXTBOOK 2C PAGE 89

Think together

WAYS OF WORKING Whole class teacher led (I do, We do, You do)

ASK
- *How can you tell how many minutes past 6 it is?*
- *Do the numbers around the edge give you a clue?*
- *What could you count in to make it easier to read the minutes?*

IN FOCUS Question ❶ will help scaffold the children's counting in five-minute intervals. To secure their understanding that this segment represents 5 minutes, ask children to match the picture to an analogue clock showing all the minute divisions.

STRENGTHEN If children are struggling to tell the time in questions ❶ and ❷, offer them an analogue clock to make the number with. As the children move the minute hand round through the correct hour, count the five-minute intervals with them. Make sure to reinforce the 'past' and 'to' elements of the clock face. As well, offer children flash cards showing different minutes past and to. Can they match the picture they are looking at with one of the flash cards? Using the flash card, can they name the time in full?

DEEPEN If children have found all of the times between the two times given in question ❸, deepen their understanding by asking if there are any times that could be labelled in more than one way. As well, ask children if all hours have the same number of solutions. Can they explain?

ASSESSMENT CHECKPOINT At this point in the lesson, children should be more confident when counting in five-minute intervals. They should be increasingly fluent in their understanding and use of 'past' and 'to', recognising and explaining when to use each. They should be able to link their understanding of the vocabulary from the previous lesson with that of this lesson.

ANSWERS

Question ❶ a): Five minutes past 6

Question ❶ b): Twenty-five minutes to 7

Question ❶ c): Ten minutes past 6

Question ❶ d): Twenty minutes to 7

Question ❷ a): Twenty minutes past 3

Question ❷ b): Ten minutes to 4

Question ❷ c): Twenty-five minutes past 3

Question ❷ d): Five minutes to 4

Question ❸ : Children should make accurate times using pictures or concrete resources.

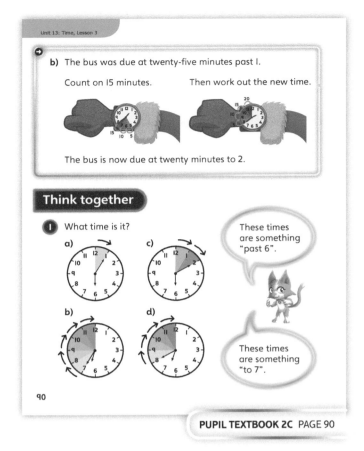

PUPIL TEXTBOOK 2C PAGE 90

PUPIL TEXTBOOK 2C PAGE 91

Practice

WAYS OF WORKING Independent thinking

IN FOCUS Question ❶ links the concept to children's real-life experience. It may be beneficial to have the pictures and vocabulary available as cutouts so children can manipulate and order them more easily. For questions ❶, ❷ and ❸, encourage children to make the times on an analogue clock so they can manipulate them.

STRENGTHEN As question ❹ is asked in a completely abstract way, ask children how they could make it easier to visualise the time on a clock. If the time is 'to' 8, what hour will they be counting within?

DEEPEN Use Ash's question in question ❺ to deepen children's thinking. How many times can children say in two different ways? Are there any times children can say in more than two ways? Is this the same for every hour?

ASSESSMENT CHECKPOINT At this point in the lesson, children should be able to confidently count around the clock in five-minute intervals. They should be able to use 'past' and 'to' fluently to describe the times they read and they should be able to link the vocabulary they have learned in previous lessons with the vocabulary learned in this lesson.

ANSWERS Answers for the **Practice** part of the lesson appear in the separate **Practice and Reflect answer guide**.

Reflect

WAYS OF WORKING Independent thinking

IN FOCUS Give children an opportunity to develop their own line of thinking. Ask them what representations of time they have worked with and how they could use them now to show the time.

ASSESSMENT CHECKPOINT Look for children recognising that, at twenty past, the minute hand should be pointing at the 4. Children's reasoning should make mention of the concepts they have covered so far. For example, they may have used a concrete representation or picture, counted in 5s on their fingers and/or looked back at their prior work.

ANSWERS Answers for the **Reflect** part of the lesson appear in the separate **Practice and Reflect answer guide**.

After the lesson ⏸

- Have children recognised how the concepts they have learned about in the past three lessons link?
- How will you reinforce this link?

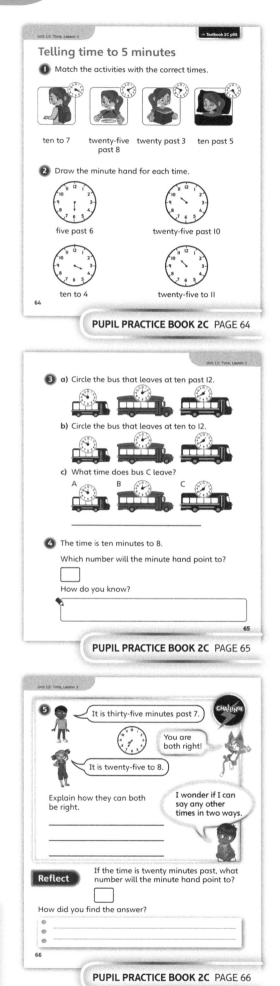

PUPIL PRACTICE BOOK 2C PAGE 64

PUPIL PRACTICE BOOK 2C PAGE 65

PUPIL PRACTICE BOOK 2C PAGE 66

Minutes in an hour

Learning focus

In this lesson, children will develop their understanding of how many minutes there are in an hour. They will use this understanding, and the representation of the bar model, to help them solve mathematical problems.

Small steps

→ Previous step: Telling time to 5 minutes
→ **This step: Minutes in an hour**
→ Next step: Finding durations of time

NATIONAL CURRICULUM LINKS

Year 2 Measurement - Time

Know the number of minutes in an hour and the number of hours in a day.

ASSESSING MASTERY

Children can recognise that there are 60 minutes in an hour and can show this understanding on an analogue clock. Children can use their understanding to calculate and convert durations expressed in minutes, or hours and minutes, up to 100 minutes.

COMMON MISCONCEPTIONS

Children may not recognise that they can continue counting in minutes once they reach the full 60 minutes in an hour. To help children understand this concept, link the representation of a clock face to the representation of a number line. Ask:
• *How are these two representations the same? How are they different? What would happen if you counted on from 60 on a number line? Could you do this on a clock face? How is the process different on a clock face to a number line? How is it similar?*

STRENGTHENING UNDERSTANDING

Offer children opportunities to count up in 5s and 10s, around a clock face with 12 interval markings but no numbers. This will help to reinforce the idea of counting around the circle, without needing to stop at the 12. When counting, ask: *Does this representation looks like anything you have met before? How is it similar to what you have seen? How is it different?*

GOING DEEPER

Challenge children to find how many minutes are in a set number of hours. Ask: *How many minutes are in one hour? Two hours? Three? Four?* Ask children to describe any patterns they find.

KEY LANGUAGE

In lesson: hour, minutes, longer, same, units

Other language to be used by the teacher: last, clock, convert

STRUCTURES AND REPRESENTATIONS

Blank clock face, number line, bar model

RESOURCES

Optional: Base 10 equipment, analogue clock manipulatives

 In the eTextbook of this lesson, you will find interactive links to a selection of teaching tools.

Before you teach 🕚

• Have children recognised that there are 60 minutes in an hour?
• How will you challenge those children in the opening part of the lesson?

Discover

Minutes in an hour

Discover

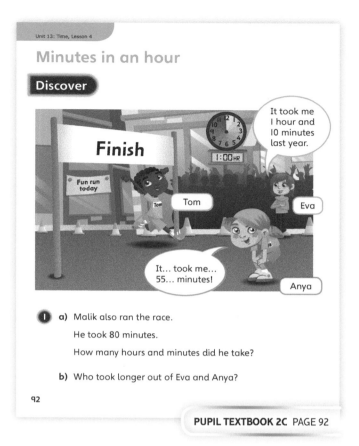

WAYS OF WORKING Pair work

ASK

- *What clocks can you see in the picture?*
- *Are there any new representations of time?*
- *How are those representations different to those you have seen before?*
- *Where would the minute hand point to if it was 55 minutes past the hour?*
- *Is a race result of 1 hour and 10 minutes faster or slower than 55 minutes?*
- *How many hours and minutes are in 80 minutes?*

IN FOCUS This picture will give children their first experience in this unit of a digital clock. Use this as an opportunity to discuss how that representation of time is different to what children have seen before. Additionally, to help children see that they can continue counting around a clock face for as long as they like, use the clock face in the picture to count the minutes in Eva's time. Children should follow the minutes with their fingers to help cement their understanding.

ANSWERS

Question ❶ a): Malik took 1 hour and 20 minutes.

Question ❶ b): Eva took longer.

❶ a) Malik also ran the race.

He took 80 minutes.

How many hours and minutes did he take?

b) Who took longer out of Eva and Anya?

92

PUPIL TEXTBOOK 2C PAGE 92

Share

WAYS OF WORKING Whole class teacher led

ASK

- *The clock says one hour. How many minutes is that?*
- *How can you prove that there are 60 minutes in one hour? Can you count in 5s to show me?*
- *If something lasts for 1 hour and 5 minutes, how many minutes is that? What about 1 hour and 10 minutes?*
- *If a whole hour is 60 minutes, can you use this to show how many minutes half of an hour is?*
- *Do you think it is easier to think of a time as 75 minutes or 1 hour and 15 minutes?*
- *How is 80 minutes less than 1 hour and 30 minutes when 80 is a bigger number than both 1 and 30?*

IN FOCUS At this point in the lesson, it is important to make sure that children are confident with the concept that minutes can continue to be counted after reaching the 60th minute. At all times during this section, make sure the link between the measurement of minutes, and hours and minutes, is made explicit. Ensure children are given sufficient opportunity to practise making this link.

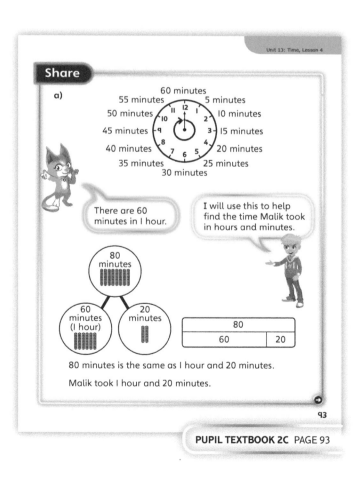

PUPIL TEXTBOOK 2C PAGE 93

Think together

WAYS OF WORKING Whole class teacher led (I do, We do, You do)

ASK

Question ① a):
• *How can you find out how many minutes are in one hour?*
• *Why is the full clock face coloured?*

Question ① b):
• *What do you need to do if you are counting the minutes in more than one hour?*
• *Why is there more than one clock face? Is that what it would look like if you were counting this in real life?*
• *How else could you represent the times?*
• *How does Base 10 equipment help you represent the times?*

IN FOCUS In question ① b), make sure children understand the image of the two clock faces as a representation of time, not to mean that there would be more than one clock face in real life. Support this idea by encouraging children to move the minute hand around a clock to match the question. Identify that this is possible on the same clock face.

STRENGTHEN If children are struggling with question ② , offer them the concrete and pictorial representations of times they have worked with so far to support their thinking. Ask children to count the minutes around a clock face. How many minutes did they count? Could they represent the minutes using another resource or picture?

DEEPEN Deepen conceptual understanding of question ③ by challenging children to create a mini lesson that explains how the part-whole model shows how many hours and minutes are in X minutes. Ask children to imagine they are going to introduce this to someone who has never seen it before. Can they prepare a short lesson that would help someone understand how the part-whole model shows how many hours and minutes are in X minutes? What concrete resources or pictures will they use? Children could be given a video recording device to record the mini lesson.

ASSESSMENT CHECKPOINT At this point in the lesson, look for children recognising they can count the minutes around a clock face, crossing the hour mark as many times as necessary. Children should be more confident at converting between hours and minutes and should be able to support their reasoning with concrete and pictorial representations, including Base 10 equipment and the bar model.

ANSWERS

Question ① a): 1 hour is the same as 60 minutes.

Question ① b): 1 hour and 5 minutes is the same as 65 minutes.

Question ② : 1 hour and 15 minutes is the same as 75 minutes.

Question ③ : 95 minutes is the same as 1 hour and 35 minutes.

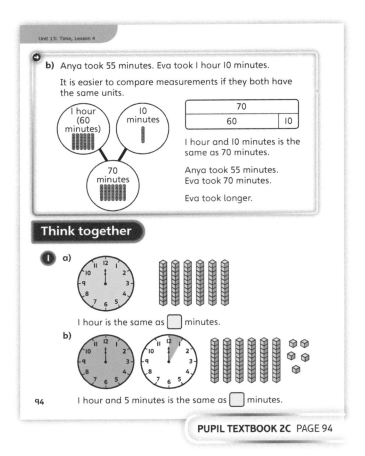

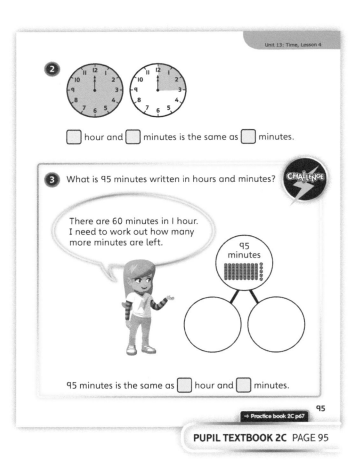

Practice

WAYS OF WORKING Independent thinking, pair work

IN FOCUS Questions **1**, **2** and **3** scaffold children's ability to find a number of minutes on the clock. To help them make the links between the part-whole model and the clock face, provide clock tools that the children can manipulate in order to count the minutes. As children move the minute hand, encourage them to colour in each five-minute segment.

STRENGTHEN If children are struggling with question **4**'s abstract representations of time, provide children with the concrete and pictorial representations they have been using thus far to create the times listed. Ask children if they could represent the minutes using another resource or picture. Which representation helped them compare times most clearly?

DEEPEN Challenge children to devise a word problem similar to question **4** and then swap problems with a partner. Can they use resources to show how they found the solution?

ASSESSMENT CHECKPOINT At this point in the lesson, children should be confident when converting hours to minutes and vice versa. Look for children to be using the concrete and pictorial representations they have worked with to support their reasoning. Children should also use these representations to help them compare and order times. Children should count the minutes around the clock confidently and fluently, and recognise when a given number of minutes will be greater or less than an hour.

ANSWERS Answers for the **Practice** part of the lesson appear in the separate **Practice and Reflect answer guide**.

Reflect

WAYS OF WORKING Pair work

IN FOCUS Introduce children to Astrid's idea and give them time to consider what their answer would be. Once they have done so, ask them to prove how many minutes are in an hour. Once children have fed back, give them time to discuss with their partner how they would help Astrid overcome her misconception.

ASSESSMENT CHECKPOINT Children should recognise that the numbers around the clock face do not directly link to the number of minutes they represent. They should be able to explain, and show, how they know there are 60 minutes in 1 hour.

ANSWERS Answers for the **Reflect** part of the lesson appear in the separate **Practice and Reflect answer guide**.

After the lesson ⏸

- Are children confident with how many minutes are in an hour?
- Are children secure converting from hours to minutes and from minutes to hours?

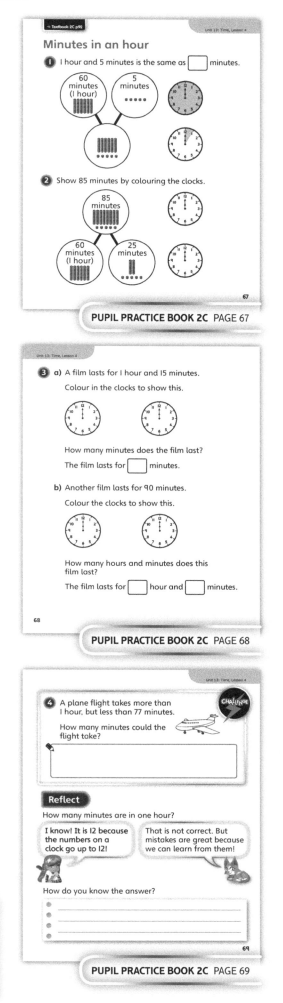

→ Textbook 2C p92

Minutes in an hour

1 I hour and 5 minutes is the same as ☐ minutes.

2 Show 85 minutes by colouring the clocks.

67

PUPIL PRACTICE BOOK 2C PAGE 67

Unit 13: Time, Lesson 4

3 a) A film lasts for I hour and I5 minutes.
Colour in the clocks to show this.

How many minutes does the film last?
The film lasts for ☐ minutes.

b) Another film lasts for 90 minutes.
Colour the clocks to show this.

How many hours and minutes does this film last?
The film lasts for ☐ hour and ☐ minutes.

68

PUPIL PRACTICE BOOK 2C PAGE 68

Unit 13: Time, Lesson 4

4 A plane flight takes more than I hour, but less than 77 minutes.
How many minutes could the flight take?

CHALLENGE

Reflect

How many minutes are in one hour?

I know! It is I2 because the numbers on a clock go up to I2!

That is not correct. But mistakes are great because we can learn from them!

How do you know the answer?

69

PUPIL PRACTICE BOOK 2C PAGE 69

Finding durations of time

Learning focus

In this lesson, children will use everything they have learned about counting time using an analogue clock to find the duration, in minutes, between two points of time.

Small steps

→ Previous step: Minutes in an hour
→ **This step: Finding durations of time**
→ Next step: Comparing durations of time

NATIONAL CURRICULUM LINKS

Year 2 Measurement – Time

Compare and sequence intervals of time.

ASSESSING MASTERY

Children can recognise two points in time and, using everything they have learned so far about counting time, find the duration between the two points of time.

COMMON MISCONCEPTIONS

When finding the duration, children may read the number of minutes past the hour as the duration. For example, thinking 'fifty minutes past 11' means 50 minutes have gone by, when in fact it depends on the start time. Ask:
• *Can you point to where you started and finished counting on the clock? Can you count again from the start point to the finish point? How many minutes did you count? Can you explain why it doesn't match what the clock says on its face?*

STRENGTHENING UNDERSTANDING

To support children before the lesson, ask children to count round the clock from different starting points. Begin by always counting to the 12 but move onto stopping the children's counting at other points. Alternatively, draw a large chalk clock face on the playground. Children all start at 12 on the clock. Roll a specially made dice to give children a number of minutes to move around the clock. Children score a point if they can say where they began, where they finished, and how many minutes they travelled.

GOING DEEPER

Children could be given the challenge of finding out the duration of the school day. Ask children how many minutes are in one lesson. How could they use this information to help them solve the problem? Once children have solved this, can they convert it to hours and minutes?

KEY LANGUAGE

In lesson: duration, how long?, left, passed, past, quarter, minute hand, start, end

Other language to be used by the teacher: amount, start time, end time, time taken, finish

STRUCTURES AND REPRESENTATIONS

Clock tool, number line

RESOURCES

Optional: analogue clock manipulatives, laminated pictures of clock faces, chalk, specially made dice

 In the eTextbook of this lesson, you will find interactive links to a selection of teaching tools.

Before you teach

• Are children confident at counting around a clock?
• Have children linked the representation of a number line with the clock face?

Discover

WAYS OF WORKING Pair work

ASK

- *Where can the children look to know when they will arrive?*
- *What will the clock look like at 5 o'clock? Can you make it?*
- *At the moment, are they closer to 4 o'clock or 5 o'clock?*
- *What is the finish time of their journey?*
- *How many minutes are left of the journey?*
- *How long will the total journey have been?*

IN FOCUS Use this picture to discuss the duration of some of the things children do. For example, when does swimming club start and finish? Show these times and discuss how long the club goes on for. What other things could we find the duration of time for?

ANSWERS

Question ❶ a): They have been travelling for 10 minutes so far.

Question ❶ b): There are 45 minutes left of the journey.

Share

WAYS OF WORKING Whole class teacher led

ASK

- *What is the start / end time? How can you work out how long it takes to get from the start to the end?*
- *Can you think of another way to work out the duration? Is there a way you can use clocks to help? Is there a way you can use a number line to help?*
- *What representations could you use to show the duration?*
- *If Mum had answered 'Nearly there. We will arrive at quarter to 5', how would the journey duration be different?*
- *Since the minute hand has ended on the 12, does that mean the duration was 60 minutes?*

IN FOCUS At this point in the lesson, children are introduced to the key vocabulary of 'duration'. It is important to scaffold the children's use of this word through your questioning and by supporting them in their explanations. Additionally, this would be a good point in the lesson to discuss how the duration can be different to the number of minutes past the hour. Provide children with times to record and find the durations between the times on either concrete or pictorial representations of analogue clocks.

125

Think together

WAYS OF WORKING Whole class teacher led (I do, We do, You do)

ASK

- *What is the start time? What is the end time?*
- *What does the shaded clock face show?*
- *How will you count the duration of time between the start and finish times?*
- *How could you show the duration in another way? Could you use a number line to show it?*
- *How will you record how many minutes the duration is?*
- *Could you record it in more than one way?*

IN FOCUS Questions ❶ and ❷ scaffold children's ability to recognise and find the duration between two times. These scaffolds are removed for question ❸ .

STRENGTHEN If children are struggling to use the representations to complete questions ❶ and ❷ , provide blank clock faces and ask children to mark the start times and the end times. They can then count the steps in between the two points to measure the duration of time.

DEEPEN In question ❸ , use Flo and Astrid's comments to help deepen the children's reasoning ability in this concept. Ask children if Astrid or Flo are correct in what they are saying. How would they show Astrid where she is getting muddled?

ASSESSMENT CHECKPOINT At this point in the lesson, children should recognise the word 'duration' as meaning the length of time between two points. When given start and end times, they should be able to find the duration of time between them. Children should also recognise how and why a measurement of duration can be different to the number of minutes the minute hand is pointing at.

ANSWERS

Question ❶ : Grandad takes 50 minutes to mow his lawn.

Question ❷ : Gran spends 45 minutes gardening.

Question ❸ : Gran plays for 30 minutes.

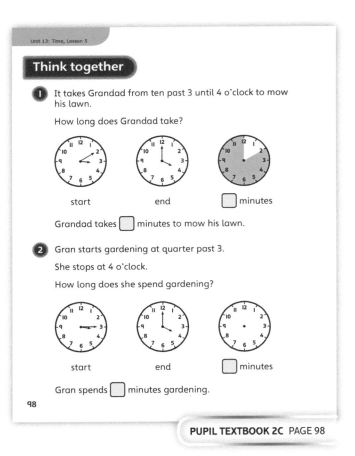

PUPIL TEXTBOOK 2C PAGE 98

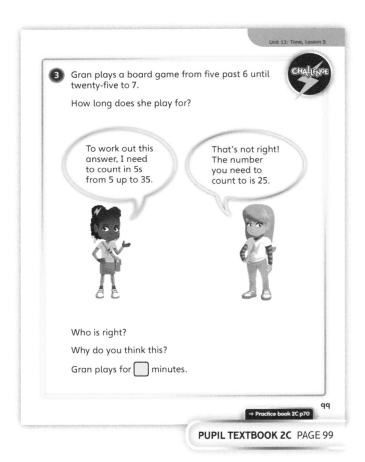

PUPIL TEXTBOOK 2C PAGE 99

Practice

WAYS OF WORKING Independent thinking

IN FOCUS Questions **1** and **2** offer children the opportunity to work with pictorial representations of time to develop their ability to find durations of time. Encourage children to use the shaded pictures in question **1** to support their thinking, although this could be further supported by allowing them to use concrete representations of an analogue clock to count the duration of time.

STRENGTHEN If children are struggling on question **3**, use Sparks' comment to help structure their thinking. Ask how converting all the times to 'something past 8' would help them find the duration. Could children use a number line to show how doing this would help? Encourage children to use an analogue clock, number line, or both, to help them find the duration of time.

DEEPEN If children are confident in finding the multiple solutions in question **5**, deepen their ability to work with durations of time by asking what the duration of the programme would be if there were 10 minutes of adverts in the middle. Children can choose the best representations to prove their ideas.

ASSESSMENT CHECKPOINT At this point in the lesson, children should be confident in finding durations of time. They should be able to use multiple representations to find and visually demonstrate durations of time. Look for children to be able to explain how they found the duration and use this understanding to independently solve problems.

ANSWERS Answers for the **Practice** part of the lesson appear in the separate **Practice and Reflect answer guide**.

Reflect

WAYS OF WORKING Pair work

IN FOCUS This question requires children to recognise a start and finish time presented in an abstract way. Give children an opportunity to independently develop their reasoning and then compare methods with a partner. Whose method was most efficient?

ASSESSMENT CHECKPOINT Children should be able to identify a start and finish time, and find the duration of time between them. Children should be fluently using the representations they have been studying over the lesson. Listen for children's reasoning as to why they have chosen the representation they did. Are they able to constructively and meaningfully critique their choice and that of their partner?

ANSWERS Answers for the **Reflect** part of the lesson appear in the separate **Practice and Reflect answer guide**.

After the lesson ⏸

- Are children confident in their use of the lesson's vocabulary?
- Can children confidently find a duration of time, when given the start and end times?

PUPIL PRACTICE BOOK 2C PAGE 70

PUPIL PRACTICE BOOK 2C PAGE 71

PUPIL PRACTICE BOOK 2C PAGE 72

Comparing durations of time

Learning focus

In this lesson, children will use their previous learning to find and compare two or more durations of time.

Small steps

→ Previous step: Finding durations of time
→ **This step: Comparing durations of time**
→ Next step: Finding the end time

NATIONAL CURRICULUM LINKS

Year 2 Measurement - Time

Compare and sequence intervals of time.

ASSESSING MASTERY

Children can find durations of time, in minutes and hours, when given start and end times. Children can use their understanding to compare the durations, explaining which is longer and which is shorter.

COMMON MISCONCEPTIONS

Children may think that a duration that ends later takes longer when, in fact, an activity may have started later and be shorter in duration. Ask:

* *Are you sure you have found the durations accurately? How could you check? Which duration is longer? What was the end point of that duration of time? Can you explain why the shorter time finishes later? What do you notice about the start times?*

STRENGTHENING UNDERSTANDING

To prepare children for this lesson, recap and reinforce their previous learning on comparing numbers. Provide children with two 2-digit numbers and ask them how they compared and ordered these numbers before. What representations did they use to show the value of the numbers and how did they use those representations to compare the numbers?

GOING DEEPER

If children are confident when ordering two durations of time, deepen their understanding by giving them the following challenge: *Joanna is planning her weekend. She has these activities to do.* [Give children a mixed timetable of hobbies and events with start and finish times. The timetable should have three or more activities on it – depending on the confidence of the child.] *She wants to know how long each activity will take and wants them put in order from the longest to the shortest activity. Can you help her?*

KEY LANGUAGE

In lesson: how long, start time, end time, minutes, hours, duration, o'clock

Other language to be used by the teacher: longer, shorter, finish, fastest, slowest, time taken

STRUCTURES AND REPRESENTATIONS

Clock, number line

RESOURCES

Optional: analogue clock manipulatives, laminated pictures of clock faces

 In the eTextbook of this lesson, you will find interactive links to a selection of teaching tools.

Before you teach ⏸

* Are children fluent at finding durations of time?
* What links between the representations and methods used in this lesson, and lessons where children have compared numbers, will you make explicit?

Discover

WAYS OF WORKING Pair work

ASK

- *Who has seen a sign like this in real life? Where would you find them?*
- *How long does it take to get from station X to station Y?*
- *What is the longest journey you could make?*
- *Could you show any of the times on the board using a resource or a picture?*
- *How many ways can you find to represent the duration of time a journey takes between station X and Y?*

IN FOCUS Use this picture as an opportunity to recap the skills learned in the previous lesson. Children will need to be secure in their ability to find durations to experience success in this lesson, so ensure this is skill is reinforced.

ANSWERS

Question ❶ a): Garforth to Hyde Park takes the longest.

Question ❶ b): It takes 55 minutes to go from Garforth to Whinmoor.

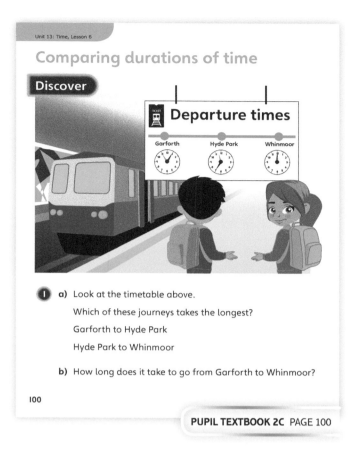

Share

WAYS OF WORKING Whole class teacher led

ASK

- *To compare two lengths of time, what information do you need to know?*
- *How can you find out how long something takes?*
- *What size jumps has Dexter used to count the minutes? Why has he counted like that?*
- *Which pair of times are easier to compare: 1 hour 15 minutes and 65 minutes or 75 minutes and 65 minutes?*
- *How has the number line helped you to compare the durations?*

IN FOCUS Use the example durations given in these problems as an opportunity to help children overcome the potential misconception. Encourage children to recognise that the second duration, while ending later, is actually shorter. To support this, encourage children to represent the duration in other, more concrete, ways, such as with Base 10 equipment.

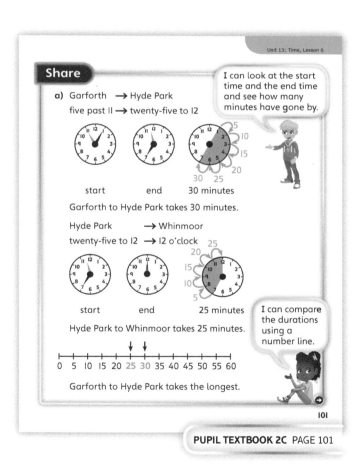

Think together

Whole class teacher led (I do, We do, You do)

ASK

- *How is finding durations in hours different to finding them in minutes?*
- *How will you find how many hours are between 3 o'clock and 6 o'clock?*
- *What will you use to compare the two durations?*
- *What resources could you use to help you?*

IN FOCUS It is important to make the distinction between question **1**, which asks for the duration in hours, and the questions that children have met so far, which have looked at durations in minutes. Ask children how the question is different to ones they have seen before. How will they use the numbers on the clock face differently?

STRENGTHEN When working on question **2**, provide children with laminated clock faces that they can draw on and colour in. Ask children to show the duration of each length of time as a picture. Their pictures should help them see which is longer and which is shorter.

DEEPEN Once children have demonstrated they can solve question **3**, deepen their understanding of this kind of time problem by challenging them to create their own. Ask children to write a similar question for a partner. Can they make a problem so their partner has to convert one of the times to match the other? Can they make a question that includes three times?

ASSESSMENT CHECKPOINT At this point in the lesson, children should have demonstrated that they are able to confidently measure durations of time in minutes and hours. Children should be able to compare durations of time, explaining which is longer and giving their reasoning. Look for children to support their reasoning with representations used in previous lessons.

ANSWERS

Question **1** : The bus takes 3 hours.

> The car takes 2 hours.

> 3 hours are more than 2 hours. The bus journey takes longer.

Question **2** : 1 hour and 30 minutes is more than 1 hour and 25 minutes, so the bicycle journey takes longer.

Question **3** : 70 minutes / 1 hour and 10 minutes is less time than 75 minutes / 1 hour and 15 minutes, so Maya ran faster.

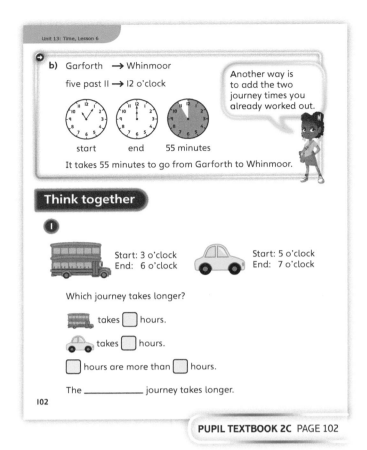

PUPIL TEXTBOOK 2C PAGE 102

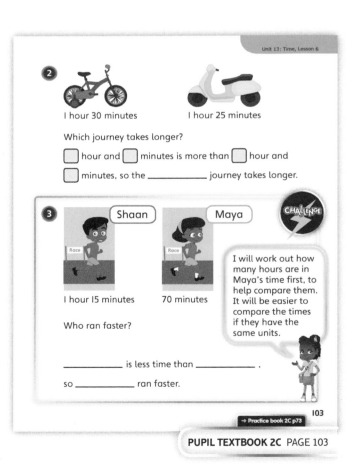

PUPIL TEXTBOOK 2C PAGE 103

Practice

WAYS OF WORKING Independent thinking

IN FOCUS It is important to note that question ① asks children to find durations in hours, not minutes. Children should be able to notice this independently by this point in the lesson through recognising the appropriate vocabulary.

For question ③, encourage children to colour the segments of time, either on the clocks shown in the question or on laminated clock faces. This will help children to cement the process of counting through a duration of time.

STRENGTHEN Questions ① and ② represent time in a purely abstract way. If children are struggling to recognise start and end times or the length of a duration of time, ask children how they could make these times easier to read and understand. How could they represent the times differently? Encourage the use of concrete resources and different representations to help children compare and order the durations.

DEEPEN Question ④ could be deepened by giving children blank clock faces to create their own start and end times. The children could then challenge each other to find the time durations between the start and end times they have chosen. When working on question ⑤, look for children to give their reasoning. Ask children to prove that they have found all possible solutions.

ASSESSMENT CHECKPOINT At this point in the lesson, children should be able to fluently measure durations of time in minutes and hours. They should be able to represent these measurements of time using concrete, pictorial and abstract representations and use these to demonstrate their conceptual understanding when comparing and ordering the times. They should be able to use their understanding to solve mathematical problems.

ANSWERS Answers for the **Practice** part of the lesson appear in the separate **Practice and Reflect answer guide**.

Reflect

WAYS OF WORKING Independent thinking

IN FOCUS Give children the opportunity to record their methods. Once children have had an opportunity to do this, ask children how they began the problem and what they compared. How did they know which was longer and which was shorter?

ASSESSMENT CHECKPOINT Look for clarity in children's explanation. They should be able to use the appropriate vocabulary to explain how they would use what they have learned to measure and compare the durations of time.

ANSWERS Answers for the **Reflect** part of the lesson appear in the separate **Practice and Reflect answer guide**.

After the lesson ⏸

- Were children able to distinguish how to use the clock to find durations in minutes and how to use the clock to find durations in hours?
- Did children make the link between comparing times and comparing the types of numbers they had compared previously?

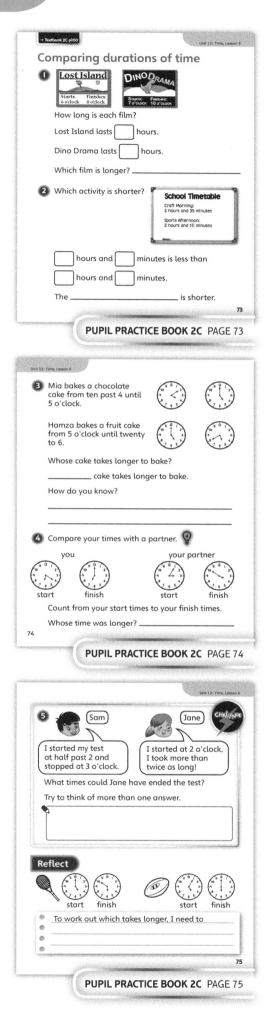

PUPIL PRACTICE BOOK 2C PAGE 73

PUPIL PRACTICE BOOK 2C PAGE 74

PUPIL PRACTICE BOOK 2C PAGE 75

Finding the end time

Learning focus

In this lesson, children will use their understanding of durations of time and counting around a clock to find an end time, when given a start time and a duration.

Small steps

→ Previous step: Comparing durations of time
→ **This step: Finding the end time**
→ Next step: Finding the start time

NATIONAL CURRICULUM LINKS

Year 2 Measurement – Time

Know the number of minutes in an hour and the number of hours in a day.

ASSESSING MASTERY

Children can recognise and confidently find a start time on an analogue clock. Children can fluently count the correct number of minutes to reliably find the end time of an event.

COMMON MISCONCEPTIONS

Children may incorrectly count a duration from a given start time. Ask:
• *Can you point to the start time? What duration have you been given? Can you count forwards in 5s?*

STRENGTHENING UNDERSTANDING

Introduce this concept by cooking with children in class. Provide children with a recipe and ask questions such as: *How long does the recipe say you should put the X in the oven for? If you put the X in at 12 o'clock, what time will you need to take it / them out?* Ask children to show how they know by using a plastic clock or by making a picture.

GOING DEEPER

To deepen children's ability and understanding of this concept, give them opportunities to work with multiple durations. For example, *Beatrice starts football club at 4:15. She warms up for 10 minutes and then plays for 15 minutes before taking a break. At what time does she have a break?*

KEY LANGUAGE

In lesson: end time, start time, taken

Other language to be used by the teacher: duration

STRUCTURES AND REPRESENTATIONS

Clock, number line

RESOURCES

Optional: analogue clock manipulatives, laminated pictures of clock faces, laminated or printed number lines

 In the eTextbook of this lesson, you will find interactive links to a selection of teaching tools.

Before you teach

• Are children confident with the vocabulary 'start time' and 'end time' from the previous lesson?
• What real-life experiences could you provide that would support the learning in this lesson?

Discover

WAYS OF WORKING Pair work

ASK

- *What time is showing on the clock?*
- *What will the time be in 20 minutes?*
- *How long does she need to wait in total for her bread to be made?*
- *Which duration of time is longer? 20 minutes or 30 minutes? How can you prove this?*

IN FOCUS Encourage children to link their learning from the previous lessons to this question. Discuss what is similar between this question and those that children have solved before, and what is different.

ANSWERS

Question ❶ a): The dough needs to go in the oven at twenty-five minutes past 1.

Question ❶ b): The bread should be taken out of the oven at fifty-five minutes past 1, or five minutes to 2.

Finding the end time

Discover

I need to leave the dough to rest for 20 minutes. Then it can go in the oven.

❶ a) What time does the dough need to go in the oven?

b) The bread needs to bake for 30 minutes. What time should it be taken out of the oven?

104

PUPIL TEXTBOOK 2C PAGE 104

Share

WAYS OF WORKING Whole class teacher led

ASK

- *What time is it in the picture? How do you know?*
- *The dough needs to be left for 20 minutes. How will the time change?*
- *What will the clock look like when the dough needs to go into the oven?*
- *Is there a way to use adding or counting on to help find the answer? How could you use a number line?*
- *Why does the number line stop at the number 60?*
- *Can you explain why fifty-five minutes past 1 is the same as five minutes to 2?*
- *Is there a way to check your solution?*
- *How is what you have done here similar to what you were doing in previous lessons? How is it different?*

IN FOCUS Ensure children are confident reading the time in the picture, and are clear that they they are being asked to work out the end time from a duration. You may want to provide plastic clocks in order to help children visualise the problem, and to draw their attention to how this question is similar to those in previous lessons.

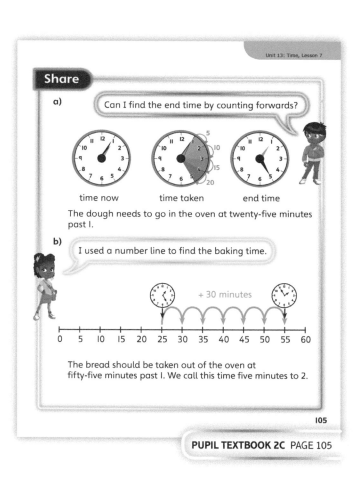

Share

a) *Can I find the end time by counting forwards?*

time now   time taken   end time

The dough needs to go in the oven at twenty-five minutes past 1.

b) *I used a number line to find the baking time.*

+ 30 minutes

0 5 10 15 20 25 30 35 40 45 50 55 60

The bread should be taken out of the oven at fifty-five minutes past 1. We call this time five minutes to 2.

105

PUPIL TEXTBOOK 2C PAGE 105

Think together

Whole class teacher led (I do, We do, You do)

ASK

- *What pieces of information do you need to find an end time?*
- *What will you find first?*
- *How will you use the start time and duration to find the end time?*
- *How can you use the number line to show how you found the end time?*

IN FOCUS Question **1** highlights the link between the analogue clock and the number line, and how children can use this link to help solve the problem. Make sure children understand this link as it will enable them to work more efficiently, using more easily recorded visual representations of time.

STRENGTHEN When children are working on question **2**, strengthen the link between the representations shown on the page and the number line. Ask children how they represented their working in question **1** and encourage the use of the number line to help with this question.

DEEPEN For children who have solved question **3**, deepen their ability to reason by asking where Lucy has gone wrong with her reasoning. What piece of learning is she missing and what advice would children give?

ASSESSMENT CHECKPOINT At this point in the lesson, children should be able to more confidently find an end time, recognising that they need a start time and duration to do so. They should be able to recognise and explain how a number line can help them find an end time.

ANSWERS

Question **1** : The pizza will be ready at quarter to 7 (forty-five minutes past 6).

Question **2** : The cookies will be ready at ten to 8 (fifty minutes past 7).

Question **3** : Filip is correct.

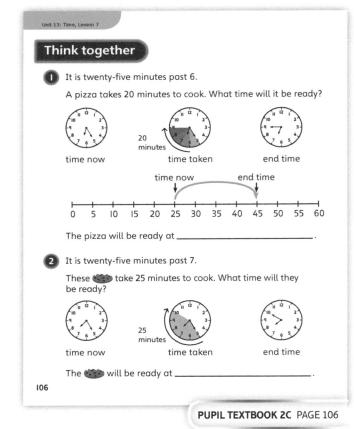

PUPIL TEXTBOOK 2C PAGE 106

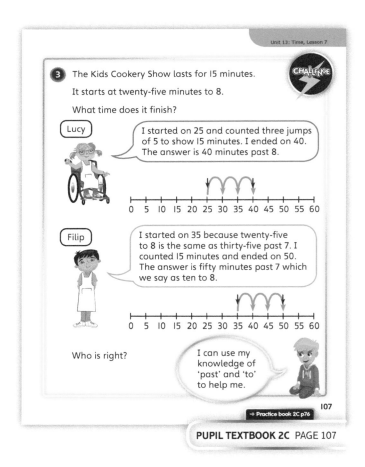

PUPIL TEXTBOOK 2C PAGE 107

Practice

WAYS OF WORKING Independent thinking

IN FOCUS When working independently on the questions in this section, children should continue to secure their understanding of the link between the analogue clock and the number line. It may be beneficial to give children number lines they can record their working on, alongside what they are recording in their workbook.

STRENGTHEN If children are struggling to know how to begin investigating question **4**, encourage them to show the two starting times on a clock face and on a number line. Ask: *How would this help you to begin finding Molly and Kasim's arrival times?*

DEEPEN When children are working on question **5**, ask them to predict how many solutions there are and then prove their predictions.

ASSESSMENT CHECKPOINT Children should be confident at finding end times when given a start time and duration. Look for children's confidence when using the various representations to help them find the end times. Children should also be able to confidently explain their thinking, using the representations and appropriate vocabulary fluently to share their ideas.

ANSWERS Answers for the **Practice** part of the lesson appear in the separate **Practice and Reflect answer guide**.

Reflect

WAYS OF WORKING Pair work

IN FOCUS Begin this activity by giving children time to discuss with their partner their method for finding the time things end. Ask children if they had a preferred way of finding an end time. *What representations did you use? What did you have to know to be able to find the end time? What was the most efficient way of finding the end time?*

Once children have discussed their methods, give them time to write their explanation.

ASSESSMENT CHECKPOINT Look for clarity in children's explanations. They should make reference to the fact that they will need a start time and duration to find an end time. Additionally, they should make mention of their chosen representations and explain how these can be used to help find an end time.

ANSWERS Answers for the **Reflect** part of the lesson appear in the separate **Practice and Reflect answer guide**.

After the lesson ⏸

- Which representation did children feel most comfortable with: the clock face or the number line?
- Are children confident finding an end time?

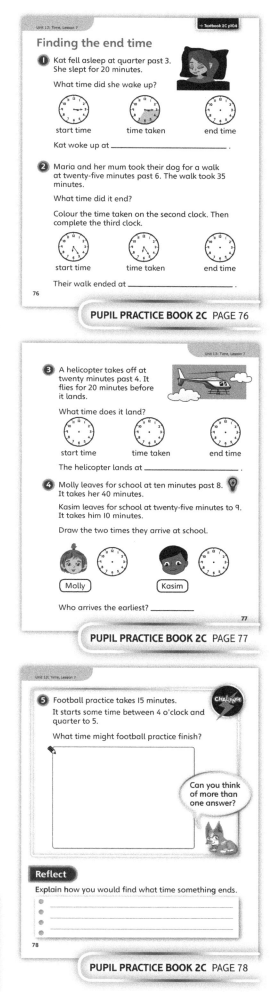

PUPIL PRACTICE BOOK 2C PAGE 76

PUPIL PRACTICE BOOK 2C PAGE 77

PUPIL PRACTICE BOOK 2C PAGE 78

Finding the start time

Learning focus

In this lesson, children will use their understanding of durations of time and counting around a clock to find a start time, when given an end time and a duration.

Small steps

→ Previous step: Finding the end time
→ **This step: Finding the start time**
→ Next step: Hours in a day

NATIONAL CURRICULUM LINKS

Year 2 Measurement – Time

Compare and sequence intervals of time.

ASSESSING MASTERY

Children can recognise and confidently find an end time on an analogue clock. They can fluently count back the correct number of minutes to reliably find the start time.

COMMON MISCONCEPTIONS

Children may incorrectly count a duration from a given end time, or may count forwards. Ask:
• *Can you point to the end time? What duration have you been given? Can you count backwards in 5s?*

STRENGTHENING UNDERSTANDING

To help children understand the concepts approached in this lesson, provide them with opportunities to count backwards along a number line and around a clock face. These concepts could be made into small games. For example, children could be positioned on a large number line or clock face drawn onto the playground. Have a dice prepared with multiples of five minutes on the faces. Children roll the dice and then jump back that many minutes. The first person around the clock or to reach the beginning of the number line wins.

GOING DEEPER

To deepen children's ability and understanding of this concept, give them opportunities to work with more than one duration. For example, *Zac watched two television programmes. One was 20 minutes long and the other was 15 minutes long. He finished watching television at 6:45. When did he start watching television?*

KEY LANGUAGE

In lesson: start time, end time, forwards, backwards, time taken

Other language to be used by the teacher: duration

STRUCTURES AND REPRESENTATIONS

Clock, number line

RESOURCES

Optional: analogue clock manipulatives, laminated pictures of clock faces, laminated or printed number lines

 In the eTextbook of this lesson, you will find interactive links to a selection of teaching tools.

Before you teach

• How confidently are the children using the vocabulary of this sequence of lessons?
• How will you ensure children get as much chance to cement their understanding of the vocabulary as possible?

Discover

Unit 13: Time, Lesson 8

WAYS OF WORKING Pair work

ASK

- *What does it mean to be late?*
- *What things have you been late for before?*
- *What time is the clock showing? How do you know?*
- *How many minutes is it to 4 o'clock?*
- *What time did the match start?*
- *How could you show the start and end times?*
- *What is the time in between called? How could you represent it?*

IN FOCUS Discuss how question ① is similar to the problems children solved in the previous lesson, and how it is different. Ask children to explain the information that was available to them in the previous lesson (start time and duration) and the information that is available to them in this problem (end time and duration). How will this change the way they solve the problems?

ANSWERS

Question ① a): The match started at five minutes past 3.

Question ① b): Children should use a number line as shown in the **Share** section.

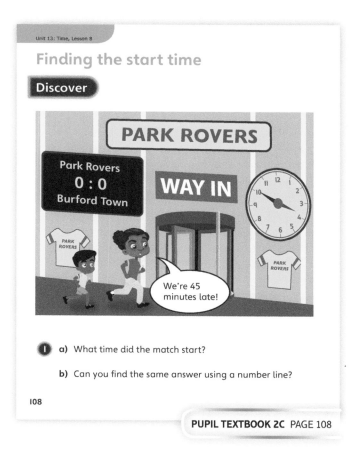

Finding the start time

Discover

① a) What time did the match start?

b) Can you find the same answer using a number line?

108

PUPIL TEXTBOOK 2C PAGE 108

Share

WAYS OF WORKING Whole class teacher led

ASK

- *What time is it in the picture? How do you know?*
- *They are 45 minutes late. How has the clock changed to get to this point?*
- *How many 5s are in 45 minutes?*
- *What did the clock look like when the match started?*
- *How could we use a number line to help us solve this?*
- *Why does the number line stop at the number 60?*
- *How is our use of the number line different for these questions?*
- *Can you explain why fifty minutes past 3 is the same as ten minutes to 4?*

IN FOCUS Make sure children understand that they are counting back on the number line to solve these questions. Use this opportunity to practise this skill, giving end times and durations to children for them to count back and find the start times.

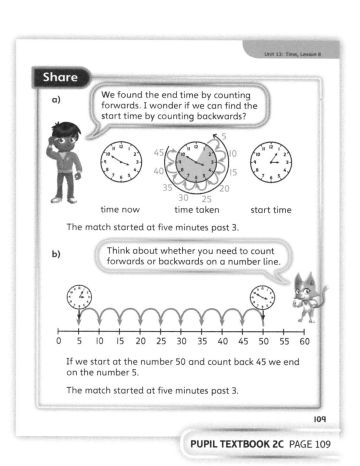

Share

a) We found the end time by counting forwards. I wonder if we can find the start time by counting backwards?

time now   time taken   start time

The match started at five minutes past 3.

b) Think about whether you need to count forwards or backwards on a number line.

If we start at the number 50 and count back 45 we end on the number 5.

The match started at five minutes past 3.

109

PUPIL TEXTBOOK 2C PAGE 109

Think together

Whole class teacher led (I do, We do, You do)

ASK

- *Where will you start counting on the clock?*
- *Which way will you need to count around the clock?*
- *How will you show this on a number line?*
- *Which way will you need to count along the number line?*

IN FOCUS Question **1** makes the link between the analogue clock and the number line explicit for children when they are solving these kinds of problems. Make sure children are clear with how the number line links to the analogue clock, as it will enable them to work more efficiently, using more easily recorded visual representations of time.

STRENGTHEN When children are working on question **2**, strengthen the link between the representations shown on the page and the number line. Ask children to explain how they will use it to help solve the problem.

DEEPEN Encourage children to use the number line to help solve question **3**. Using previous learning, and the number line, can children think of a way to prove that their answer is right?

ASSESSMENT CHECKPOINT At this point in the lesson, children should be able to more confidently find a start time, recognising that they need an end time and duration to do so. They should be able to recognise and explain how a number line can help them find a start time.

ANSWERS

Question **1** : Assembly started at twenty-five past 10.

Question **2** : Playtime started at twenty past 11.

Question **3** : Janet started at quarter past 11.

Tim started at twenty-five past 11.

Janet started first.

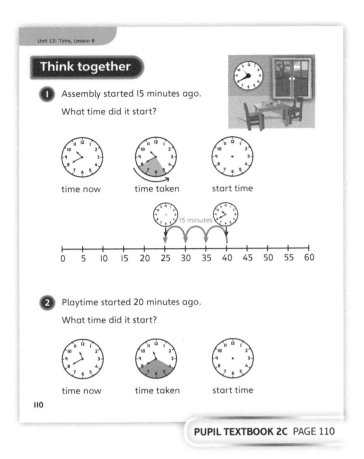

PUPIL TEXTBOOK 2C PAGE 110

PUPIL TEXTBOOK 2C PAGE 111

Practice

WAYS OF WORKING Independent thinking

IN FOCUS At this point in the lesson, children should have access to number lines to help support their working out for each question.

STRENGTHEN To help children use the number line model when solving the questions in this part of the lesson, ask:
• *What time will you start at on the number line?*
• *How could you record the duration of time?*
• *Can you show me the jumps of five minutes?*
• *Could you group some of those jumps into bigger jumps?*
• *How could you record the time more efficiently?*
• *What size jumps could you use?*

DEEPEN When children are working on question **5**, ask them to work systematically to find all possible solutions.

ASSESSMENT CHECKPOINT Children should be confident at finding start times when given an end time and duration. Look for children's confidence when using the various representations to help them find the start times. Children should also be able to confidently explain their thinking, using the representations and appropriate vocabulary fluently to share their ideas.

ANSWERS Answers for the **Practice** part of the lesson appear in the separate **Practice and Reflect answer guide**.

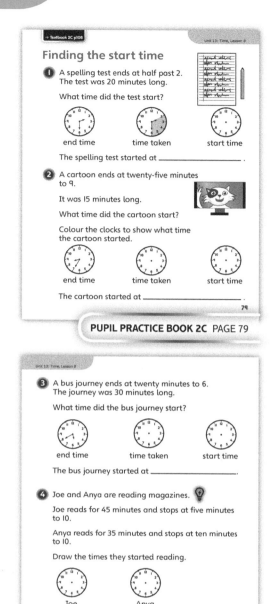

PUPIL PRACTICE BOOK 2C PAGE 79

PUPIL PRACTICE BOOK 2C PAGE 80

Reflect

WAYS OF WORKING Pair work

IN FOCUS Begin this activity by giving children time to discuss with their partner their method for finding the time things start. Ask them to convince their partner that their method is better. Once children have discussed their methods, give them time to write their explanation.

ASSESSMENT CHECKPOINT Look for clarity in children's explanations. They should make reference to the fact that they will need an end time and duration to find a start time. Additionally, they should make mention of their chosen representations and explain how these can be used to help find a start time.

ANSWERS Answers for the **Reflect** part of the lesson appear in the separate **Practice and Reflect answer guide**.

After the lesson ⏸

• Was finding the start time easier or more difficult for children than finding the end time?
• How could you offer children opportunities to practise finding the start and end times in other contexts or lessons?

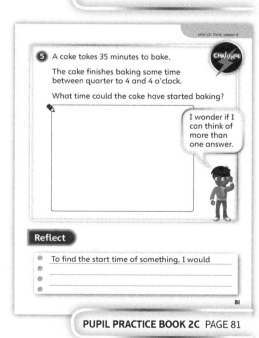

PUPIL PRACTICE BOOK 2C PAGE 81

Hours in a day

Learning focus

In this lesson, children will learn that there are 24 hours in a day. They will learn how there are morning and afternoon times, and use this to solve simple problems.

Small steps

→ Previous step: Finding the start time
→ **This step: Hours in a day**
→ Next step: Comparing mass

NATIONAL CURRICULUM LINKS

Year 2 Measurement – Time

Know the number of minutes in an hour and the number of hours in a day.

ASSESSING MASTERY

Children can demonstrate their understanding that there are 24 hours in a day. Children can recognise that 2 o'clock in the morning is different from 2 o'clock in the afternoon, and can use this to solve mathematical problems.

COMMON MISCONCEPTIONS

Children may think that one day is shown by the hour hand moving once around the clock to the next instance of the same time (for example, 11 o'clock to 11 o'clock). Ask:
- *How many hours are there in a day? How many hours have you counted? Do those two amounts match? Which is greater? How many more hours do you need to count until you have counted a full day?*

Children may have a lack of understanding of the parts of the day they have little experience of (for example, very late at night) and may associate the start of the day with dawn and the end of the day with sunset. Ask:
- *If the sun comes up at 5 am and goes down at 9 pm, how many hours has it been daylight?*
- *Is that a full 24 hours? What happens with the other hours? How many hours pass while you are asleep?*

STRENGTHENING UNDERSTANDING

Prepare children for this lesson by giving them opportunities to count around the clock face in hours. Children could role play what they would be doing at different times during the day as they count around a clock. Alternatively, they could use a teddy bear to act out the situations, to allow them to concentrate on counting hours.

Children could also be given 24 pictures of activities done during the day. Ask them to order these around a clock. Use this as an opportunity to discuss why there are 24 pictures and not 12. (For suggestions, see **Share: In focus** on page 141.)

GOING DEEPER

Children could be given the challenge of investigating how many hours there are in a week; in two weeks; in a month. Ask children if they can they prove their responses.

KEY LANGUAGE

In lesson: hours, day, o'clock, midday, daytime, midnight, around the clock

Other language to be used by the teacher: morning, afternoon, twice, nighttime, am, pm, duration

STRUCTURES AND REPRESENTATIONS

Clock

RESOURCES

Optional: analogue clock manipulatives, laminated pictures of clock faces, weekday timeline (noting hours and weekdays), 24 pictures of activities linked to each hour on the clock, soft toys for role play

 In the eTextbook of this lesson, you will find interactive links to a selection of teaching tools.

Before you teach ⏸

- What other experiences could you offer children to help them engage with and understand times of day that they may not have real-life experience of?

Discover

WAYS OF WORKING Pair work

ASK

- *What times do the two clocks show?*
- *How long does Sunil have to drink his smoothie?*
- *How many times does the minute hand travel around the clock in one day?*

IN FOCUS The picture in this part of the lesson offers an interesting opportunity to discuss the duration of time between the two pictures. Emphasise that the second picture says 'Next day' to encourage children to realise that at least 24 hours have passed.

ANSWERS

Question ❶ a): The hour hand travels twice around the clock. There are 24 hours in one day.

Question ❶ b): He should not drink the smoothie as it is past the safe time to use it.

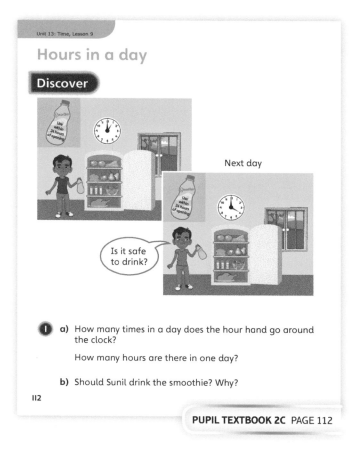

PUPIL TEXTBOOK 2C PAGE 112

Share

WAYS OF WORKING Whole class teacher led

ASK

- *How can you show how many hours there are in a day? Can you say each o'clock time as I turn the hand and tell me to stop when you think a day has gone past? Let's do the same activity again – this time tell me what you would be doing at each o'clock time.*
- *How many 8 o'clock times are in a whole day?*
- *When will 24 hours from now be?*
- *Give me a time that is more or less than 24 hours from now.*
- *Where have you seen the words '24 hours' written in real life? (For example: '24 hour cash', 'open 24 hours'.) What does it mean when you see it?*

IN FOCUS To help children relate to the times they will have little experience of, likely to be 9 pm – 5 am, it may be worthwhile to discuss what might be happening during these times. You could provide pictures of nocturnal animals, motorway workers, street cleaners, and so on, and link them to the times as you count through the clock.

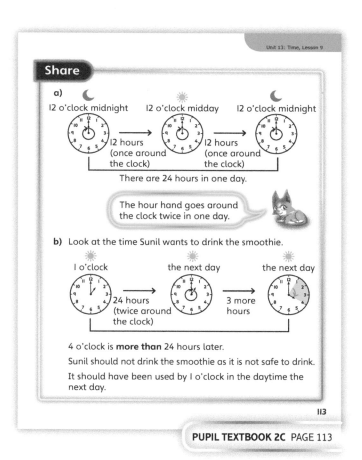

PUPIL TEXTBOOK 2C PAGE 113

Think together

Whole class teacher led (I do, We do, You do)

ASK

- *How do you know when to start counting in hours?*
- *What time will it be after 1 hour? 2 hours? Do you notice a pattern?*
- *To move through 24 hours, how many times will the hour hand travel around the clock?*
- *What do you need to know to begin working out 24 hours from now?*

IN FOCUS Question ❶ offers a good opportunity to reinforce the understanding that a day is composed of 24 hours, which is twice around the clock. Use the images of the clocks, coupled with the day and night symbols, to reinforce and cement this understanding. Encourage children to use analogue clock manipulatives to move through 24 hours, counting the hours as they do so.

STRENGTHEN If children are struggling to count the hours between the two times in question ❷, ask them to describe how the two times are shown in each part of the question. How could they make it easier to compare the two times? Can they show how they would count 24 hours from twenty-five past 1? If children solve this, extend their learning by asking how many more minutes the patient needs to wait.

DEEPEN Once children have explained what information is missing in question ❸, deepen the investigation by asking whether there are any potential solutions they could find with the information they have. Can they explain how they came to their solutions?

ASSESSMENT CHECKPOINT At this point in the lesson, children should be able to recognise that there are 24 hours in a day. They should be able to recognise and explain how they can find 24 hours from a given time by counting 24 hours from the start time. The children should recognise that while the finish time matches the start time, the day has changed.

ANSWERS

Question ❶ : The postman will be back at quarter past 9 tomorrow (Wednesday).

Question ❷ : 24 hours after twenty-five past 1 on Monday, the time will be twenty-five past 1 and the day will be Tuesday. She cannot take the bandage off now (she must wait another 10 minutes).

Question ❸ : We need to know the day he started and the day he finished and whether he started and finished in the morning or at night.

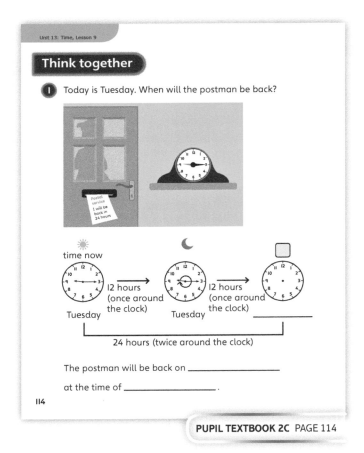

PUPIL TEXTBOOK 2C PAGE 114

PUPIL TEXTBOOK 2C PAGE 115

Practice

WAYS OF WORKING Independent thinking

IN FOCUS Questions **1**, **2** and **3** give children pictorial representations of the time to scaffold their independent learning. Provide plastic clocks or laminated clock pictures to support children's work.

STRENGTHEN If children are struggling to remember to move into a new day when counting 24 hours, offer them a timeline with the hours and weekdays recorded on it. Ask children to find the day and time on the timeline and then count on another 24 hours.

DEEPEN When solving question **4**, deepen children's reasoning by asking them to find two ways to prove when Ella can or cannot eat a biscuit.

ASSESSMENT CHECKPOINT At this point in the lesson, children should be able to confidently recognise and explain that there are 24 hours in a day. They should be able to, given any starting time, find 24 hours in the future and explain how the time stays the same and the day changes. Children should be able to use this understanding to solve simple problems confidently.

ANSWERS Answers for the **Practice** part of the lesson appear in the separate **Practice and Reflect answer guide**.

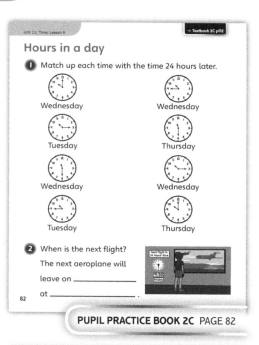

PUPIL PRACTICE BOOK 2C PAGE 82

PUPIL PRACTICE BOOK 2C PAGE 83

Reflect

WAYS OF WORKING Pair work

IN FOCUS Once children have discussed what Astrid should have said, ask them what advice they would give Astrid to correct her mistake. How would they prove to her that there are 24 hours in a day, not 12?

ASSESSMENT CHECKPOINT Look for children recognising how the misconception of 12 hours in a day could be made. Children should be able to explain that Astrid should have travelled around the clock twice and give ways of explaining this, based on the models and representations used in the lesson. Finally, children should be able to work out and recognise that there are 48 hours in 2 days.

ANSWERS Answers for the **Reflect** part of the lesson appear in the separate **Practice and Reflect answer guide**.

After the lesson ⏸

- Are children confident that there are 24 hours in a day?
- How did you challenge children's assumptions about the times they were not familiar with?

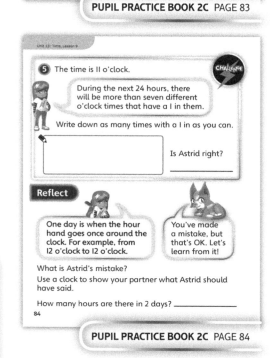

PUPIL PRACTICE BOOK 2C PAGE 84

End of unit check

Don't forget the *Power Maths* unit assessment grid on p26.

WAYS OF WORKING Group work – adult led

IN FOCUS Question **1** assesses children's ability to recognise times on an analogue clock and use the terminology of 'minutes past' and 'minutes to'.

Question **2** assesses children's ability to recognise, measure, convert and compare durations of time.

Question **3** assesses children's ability to count forward fluently from a given time.

Question **4** assesses children's ability to find durations of time when given starting and ending times, and use these to compare and order lengths of time.

Question **5** assesses children's ability to count through 24 hours and recognise that the day has changed.

Think!

WAYS OF WORKING Pair work

IN FOCUS This question assesses children's ability to read time on an analogue clock and in written form and to explain why the time in the picture matches the written time beneath. Ask: *What are the important words in the written times? Which hand shows the minutes? The hours? Can you match the hours in words to those in the picture?*

This question provides an opportunity to discuss the similarities and differences between times such as 'twenty minutes to 3' and 'forty minutes past 2'. Ask: *How are these times the same? How are they different?*

Encourage children, in pairs, to think through or discuss how they know that the times are right, before writing their answer in **My journal**.

ANSWERS AND COMMENTARY Children will demonstrate mastery by counting in steps of five minutes and recognising at what times 'past' and 'to' should be used. They will be able to explain how the hour and minute hands show the written time.

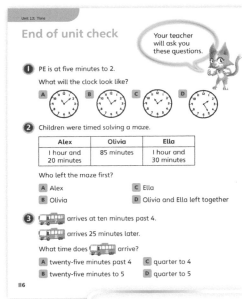

PUPIL TEXTBOOK 2C PAGE 116

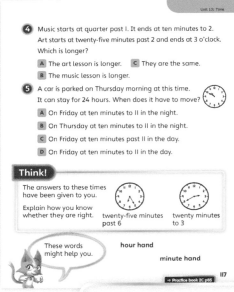

PUPIL TEXTBOOK 2C PAGE 117

Q	A	WRONG ANSWERS AND MISCONCEPTIONS	STRENGTHENING UNDERSTANDING
1	B	A or C suggests that children have misread the hands on the clock. D may suggest that children lack understanding of how the numbers on the clock face represent minutes.	Make sure any representations of analogue clocks are labelled clearly. Tell the story of your day using times. Children should show the times mentioned using analogue clocks. Depending on the fluency of the children, you can adapt this activity by: using only o'clock times; including 'half past' and 'quarter past/to'; giving start and end times and asking for the duration; giving duration and either a start or end time and asking for the other.
2	A	B suggests children have assumed that the time shown in minutes is less than that shown in hours. It could also indicate that they have converted the times inaccurately.	
3	B	A suggests children have ignored the minutes in the initial time. C indicates miscounting. D suggests children have muddled their 'past' and 'to' vocabulary.	
4	C	A suggests children have assumed that as the end time is in a different hour from the start time, the lesson is longer. B may indicate miscounting.	
5	D	A indicates children have only counted 12 hours. B suggests children have not moved through to the next day. C suggests children have misread the clock's hands.	

My journal

WAYS OF WORKING Independent thinking

ANSWERS AND COMMENTARY

For each time, children may record answers such as those shown below.
- I know the time is twenty-five minutes past 6 because:
  - The hour has just passed 6.
  - The minute hand is pointing at 5 which means 25 minutes.
  - The minute hand is in the 'past' section of the clock.
- I know the time is twenty minutes to 3 because:
  - The hour hand is almost at 3.
  - The minute hand is pointing to 8 which means 'twenty to' in minutes.
  - The minute hand is in the 'to' section of the clock.

If children are struggling to give reasons, ask:
- *Where is the minute hand pointing to? Can you count the minutes?*
- *What part of the clock is the minute hand in: 'to' or 'past'? How do you know?*
- *What do the hour hands tell you on each clock face?*

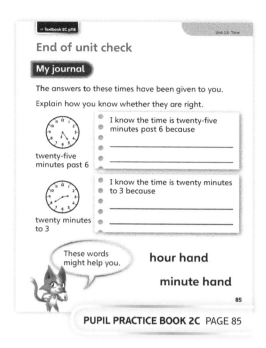

PUPIL PRACTICE BOOK 2C PAGE 85

Power check

WAYS OF WORKING Independent thinking

ASK
- *What did you know about reading time before you started this unit?*
- *What new things have you learned?*
- *Do you think you could look at a clock at home and tell the time by yourself?*

Power puzzle

WAYS OF WORKING Independent thinking

IN FOCUS This puzzle will assess children's recognition of written time and the start and end times of 20-minute durations. Children should be able to recognise where 20 minutes have passed between their start time and end time, although it may help them to have a selection of the representations used in this unit at hand, to support their thinking.

ANSWERS AND COMMENTARY If children are unable to follow the route accurately, it may be beneficial to give them opportunities to practise:
- matching written times with pictorial and concrete representations of an analogue clock
- moving forwards and backwards through time, using the analogue clock
- recognising and using the key vocabulary appropriate to measuring time.

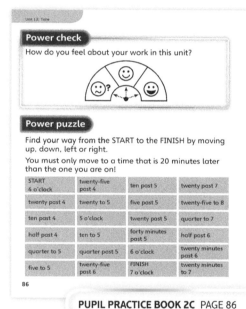

PUPIL PRACTICE BOOK 2C PAGE 86

After the unit ⏸

- Measuring time is such a commonplace activity that it can be taken for granted. How will you encourage children to regularly measure time outside of this unit of work? Some ideas might include: using time within children's role play, giving children time-keeping responsibilities, asking children what the time is, and so on.
- Is your classroom a 'time-rich' environment? How many reminders or opportunities are there for children to engage with time around the school environment? Is there a clock in each room? How could the resources be improved to deepen children's understanding of and fluency with time?

Strengthen and **Deepen** activities for this unit can be found in the *Power Maths* online subscription.

145

Unit 14
Weight, volume and temperature

Mastery Expert tip! "When I taught this unit, I made sure I backed up the examples in the pupil book with lots of practical and hands-on activities relating to mass, capacity, volume and temperature. This really helped children make connections to real-life experience and helped them secure their skills at reading scales and using standard units. It was also a great, fun, way to end the school year in maths!"

Don't forget to watch the Unit 14 video!

WHY THIS UNIT IS IMPORTANT

This unit focuses on children accurately measuring mass, volume, capacity and temperature. It is the first time that children have been introduced to the standard units for these measures, which provides the foundation for using measures in day-to-day life and for subsequent learning in Key Stage 2.

Within this unit, children are also introduced to making chains of linked reasoning about measures, and they get the opportunity to apply their ordering, comparing and estimating skills to a different area of maths. Children are also introduced to the use of different scales (such as scales that increase in 2s, 5s and 10s) and how to work out the value of each increment on the scale. This is important as it provides children with the skills they need in order to use a wide range of scales on different measuring equipment in day-to-day life.

WHERE THIS UNIT FITS

→ Unit 13: Time
→ **Unit 14: Weight, volume and temperature**

This unit builds upon the previous work children have done on mass, volume and capacity in Year 1, and the work using standard units of measure for length and height in Year 2 Unit 8. It also builds upon children's ability to count in steps of 2, 5 and 10 covered in Units 5 and 6 in Year 2. This unit also develops the reasoning skills that children have acquired throughout the year.

Before they start this unit, it is expected that children:
- know how to count in steps of 2, 5 and 10
- understand the concept of measuring mass, capacity and volume using non-standard units
- know how to read basic scales.

ASSESSING MASTERY

Children who have mastered this unit will be able to use the standard units of g, kg, ml, l and °C to measure and solve problems relating to mass, volume, capacity and temperature. They will be able to order and compare using each type of measure, and will be able to make sensible approximations as to the mass, volume, capacity or temperature of different objects or real-life situations. Children will be able to reason using measures, including making chains of connected reasoning when ordering and comparing measures.

COMMON MISCONCEPTIONS	STRENGTHENING UNDERSTANDING	GOING DEEPER
Children may not accurately work out the value of each increment on a scale which does not increase in 1s, and may therefore incorrectly read the value.	Ensure children have practical experiences measuring with a range of equipment with different scales, including, if possible, examples of the same unit on different scales. Draw children's attention to the known steps on the scale, and the number of steps between them, asking them to try counting in 2s, 5s or 10s to see which 'fits'.	Encourage children to make increasingly accurate approximations of the mass, volume, capacity and temperature of different objects or situations. Encourage them to draw upon their practical experience of each measure, and to build a set of common reference points. For example: a bag of sugar is 1 kg; the temperature in a fridge is about 3 °C.
Children may not link scales on measuring equipment to their experience of number lines.	Use a range of different number lines. Draw children's attention to how the scales are just a number line presented in a different way, for example by turning a thermometer or measuring jug on its side to liken the scale to a number line.	

Unit 14: Weight, volume and temperature

WAYS OF WORKING

Use these pages to introduce the unit focus to children as a whole class. You can use the different characters to explore different ways of working, and to begin to discuss and develop children's reasoning skills relating to measures.

STRUCTURES AND REPRESENTATIONS

Number line: This model helps children to understand and use different scales on a variety of measuring equipment. Draw children's attention to how a scale is effectively a number line in 'disguise'.

0 °C   10 °C   20 °C   30 °C   40 °C   50 °C   60 °C   70 °C   80 °C   90 °C   100 °C

Base 10 equipment: This model is useful for helping children to compare and order different measures, and also for when numbers over 100 are introduced for the first time.

10 g + 25 g = 35 g

Balance scales

Measuring jugs

Weighing scales

Thermometers

KEY LANGUAGE

There is some key language that children will need to know as part of the learning in this unit:

→ balance, comparing, estimating, reasoning, accurately, total, scale, interval

→ 100s, 100, 200, 300, 400, 500, 600, 700, 800, 900, 1,000

→ mass, weight, grams (g), kilograms (kg), kilos

→ volume, capacity, millilitres (ml), litres (l)

→ temperature, thermometer, degrees Celsius (°C)

→ more than, (>), less than (<), identical (=), divide (÷)

→ heavier, heaviest, lighter, lightest

→ greater, greatest, least, smaller, smallest, full, half, three-quarters, quarter, nearest to, X times as much

→ hotter, hottest, warmer, warmest, colder, coldest, cooler, coolest

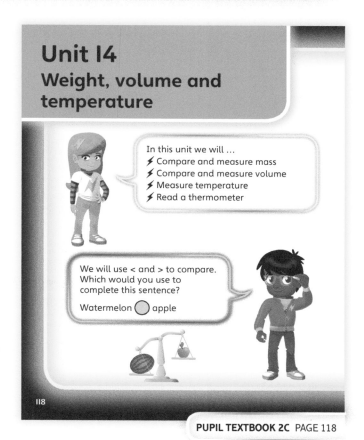

Unit 14
Weight, volume and temperature

In this unit we will …
- Compare and measure mass
- Compare and measure volume
- Measure temperature
- Read a thermometer

We will use < and > to compare. Which would you use to complete this sentence?

Watermelon ◯ apple

118

PUPIL TEXTBOOK 2C PAGE 118

We will need some maths words. Which of these have you heard before?

mass   balance   weighing scales

grams, g   kilograms, kg

litres, l   millilitres, ml   volume   capacity

temperature   thermometer

degrees Celsius, °C   estimate

approximation

We will use different things to measure. Have you used any of these? Can you match the names?

thermometer
balance scale
measuring jug
weighing scale

119

PUPIL TEXTBOOK 2C PAGE 119

Comparing mass

Learning focus

In this lesson, children will use balance scales to compare the mass of two or more objects, and use chains of reasoning to order the mass of more than two objects.

Small steps

→ Previous step: Hours in a day
→ **This step: Comparing mass**
→ Next step: Measuring mass in grams (1)

NATIONAL CURRICULUM LINKS

Year 2 Measurement – Weight, volume and temperature

Compare and order lengths, mass, volume/capacity and record the results using >, < and =.

ASSESSING MASTERY

Children can use balance scales to compare the mass of two objects and use chains of reasoning, as well as direct comparison using balance scales, to compare and order the mass of more than two objects.

COMMON MISCONCEPTIONS

Children may not understand that if $a > b$ and $b > c$, then a must be greater than c. Provide children with practical and real-life examples to help them order the mass of three objects using balance scales. Ask:
• *Do you need to measure the mass of 'a' against 'c' or can you know if 'a' is heaver or lighter than 'c' by comparing other objects?*

STRENGTHENING UNDERSTANDING

Support children by giving them plenty of practical opportunities to use balance scales to compare objects, and then put them in order based on their mass and the comparisons made.

GOING DEEPER

Children should be able to use more advanced chains of reasoning to compare the mass of more than three objects. Provide children with four or more objects and ask them to compare the masses. Can they order the objects from lightest to heaviest? Can they then write a corresponding number sentence using < or >?

KEY LANGUAGE

In lesson: mass, lightest, heavier than, heaviest, **lighter than,** balance, comparing, >, <, =

Other language to be used by the teacher: comparison, reasoning, weight

STRUCTURES AND REPRESENTATIONS

Balance scales

RESOURCES

Mandatory: balance scales, range of objects of different masses

 In the eTextbook of this lesson, you will find interactive links to a selection of teaching tools.

Before you teach ⏸

• Are children confident with using < and > to compare values?
• What exposure have children had previously to comparing the mass of different objects?

Discover

Pair work

ASK

- *What do you think the heaviest item is? What about the lightest?*
- *What could you use to find out?*

IN FOCUS This part of the lesson introduces children to comparing and ordering mass by making direct comparisons, and using this information to form chains of reasoning.

ANSWERS

Question **1** a): You can find out which items each person should carry by balancing them and comparing the mass.

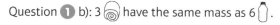

Question **1** b): 3  have the same mass as 6 .

Comparing mass

Discover

You should carry the lightest.

I will carry the heaviest.

Tent   Sleeping bags   Food

1 a) How can you find out what each person should carry?

b) 1 has the same **mass** as 2 . What is the mass of 3 in bottles?

120

PUPIL TEXTBOOK 2C PAGE 120

Share

WAYS OF WORKING Whole class teacher led

ASK

- *What could you use to help you compare mass?*
- *How did you work out which was the heaviest?*
- *Which two items do you need to compare to work out which is the lightest?*
- *How did you work out how many bottles have the same mass as 3 sleeping bags? What information did you use to help you?*

IN FOCUS In this section, children are reminded that they can use inequality signs < and > to help them when they are comparing mass.

ASSESSMENT CHECKPOINT Correct answers to these questions will help you assess whether children are able to use chains of reasoning to solve problems.

Share

You should use a balance to be exact when comparing mass.

a)

We know the heaviest, but we don't know which is **lightest** yet.

I remember that we can use > to mean **heavier than**, and < to mean **lighter than**.

b)

3 have the same mass as 3 lots of 2 , which is 6 .

121

PUPIL TEXTBOOK 2C PAGE 121

Think together

WAYS OF WORKING Whole class teacher led (I do, We do, You do)

ASK

- Question **1** : *Which is the heaviest? Do you need to compare the mass of the torch and the tent?*
- Question **1** : *What do the < and > signs mean?*
- Question **2** a): *If you know that you need 1 mallet and 2 bottles to have the same mass as the stove, what else do you know?*
- Question **2** b): *What is the mass of the mallet? How can you use information to help you work out the mass of the tent?*

IN FOCUS This section develops children's use of connected chains of reasoning to solve problems. For example, in question **1**, children need to use the fact that the mallet is heavier than the torch, but lighter than the tent, to work out that the tent is the heaviest and the torch is the lightest.

In question **2** a), children are expected to reason that, as the mallet and 2 bottles have the same mass as the stove, and the stove has the mass of 10 bottles, then the mallet by itself has the mass of 8 bottles. In part b) children can then reason that as 2 mallets have the same mass as the tent, then the tent has the mass of 8 bottles + 8 bottles = 16 bottles.

STRENGTHEN If children are struggling to make the chains of reasoning required for them to solve these problems, help them by breaking the problems down into smaller steps. For example, in question **1** you could help children create inequality statements to represent the two balance scales shown (such as mallet > torch, tent > mallet) and then use these to construct the inequality statements required to answer the problem which compares all three items.

DEEPEN Question **3** introduces children to using proportional language about mass such as 'twice as heavy as' and 'half as heavy as'. Consider whether children can use this language when discussing other questions in this section. For example, in question **2** can they express that the tent is twice as heavy as the mallet?

ASSESSMENT CHECKPOINT Question **1** should help you assess whether children are able to accurately use the inequality signs when comparing mass. Question **2** should help you assess whether children are able to make more complex chains of reasoning.

ANSWERS

Question **1** : Torch < mallet, mallet < tent

Mallet > torch, tent > mallet

Question **2** a): ⟍🔨 has the same mass as 8 🍾

Question **2** b): 🎒 has the same mass as 16 🍾

Question **3** a): Dad's bag is heaviest (because Dad's bag is 5 times as heavy as Molly's bag and Jack's bag is lighter than Molly's).

Question **3** b): Jack's bag is lightest (because Jack's bag is half as heavy as Molly's bag which is lighter than Dad's bag).

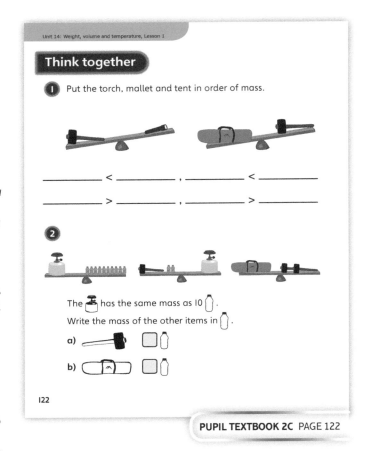

Unit 14: Weight, volume and temperature, Lesson 1

Think together

1 Put the torch, mallet and tent in order of mass.

_____ < _____ , _____ < _____

_____ > _____ , _____ > _____

2

The 🔥 has the same mass as 10 🍾.
Write the mass of the other items in 🍾.

a)

b)

122

PUPIL TEXTBOOK 2C PAGE 122

3 Another family go camping.

Molly says, 'My bag is twice as heavy as a tent.'

Jack says, 'My bag is half as heavy as Molly's.'

Dad says, 'My bag is five times as heavy as Molly's.'

a) Whose bag is heaviest?

_____'s bag is heaviest.

b) Whose bag is lightest?

_____'s bag is lightest.

I wonder how many tents balance each bag.

→ Practice book 2C p87

123

PUPIL TEXTBOOK 2C PAGE 123

Practice

WAYS OF WORKING Independent thinking

IN FOCUS Question **3** provides children with further practice at using proportional language to order and compare mass.

STRENGTHEN If children are struggling with using the comparison language required in questions **1** and **3**, begin by modelling similar situations using practical apparatus, such as a balance scale and objects around the classroom, and ask children to make similar comparison statements, for example: *Is the cube or the sphere heavier? Which item is twice as heavy as the sphere?*, before applying this to the information given in the questions.

DEEPEN Question **4** extends children to having to make chains of reasoning involving four different direct comparisons. Can children express a given object in terms of another, to work out its mass in cubes, and thus order the items from lightest to heaviest?

ASSESSMENT CHECKPOINT Question **1** will help you assess whether children are comfortable with using basic comparison language that is connected to mass (heavier and lighter).

Question **2** will help you assess whether children can use chains of inequality signs to order mass.

ANSWERS Answers for the **Practice** part of the lesson appear in the separate **Practice and Reflect answer guide**.

Reflect

WAYS OF WORKING Pair work

IN FOCUS This section focuses on children being able to explain the meaning of the inequality signs and use these to make chains of reasoning.

ASSESSMENT CHECKPOINT The question asked by Sparks will help you assess whether children are able to construct their own chains of reasoning. Can they identify that the tin is heavier than the box?

ANSWERS Answers for the **Reflect** part of the lesson appear in the separate **Practice and Reflect answer guide**.

After the lesson ⏸

• Are children secure with using < and > to compare mass?
• How can you incorporate comparing mass (and other units of measure) into day-to-day classroom life?

PUPIL PRACTICE BOOK 2C PAGE 87

PUPIL PRACTICE BOOK 2C PAGE 88

PUPIL PRACTICE BOOK 2C PAGE 89

Measuring mass in grams ①

Learning focus

In this lesson, children will explore the use of standard units of mass (grams), and how they can measure these using both balance scales and weighing scales.

Small steps

→ Previous step: Comparing mass
→ **This step: Measuring mass in grams (1)**
→ Next step: Measuring mass in grams (2)

NATIONAL CURRICULUM LINKS

Year 2 Measurement – Weight, volume and temperature

Choose and use appropriate standard units to estimate and measure length/height in any direction (m/cm); mass (kg/g); temperature (°C); capacity (litres/ml) to the nearest appropriate unit – using rulers, scales, thermometers and measuring vessels.

ASSESSING MASTERY

Children can understand the need to use standard metric units of mass in order to accurately measure, and can accurately find the mass of items in grams, such as a book, and weigh out a certain mass, such as 30 g of salt.

COMMON MISCONCEPTIONS

Children may not understand or accurately use the term 'grams' and its symbol 'g'. Draw parallels with more familiar units of measurement and their symbols, such as 'centimetre' and 'cm'. Ask:
• *What other symbols do you use when measuring?*

Children may think they cannot find the mass of items using a balance scale that does not directly correspond to the weights they have. For example, they may think that when using 10 g and 5 g weights they can only find the mass of items that are 10 g and 5 g. Ask:
• *How could you tell if something was heavier or lighter than 5 g or 10 g?*

STRENGTHENING UNDERSTANDING

This is the first time children are exposed to metric units for mass. Therefore, they will benefit from plenty of hands-on practical experience in measuring the mass of items (using weights, balance scales and weighing scales) to build confidence in using grams (g) accurately. Expose children to balance scales and weighing scales that have a range of different scales on them.

GOING DEEPER

Challenge children to use proportional relationships and language to help them predict and express the mass of other items. For example, ask: *If the mass of an apple is twice the mass of an orange, and an orange has a mass of 20 g, what is the mass of the apple?*

KEY LANGUAGE

In lesson: grams, measure, accurately, mass, weighing, balance, heavy, weights, weighing scales, total

Other language to be used by the teacher: metric units of measure, heavier, heaviest, lighter, lightest, balance scales

STRUCTURES AND REPRESENTATIONS

Base 10 equipment, balance scales, weighing scales

RESOURCES

Mandatory: balance scales, weighing scales, weights, range of objects to weigh

Optional: Base 10 equipment, cubes

 In the eTextbook of this lesson, you will find interactive links to a selection of teaching tools.

Before you teach ⏸

• What exposure have children had to standard units of measure before this unit?
• Are children able to accurately read a range of scales and interpret a range of number lines?

Discover

ASK

- *What can you see? What is the problem asking you?*
- *What does it mean when two things balance on a balance scale?*
- *What does 100 g mean? What does 10 g mean?*

IN FOCUS This part of the lesson introduces children to measuring the mass of items in grams, a standard unit of measure. Strengthen understanding by providing children with a range of familiar items labelled in grams, such as bags of flour, sugar and salt.

ANSWERS

Question ❶ a): They can measure mass accurately by weighing the flour and salt using a standard unit of measure, grams (g).

Question ❶ b): The mass of the flour is 35 g.

PUPIL TEXTBOOK 2C PAGE 124

Share

WAYS OF WORKING Whole class teacher led

ASK

- Question ❶ a): *What could you use to measure the mass accurately? What units of measure could you use?*
- Question ❶ a): *How could you make sure you were using the balance scales accurately?*
- Question ❶ b): *What mass of weights is balancing the flour?*
- Question ❶ b): *How could you use numbers and units of measure to write down the weight of flour?*

IN FOCUS Through the discussion in this part of the lesson, children are introduced to grams as the standard unit of measure for mass, and how measuring mass accurately can be achieved using a balance scale and weights. Ensure children are provided with lots of practical experience of handling weights alongside the discussion in this section of the lesson.

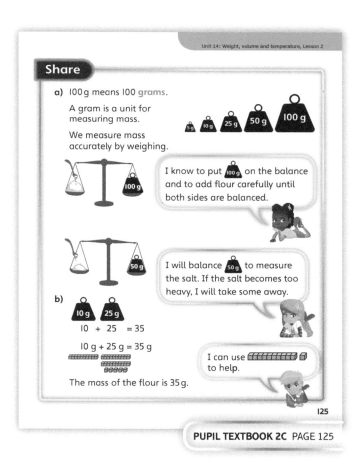

PUPIL TEXTBOOK 2C PAGE 125

Think together

WAYS OF WORKING Whole class teacher led (I do, We do, You do)

ASK

- Question ❶ : *Is there a single weight with the mass of 60 g or 30 g? How could you use more than one weight at the same time to make 60 g and 30 g?*
- Question ❷ : *What is the mass of the heart model? How do you know?*
- Question ❷ : *How can you use the mass of the heart model to work out the mass of the star model?*

IN FOCUS Question ❷ focuses on children using and understanding proportional language and relationships in order to use the mass of one item to find the mass of another item.

STRENGTHEN In order to further support children with combining weights to measure the mass of items using a balance scale (as required by question ❶), provide them with practical experience of using this type of scale to find the mass of classroom items. If children are struggling with the calculation element of question ❷ (35 + 35, or double 35), provide access to a range of representations, such as Base 10 equipment, in order to support their calculations.

DEEPEN Question ❸ introduces children to an additional way of measuring mass by using weighing scales. Children should also be expected to reason using mass, and this question provides opportunity for them to practise this. They have to identify that the difference between the mass of the two items is 10 g, and therefore this must be the mass of the salt dough leaf.

ASSESSMENT CHECKPOINT Question ❶ will help you assess whether children are able to understand how they can use weights and a balance scale to measure the mass of items. Question ❷ will help you assess whether children can use proportional language and relationships when reasoning about mass.

ANSWERS

Question ❶ : 50 g + 10 g balances the flour.

25 g + 5 g balances the salt.

Question ❷ : The ♡ has a mass of 35 g.

The ☆ has a mass of 70 g.

Question ❸ : The 🧍 has a mass of 30 g.

The 🍃 has a mass of 10 g.

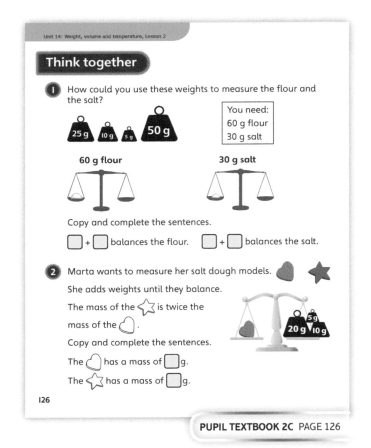

Think together

❶ How could you use these weights to measure the flour and the salt?

25 g   10 g   5 g   50 g

You need:
60 g flour
30 g salt

60 g flour   **30 g salt**

Copy and complete the sentences.

☐ + ☐ balances the flour.   ☐ + ☐ balances the salt.

❷ Marta wants to measure her salt dough models.

She adds weights until they balance.

The mass of the ☆ is twice the mass of the ♡ .

Copy and complete the sentences.

The ♡ has a mass of ☐ g.

The ☆ has a mass of ☐ g.

126

PUPIL TEXTBOOK 2C PAGE 126

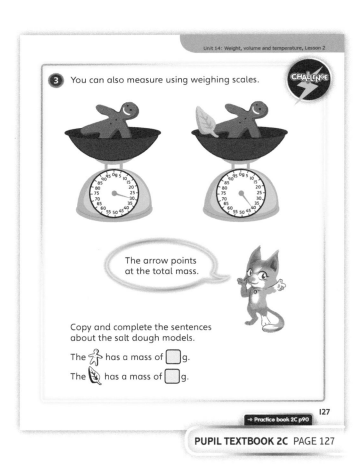

❸ You can also measure using weighing scales.   CHALLENGE

The arrow points at the total mass.

Copy and complete the sentences about the salt dough models.

The 🧍 has a mass of ☐ g.

The 🍃 has a mass of ☐ g.

→ Practice book 2C p90

127

PUPIL TEXTBOOK 2C PAGE 127

Practice

WAYS OF WORKING Independent thinking

IN FOCUS Throughout this section of the lesson children are exposed to different ways of measuring mass using the standard unit of grams. In question ❸, they are introduced to a range of different scales. In question ❹, children are invited to explore proportional relationships themselves. For this to be effective, it is important that the cubes provided each have the same mass.

STRENGTHEN If children need further support with question ❶ or ❷, it is important that they are provided with practical experience of measuring the mass of different items so they can see how different weights can be combined to achieve this accurately.

DEEPEN Question ❹ provides further opportunity for children to practise and develop their reasoning skills using mass. Encourage children to make a connection between the masses of different models made from cubes and the numbers of cubes they contain, either by looking at the proportional relationship between the models (20-cube model is twice as heavy as 10-cube model) or by working out the mass of each cube (mass of 10-cube model ÷ 10 = 1 cube). Children should then be expected to check their predictions, and this could be extended to predicting the masses of models made from different numbers of cubes.

ASSESSMENT CHECKPOINT Questions ❶ and ❷ should help you assess whether children understand how they can use weights and a balance scale to find the mass of items. Question ❸ should help you assess whether children can read a range of different scales.

ANSWERS Answers for the **Practice** part of the lesson appear in the separate **Practice and Reflect answer guide**.

Reflect

WAYS OF WORKING Whole class

IN FOCUS This section draws children's attention to the difference between the two common types of measurement problems: measuring to find the mass (Rav's statement) and measuring a certain mass of an item (Alia's statement).

ASSESSMENT CHECKPOINT Use the discussions resulting from this section to assess whether children understand the difference in approaches needed for the two different types of problem. For example, to solve Rav's problem you would need to add weights to balance scales until the scales balanced, and to solve Alia's problem you would need to add 30 g in weights and then add cheese until the scale was balanced.

ANSWERS Answers for the **Reflect** part of the lesson appear in the separate **Practice and Reflect answer guide**.

After the lesson ⏸

- Are children confident in using weights and a balance scale to find the mass of items?
- Can children read a range of different weight scales?

PUPIL PRACTICE BOOK 2C PAGE 90

PUPIL PRACTICE BOOK 2C PAGE 91

PUPIL PRACTICE BOOK 2C PAGE 92

Measuring mass in grams ②

Learning focus

In this lesson, children will measure and compare the mass of objects that are over 100 g using scales, giving the mass to the nearest 100 g.

Small steps

→ Previous step: Measuring mass in grams (1)
→ **This step: Measuring mass in grams (2)**
→ Next step: Measuring mass in kilograms

NATIONAL CURRICULUM LINKS

Year 2 Measurement – Weight, volume and temperature

- Choose and use appropriate standard units to estimate and measure length/height in any direction (m/cm); mass (kg/g); temperature (°C); capacity (litres/ml) to the nearest appropriate unit, using rulers, scales, thermometers and measuring vessels.
- Compare and order lengths, mass, volume/capacity and record the results using >, < and =.

ASSESSING MASTERY

Children can count in increments of 100 and use weighing scales to give the mass of items to the nearest 100 g. Children can compare the mass of objects over 100 g.

COMMON MISCONCEPTIONS

Children may count in 100s after 100, for example, they may count 98, 99, 100, 200, 300, 400… Display a range of number lines, including some marked in increments of 1 above 100 and others marked in increments of 100. Ask:
- *What numbers are missing between 100 and 200? Between 200 and 300?*

When estimating items, children may think that physically bigger items always have a larger mass than smaller items. Provide a range of items for children to estimate and measure the mass of, including light big objects, such as an empty box, and heavy small objects, such as a box of staples. Ask:
- *Which item do you think is heavier? Why?*

STRENGTHENING UNDERSTANDING

To help support with numbers above 100, use a range of practical representations, including Base 10 equipment. This lesson requires children to understand that 200 g is twice as heavy as 100 g, rather than just a bit more than 100. This should not only give a deeper understanding of measuring mass, and help children measure usefully for recipes, but will also prepare them for developing their understanding of place value.

GOING DEEPER

It is important that children develop the ability to estimate the mass of items. Provide children with the opportunity to do this initially by holding a 100 g weight in one hand and an item in the other, and comparing their mass. You can then support children to extend this by asking them to estimate the mass of items without first comparing them with a 100 g weight.

KEY LANGUAGE

In lesson: 100, 200, 300, 400, 500, 600, 700, 800, 900, 1,000, mass, **hundreds**, to the nearest, grams (g), heavier, heaviest, lighter, lightest, estimate

Other language to be used by the teacher: compare

STRUCTURES AND REPRESENTATIONS

Number lines, Base 10 equipment, balance scales, weight scales

RESOURCES

Mandatory: number lines, balance scales, 100 g weights, classroom objects

Optional: weighing scales, Base 10 equipment

 In the eTextbook of this lesson, you will find interactive links to a selection of teaching tools.

Before you teach ⏸

- Are there any common misconceptions from the previous lesson that need addressing?
- Are children confident at reading scales?

Discover

WAYS OF WORKING Pair work

ASK

- *What can you see? Look at the scales closely.*
- *What do you think the scales go up in?*
- *Question* **1** *b): What could the fourth guinea pig weigh? How do you know?*

IN FOCUS This part of the lesson introduces children to counting beyond 100 for the first time. It may initially be unclear to children what the un-numbered marks on the scales stand for, so spend some time ensuring they understand that the marks increase by 100 each time.

ANSWERS

Question **1** a): The smallest guinea pig has a mass of 300 g.

The middle guinea pig has a mass of 700 g.

The largest guinea pig has a mass 800 g to the nearest 100 g.

Question **1** b): The other guinea pig could have a mass of more than 300 g and less than 700 g.

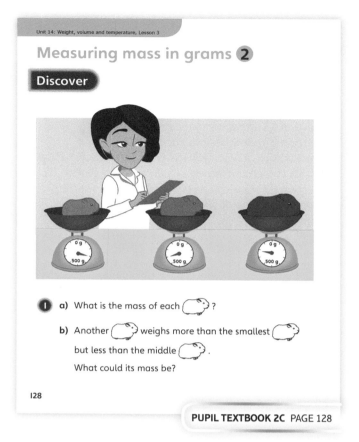

Share

WAYS OF WORKING Whole class teacher led

ASK

- *Listen to the numbers I say. What am I counting in? 100, 200, 300...*
- *Can you count in 100s?*
- *Question* **1** *a): What does each line on the scales stand for?*
- *Question* **1** *a): Do you know exactly how heavy the third guinea pig is?*
- *Question* **1** *a): What 100s number is it closest to? What could you say about its mass?*

IN FOCUS Children are introduced to counting in 100s during this part of the lesson. It is important to draw their attention to the patterns, and to compare the counting and scales to a number line, which is marked in 100s.

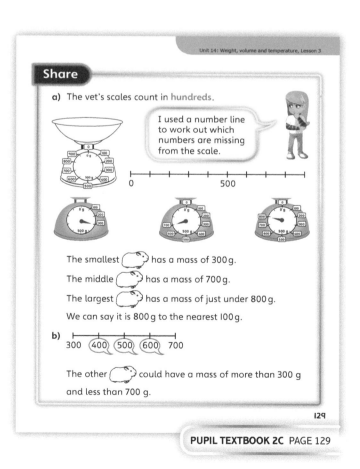

Think together

Whole class teacher led (I do, We do, You do)

ASK

- Question **1** : *What are the scales counting in?*
- Question **1** : *How heavy is each item?*
- Question **2** : *How can you use balance scales and 100 g weights to measure the mass of items to the nearest 100 g?*
- Question **2** : *How can you work out the mass of the rat? What do you know about its mass?*

IN FOCUS Question **2** introduces children to measuring in 100 g increments using balance scales. It asks children to compare the mass of items, and gives them opportunity to rehearse the terms lightest and heaviest, which were used in lessons 1 and 2 of this unit. Children also need to use the proportional reasoning skills they developed in lessons 1 and 2 to work out that the rat is twice as heavy as the hamster and must therefore weigh 400 g.

STRENGTHEN To support children with counting in 100s, you can use a range of practical and pictorial representations, including Base 10 equipment and number lines that are marked in increments of 100.

DEEPEN As well as accurately measuring mass to the nearest 100 g, it is important that children also develop the skill of estimating the mass of items. For question **3** , provide children with a range of items, including those whose mass does not correspond to its size, such as small, heavy items and large, light items, and ask children to estimate whether the mass of each item is more or less than 100 g. They can then use balance scales to check their predictions. Ask: *How many of your estimates were correct?*

ASSESSMENT CHECKPOINT Question **1** will help you assess whether children can accurately read scales that go up in increments of 100 g. If children struggle with this, check whether this is a difficulty in counting in 100s or in reading scales.

ANSWERS

Question **1** a): The tortoise has a mass of 400 g.

Question **1** b): The parrot has a mass of 800 g.

Question **2** a): The hamster is the lightest. The squirrel is the heaviest.

Question **2** b): hamster < rat < squirrel

Question **3** : Answer will depend on the items that children estimate the mass of. Their estimates should be checked using balance scales and a 100 g weight.

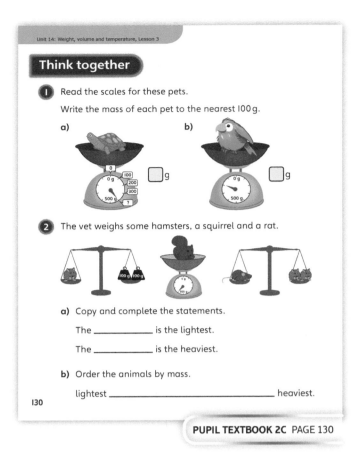

PUPIL TEXTBOOK 2C PAGE 130

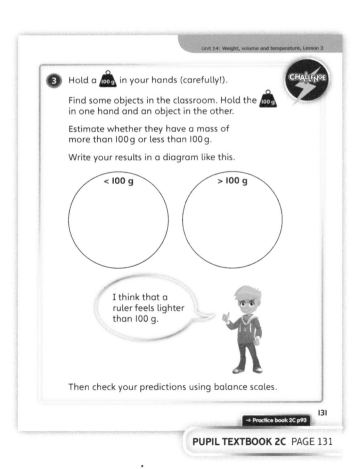

PUPIL TEXTBOOK 2C PAGE 131

Practice

WAYS OF WORKING Independent thinking

IN FOCUS Question ❶ b) involves children counting back from 100 and understanding that 100 less than 100 is 0. Questions ❷ and ❸ introduce children to scales that are not marked in single increments of 100, but are instead only numbered at 200 g increments, as well as different styles of scales. Draw children's attention to these scales, and ask them to work out what the un-numbered lines stand for. In question ❸ b), ensure children understand that 0 is marked instead of 1000 on the last two scales.

STRENGTHEN To support children in giving the mass to the nearest 100 g, provide them with plenty of practical and real-life experiences of measuring mass using scales, to the nearest 100 g. You can also provide them with 100 g and 200 g weights to (carefully) hold, and ask them to estimate if items are closer to 100 g or 200 g in weight, and to check this using weighing scales.

DEEPEN It is important that children are able to use and apply their relative reasoning skills and make chains of reasoning that involve masses over 100 g. Deepen understanding of question ❹ by providing children with three different objects, each of a different mass. Can they order the objects from lightest to heaviest, and from heaviest to lightest? What other objects around the classroom would fall between the lightest and heaviest weights?

ASSESSMENT CHECKPOINT Question ❷ will help you assess whether children are able to give masses to the nearest 100 g, which is an important skill, as when measuring items in real life they are unlikely to have objects with masses that fall in exactly 100 g increments.

ANSWERS Answers for the **Practice** part of the lesson appear in the separate **Practice and Reflect answer guide**.

Reflect

WAYS OF WORKING Pair work

IN FOCUS This question draws children's attention to the fact that even though two objects may have the same mass when measured to the nearest 100 g, they may in fact have different actual masses.

ASSESSMENT CHECKPOINT Use this question to assess whether children understand that the further past a marking on a scale (such as the 600 g mark) the pointer is, the heavier the item.

ANSWERS Answers for the **Reflect** part of the lesson appear in the separate **Practice and Reflect answer guide**.

After the lesson ⏸

- Are children secure using numbers above 100?
- How can you incorporate measuring and estimating the mass of objects above 100 g into day-to-day classroom life?

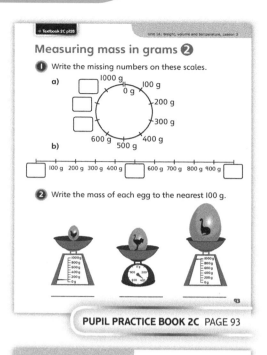

PUPIL PRACTICE BOOK 2C PAGE 93

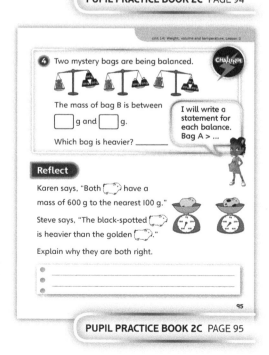

PUPIL PRACTICE BOOK 2C PAGE 94

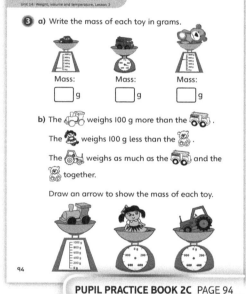

PUPIL PRACTICE BOOK 2C PAGE 95

Measuring mass in kilograms

Learning focus

In this lesson, children will be introduced to kilograms, their second standard unit of mass, and will explore measuring and estimating mass using both grams and kilograms.

Small steps

→ Previous step: Measuring mass in grams (2)
→ **This step: Measuring mass in kilograms**
→ Next step: Comparing volume

NATIONAL CURRICULUM LINKS

Year 2 Measurement – Weight, volume and temperature

- Choose and use appropriate standard units to estimate and measure length/height in any direction (m/cm); mass (kg/g); temperature (°C); capacity (litres/ml) to the nearest appropriate unit, using rulers, scales, thermometers and measuring vessels.
- Compare and order lengths, mass, volume/capacity and record the results using >, < and =.

ASSESSING MASTERY

Children can accurately measure the mass of objects in both kilograms and grams, and make sensible estimations for the mass of different items. Children can compare the mass of objects in kilograms.

COMMON MISCONCEPTIONS

Children may think that 1 kg and 1 g are the same. Emphasise that heavier objects are weighed in kilograms and lighter objects are weighed in grams. Compare an object weighing 1 kg, such as a bag of flour, with a smaller object, such as a packet of butter, and ask:
- *Which do you think is heavier? Do you think it is measured in grams or kilograms?*

STRENGTHENING UNDERSTANDING

Support children by providing plenty of practical opportunities for them to measure objects in kilograms using both weighing scales and balance scales. Ensure children measure the weight of a variety of different objects, including light big objects and heavy small objects, to cement understanding that a bigger object does not necessarily mean a heavier object.

GOING DEEPER

Children should begin to understand the equivalence between 1,000 g and 1 kg. Challenge children to choose a classroom object and then estimate how many of them it would take to make a mass of 1 kg. Ask them to prove their predictions by weighing the objects.

KEY LANGUAGE

In lesson: **kilogram** (kg), kilo, heavier, heaviest, lighter, lightest, mass, total, estimate, <, >, =

STRUCTURES AND REPRESENTATIONS

Number lines, Base 10 equipment, balance scales, weighing scales

RESOURCES

Mandatory: various kilogram weights, 100 g weights, balance scales, weighing scales

Optional: Base 10 equipment, number lines

 In the eTextbook of this lesson, you will find interactive links to a selection of teaching tools.

Before you teach ⏸

- Are children confident with measuring the mass of items in grams?
- Are children able to make sensible estimations for the mass of items in grams?

Discover

WAYS OF WORKING Pair work

ASK

- *What can you see in this picture?*
- *How can you work out the mass of everyone's fruit?*

IN FOCUS This section introduces children to the symbol 'kg', and the term 'kilogram' for the first time. Children may at first be unsure as to what kg stands for. Establish with them what they are measuring (mass) and that kilogram is another standard unit of mass that is larger than grams.

ANSWERS

Question ❶ a): Anya will need a stronger bag for the 🍍.

Question ❶ b): The mass of the 🍌 is 2 kg.

Share

WAYS OF WORKING Whole class teacher led

ASK

- *What could kilogram mean?*
- *Hold this kilogram weight carefully. Is it heavy or light?*
- *Is a kilogram heavier than a gram?*
- *Which of the objects are heavier than a kilogram? How can you tell?*
- *What is the mass of each weight on the balance scale?*
- *How far between the 0 and 5 is the arrow pointing to on the scales for the bananas?*
- *How many numbers are there between 0 and 5?*
- *Can you put the missing numbers on the scale?*

IN FOCUS Children are introduced to kilograms through the discussion resulting from this section. It is important that children have practical experience of the mass of a kilogram, by holding a 1 kg weight. They should compare this with their experience of holding weights that are measured in grams. Establish with children that 1 kg is heavier than any of the gram weights that they have held previously.

Think together

WAYS OF WORKING Whole class teacher led (I do, We do, You do)

ASK

- Question ❶ : *What mass balances each of the items on the balance scale?*
- Question ❶ c): *What balances the apples? Do you know the mass of the potatoes?*
- Question ❷ : *How can you work out the mass of crate A?*
- Question ❷ : *What is 5 times the mass of crate A? How could you work this out?*
- Question ❷ : *Where would these numbers go on the number line?*

IN FOCUS Questions ❶ c) and ❷ ask children to reason using their knowledge of kilograms and direct comparison of the mass of different objects. In question ❶ c), children need to realise that as the mass of a bag of potatoes is balanced by 5 kg, and the apples are balanced by a bag of potatoes *and* 1 kg, that the mass of the apples must be 6 kg.

STRENGTHEN In question ❷ , children may benefit from using practical representations, such as Base 10 equipment, to help them work out 5 x 4 and half of 20. Encourage children to use the calculation skills that they have developed throughout Year 2.

DEEPEN Children should begin to develop an awareness of the equivalence between 1,000 g and 1 kg. The activity in question ❸ helps them to establish this through the use of a comparison exercise, similar to those that they have been exposed to in previous lessons in this unit. Ask children how many grams one chocolate bar is, and then how many chocolate bars are the same as 1 kg, and therefore how many grams are the same as 1 kg. Children may need support with the vocabulary for 1,000 as this is the first time they will have encountered it, and they may initially say '10 hundreds'. A number line marked in 100 increments up to 1,000 would be a useful representation for children to support this understanding.

ASSESSMENT CHECKPOINT Question ❶ will help you assess whether children are confident using the term kilogram and the symbol kg.

Question ❷ will help you assess whether children can apply their proportional reasoning skills, which they have developed in Lessons 2 and 3 of this unit using grams, to a different standard unit of measure.

ANSWERS

Question ❶ a): 1 kg

Question ❶ b): 5 kg

Question ❶ c): 6 kg

Question ❷ : Mass of crate A shown at 4 kg on the scale. Mass of crate B shown at 20 kg on the scale (4 x 5 = 20). Mass of crate C shown at 10 kg on the scale (20 ÷ 2 =10).

Question ❸ : 1,000 g has the same mass as 1 kg.

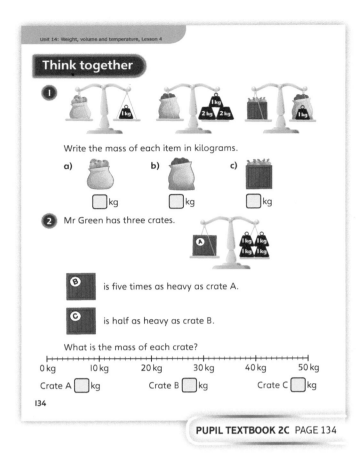

PUPIL TEXTBOOK 2C PAGE 134

PUPIL TEXTBOOK 2C PAGE 135

Practice

WAYS OF WORKING Independent thinking

IN FOCUS Question ② further develops children's use and understanding of different scales, as it asks them to draw on the arrows to show the given mass. Question ② b) involves children combining different stated masses to find the total mass and then recording this on the scales.

Question ③ requires pupils to make estimates based on their understanding of grams and kilograms from the whole of the unit so far.

STRENGTHEN If children are struggling to identify a sensible estimate for the mass of items in question ③ , they will benefit from practical experience of comparing the masses of similar items with different weights. For example, they could hold a book and a 1 kg weight. Ask: *Is the book heavier or lighter? So would the book be heavier or lighter than 20 kg?*

DEEPEN Children should be expected to build increasingly complex chains of reasoning about mass, a skill that has been developed gradually so far in this unit. Question ④ provides an opportunity to apply this skill to a more challenging problem, requiring children to work out the difference between the masses of different combinations of suitcases in order to work out the actual mass of each:

42 kg – 25 kg = mass of suitcase B, 60 kg – 42 kg = mass of suitcase C

ASSESSMENT CHECKPOINT Question ③ will help you assess children's practical understanding of the relative sizes of grams and kilograms. Do they understand, for example, that the book is unlikely to be 20 kg, as this would be 20 lots of 1,000 grams?

ANSWERS Answers for the **Practice** part of the lesson appear in the separate **Practice and Reflect answer guide**.

Reflect

WAYS OF WORKING Pair work

IN FOCUS This **Reflect** activity provides further opportunity for children to estimate the mass of different objects. Ask children to convince their partner of their answers. For example, how do they know that a book has a mass of less than 1 kg?

ASSESSMENT CHECKPOINT This question will help you further assess if children can accurately estimate the mass of different objects, building on their work so far throughout this unit. Listening to children's discussions with their partner will help you understand their reasoning and identify any misconceptions that they may still have.

ANSWERS Answers for the **Reflect** part of the lesson appear in the separate **Practice and Reflect answer guide**.

After the lesson ⏸

- Are children secure at estimating the mass of different objects?
- Have children understood the equivalence of 1,000 g and 1 kg?

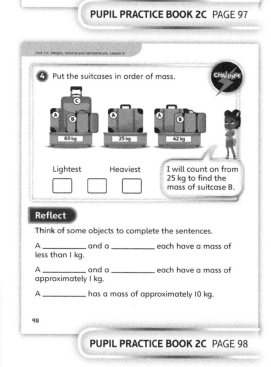

PUPIL PRACTICE BOOK 2C PAGE 96

PUPIL PRACTICE BOOK 2C PAGE 97

PUPIL PRACTICE BOOK 2C PAGE 98

Comparing volume

Learning focus

In this lesson, children will explore, measure and compare volume and capacity.

Small steps

→ Previous step: Measuring mass in kilograms
→ **This step: Comparing volume**
→ Next step: Measuring volume in millilitres (1)

NATIONAL CURRICULUM LINKS

Year 2 Measurement – Weight, volume and temperature

Compare and order lengths, mass, volume/capacity and record the results using >, < and =.

ASSESSING MASTERY

Children can explain the difference between volume and capacity, and use non-standard units and proportional reasoning to order and compare the volume or capacity of different objects.

COMMON MISCONCEPTIONS

Children may think that the taller the object, the greater the capacity. Provide children with a range of different practical experiences to help them explore this misconception. Show children a long tall measuring cylinder and a low wide bowl. Ask:
• *Which object has the greater capacity?*

Children may think that a larger capacity object always has a larger volume within it. Provide children with a large capacity object that has only a small amount of water in it, and a small capacity object that is full. Ask:
• *Which one contains the greater volume of water?*

STRENGTHENING UNDERSTANDING

Strengthen understanding by providing children with a wide range of practical experiences comparing and ordering both volume and capacity. Ensure children are exposed to a variety of containers, both tall and short, wide and narrow.

GOING DEEPER

Encourage children to estimate the volume and capacity of different items and use their estimates to order the items. Ask: *Do you think container A has a higher capacity than container B? Why?*

KEY LANGUAGE

In lesson: volume, capacity, larger, largest, smaller, smallest, fills, holds, less, more, left, >, <, =, full, half, three-quarters, a quarter, identical, hold

STRUCTURES AND REPRESENTATIONS

Base 10 equipment, number lines

RESOURCES

Mandatory: a variety of different objects that can be filled

Optional: paper and sticky tape to make cones, practical apparatus to help support calculation, Base 10 equipment

 In the eTextbook of this lesson, you will find interactive links to a selection of teaching tools.

Before you teach ⏸

• Have children had any exposure to volume and capacity before?
• Are children secure at using the inequality signs?

Discover

ASK

- *What can you see in this picture?*
- *Which cone looks like it will hold more popcorn? What makes you think this?*
- *Does a taller object always have a larger capacity?*
- *Could you make cones and test this out in real life? How might you compare the cones?*

IN FOCUS This part of the lesson introduces children to the concept of volume (the measure of how much 3D space is filled) and reintroduces them to capacity (the maximum volume a container can hold).

ANSWERS

Question ① a): You could start with both cones empty. Now fill one cone up, and tip the popcorn into the other cone. If the second cone overflows, the first cone is larger. If the second cone doesn't quite fill up, the first cone is smaller.

Question ① b): You could test how many spoonfuls of rice it takes to fill up each glass.

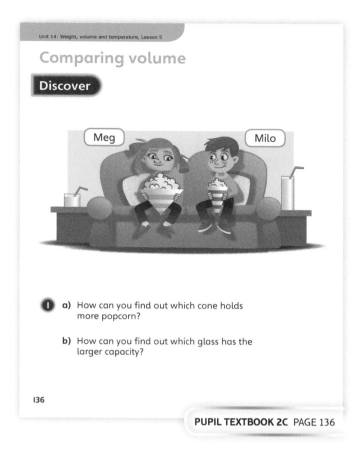

PUPIL TEXTBOOK 2C PAGE 136

Share

WAYS OF WORKING Whole class teacher led

ASK

- *How could you practically compare how much popcorn each cone holds?*
- *Could you use the < and > signs to make a statement about the cones?*
- *Is there another way you could compare the amount of popcorn each cone holds?*
- *Does anyone know what you call the measure of how much 3D space is taken up?*
- *How could you compare the capacity of the different glasses?*
- *If the tall glass holds 10 spoons of rice, and the short glass holds 5 spoons of rice, which has the larger capacity?*

IN FOCUS Children are introduced to different ways to work out the volume of an object, and to compare the capacity of objects using non-standard units, for example popcorn and rice. This part of the lesson could be very practical, with children making their own different-sized cones and exploring how they could compare the volume, and using rice (or another similar substance) and a spoon to compare the capacity of different glasses.

PUPIL TEXTBOOK 2C PAGE 137

Think together

WAYS OF WORKING Whole class teacher led (I do, We do, You do)

ASK

- Question **1** : *Which container has the least or greatest volume of tea in it? How can you tell?*
- Question **1** : *Did the size of the teapot change the volume of tea that it held? Did the largest teapot have the largest volume of tea in it?*
- Question **2** : *How can you use the capacity of the cylinder to help you work out the capacity of the cone?*
- Question **2** : *What non-standard unit will our capacity be in?*

IN FOCUS Questions **2** and **3** continue to develop children's ability to create chains of proportional reasoning, which has been developed throughout this unit. This skill is important, as proportional reasoning is the basis for all metric measures.

STRENGTHEN The calculation elements of questions **2** and **3** may present an additional challenge to some children. Encourage them to make use of the methods and approaches taught throughout Year 2, and to use a range of practical and pictorial representations, such as Base 10 equipment and number lines.

DEEPEN Children should continue to develop more advanced chains of proportional reasoning. Question **3** provides them with an opportunity to do this, by interpreting the information given in the picture and using their proportional reasoning to state the capacity (in spoonfuls) of each container. Challenge children to devise a similar question and then exchange questions with a partner.

ASSESSMENT CHECKPOINT Use the questions and discussion from this section to assess whether children are able to use the terms capacity and volume correctly.

ANSWERS

Question **1** a): A had the least tea.

Question **1** b): B had the most tea.

Question **1** c): The jug for C is half full.

Question **2** a): The has a capacity of 5 spoonfuls.

Question **2** b): The has a capacity of 25 spoonfuls.

Question **3** a): The big holds 10.

Question **3** b): The holds 30.

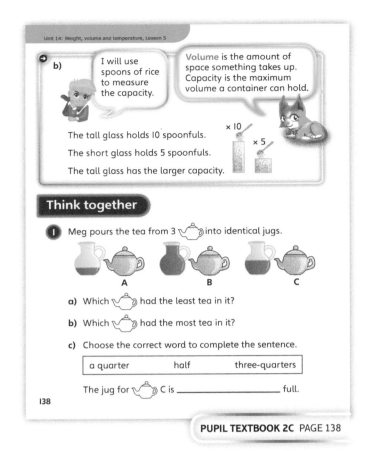

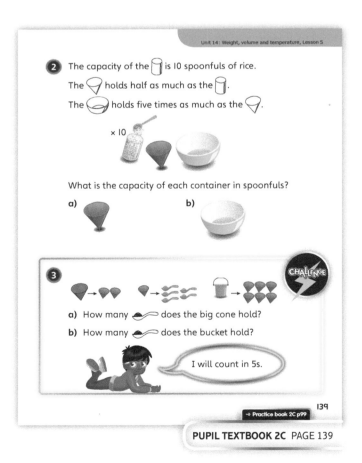

Practice

WAYS OF WORKING Independent thinking

IN FOCUS Question **2** asks children to compare the capacity of three different bowls and to apply their knowledge of inequality signs to capacity. This is a good opportunity to explore the difference between capacity and volume. This question shows the total capacity of each bowl in teacups, but that does not necessarily show the volume that each bowl is holding. A larger bowl may have a smaller volume in it than a smaller bowl.

STRENGTHEN Children will benefit from practical experience of comparing capacity using non-standard units. For example, set up a similar practical activity to that shown in question **3** , where children have to use small glasses to state the capacity of a range of larger containers. Practical and pictorial resources can be provided to help children with the calculation elements of questions **3** and **5** .

DEEPEN Children should begin to apply their proportional reasoning skills to a multi-step problem. Question **5** provides an opportunity for them to begin to do this. In this example, they have to first work out the volume of rice put into each container, and then take this total away from 20. Challenge children to complete the same problem, but with different numbers. For example, what if Milo put 2 spoonfuls in the pan? 4 spoonfuls?

ASSESSMENT CHECKPOINT Questions **2** and **3** will help you assess whether children can apply their proportional reasoning skills to capacity (question **2**) and volume (question **3**).

ANSWERS Answers for the **Practice** part of the lesson appear in the separate **Practice and Reflect answer guide**.

Reflect

WAYS OF WORKING Independent thinking

IN FOCUS This activity asks children to find and explain their own ways of working out the volume (not capacity) of the different objects. Encourage children to reflect on the use of non-standard units to compare volume and capacity throughout this lesson.

ASSESSMENT CHECKPOINT Use this activity to assess whether children are able to find the volume of rice held by the different objects using non-standard units.

ANSWERS Answers for the **Reflect** part of the lesson appear in the separate **Practice and Reflect answer guide**.

After the lesson ⏸

- How could you use day-to-day experiences and objects within the classroom to continue rehearsing the language of capacity and volume?
- Are children secure about the difference between capacity and volume?

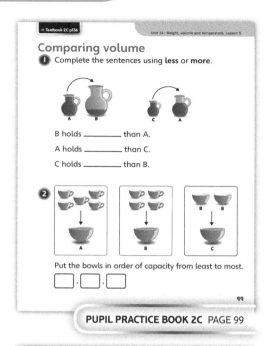

PUPIL PRACTICE BOOK 2C PAGE 99

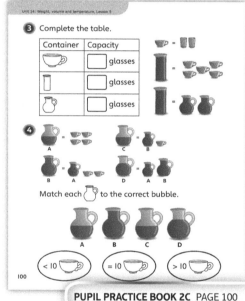

PUPIL PRACTICE BOOK 2C PAGE 100

PUPIL PRACTICE BOOK 2C PAGE 101

Measuring volume in millilitres

Learning focus

In this lesson, children will explore and use millilitres (ml) as a standard unit of measuring capacity and volume.

Small steps

→ Previous step: Comparing volume
→ **This step: Measuring volume in millilitres (1)**
→ Next step: Measuring volume in millilitres (2)

NATIONAL CURRICULUM LINKS

Year 2 Measurement – Weight, volume and temperature

Choose and use appropriate standard units to estimate and measure length/height in any direction (m/cm); mass (kg/g); temperature (°C); capacity (litres/ml) to the nearest appropriate unit, using rulers, scales, thermometers and measuring vessels.

ASSESSING MASTERY

Children can explain and demonstrate different ways in which they can accurately measure capacity and volume using the standard unit of measure of millilitres and its associated symbol (ml).

COMMON MISCONCEPTIONS

Children may think that the taller the item, the greater the capacity. Provide children with a range of different measuring jugs to compare. Ask:
• *Which measuring jug has the greatest capacity?*

Children may misread scales when the volume lies in between numbered scale points. Turn an empty measuring jug sideways to illustrate how the vertical scale is really a number line in disguise and ask:
• *What does the scale look like now? Does that help you read the value?*

STRENGTHENING UNDERSTANDING

Provide plenty of practical experience with measuring, including using teaspoons and measuring jugs. Many of the questions in this lesson could be solved practically using equipment in the classroom.

GOING DEEPER

Encourage children to consider the most efficient and accurate way of measuring different volumes. For example, is it more efficient and accurate to measure 60 ml using teaspoons or a measuring jug?

KEY LANGUAGE

In lesson: millilitres, ml, accurately, volume, divide, ÷, left, full

Other language to be used by the teacher: capacity

STRUCTURES AND REPRESENTATIONS

Number lines

RESOURCES

Mandatory: measuring jugs, teaspoons, number lines

 In the eTextbook of this lesson, you will find interactive links to a selection of teaching tools.

Before you teach ⏸

• Are children confident at reading scales on measuring jugs?
• Do children know what is meant by capacity and volume?

Discover

Pair work

ASK

- *What can you see in this picture? What do the children need to do?*
- *What does ml mean? Could this be a unit of measure?*
- *How could you measure out 10 ml of vinegar? How about 100 ml?*

IN FOCUS This activity introduces children to the standard unit of measure of millilitres, and its symbol ml, for the first time. Link question **1** b) to the questions in the previous lesson (spoonfuls of rice). Which way of measuring is more accurate?

ANSWERS

Question **1** a): You could use teaspoons ◐━━, which have a 5ml capacity, to measure out the vinegar.
5 ml = 1 ◐━━ , 10 ml = 2 ◐━━ ,
15 ml = 3 ◐━━ and 20 ml = 4 ◐━━ .
Children may realise that 100 ml would be a lot of ◐━━ (20), and therefore suggest they could use a measuring jug to measure 100 ml.

Question **1** b): 30 ml is the same as 6 teaspoons.

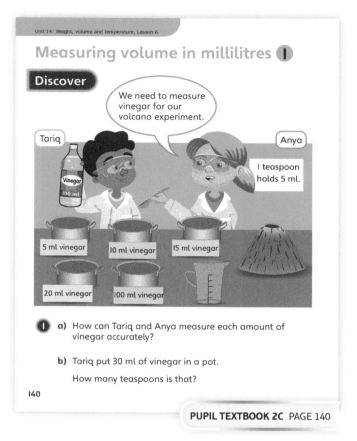

PUPIL TEXTBOOK 2C PAGE 140

Share

Whole class teacher led

ASK

- *How could you accurately measure the different volumes of vinegar?*
- *How many teaspoons would you need to make 10 ml? How do you know?*
- *What number could you count in to help you? Could you use anything to help you represent the counting?*
- *How many teaspoons would 100 ml be? Is there a better way to measure 100 ml?*

IN FOCUS In this part of the lesson, children are introduced to the idea that they can combine small standard unit measures, such as a teaspoon which holds 5 ml, to accurately measure larger volumes. Children should also consider the efficiency of using spoons to measure larger volumes. Draw their attention to Flo's statement and discuss. Ask: *Why does she need to use a measuring jug?*

STRENGTHEN Support children to use number lines and practical apparatus to help with counting in 5s.

PUPIL TEXTBOOK 2C PAGE 141

Think together

WAYS OF WORKING Whole class teacher led (I do, We do, You do)

ASK

- Question **1** b): *The level of this vinegar is on a line without a number on it. How can you work out what the volume of this vinegar is?*
- Question **2** a): *How could you combine the volume of vinegar from both jugs?*
- Question **2** b): *How can you work out how many teaspoons it is? What operation do you need to use?*

IN FOCUS Questions **1** and **2** involve reading the volume from points on the scale that are not numbered. Children need to apply their knowledge of scales from earlier work to be able to work out what each mark stands for and therefore read the volume accurately.

STRENGTHEN Provide children with plenty of practical, hands-on experiences of measuring capacity, using both teaspoons and measuring jugs. For example, for question **2**, ask children to measure water out in teaspoons into a measuring jug until they have measured out 55 ml, and count how many teaspoons it took. If it takes more than 11 teaspoons you may need to discuss why that was – did some get left in the spoon each time, or get spilt?

DEEPEN Children should begin to be able to read scales where the volume lies between two marked points. For example, in question **3** children have to reason that as the level of liquid is half-way between the 40 ml and 50 ml marks, so the volume will also be half-way between 40 ml and 50 ml (45 ml).

ASSESSMENT CHECKPOINT Use questions **1** and **2** to help you assess whether children can accurately read scales that are marked in ml.

ANSWERS

Question **1** a): 50 ml

Question **1** b): 40 ml

Question **2** a): 55 ml

Question **2** b): 55 ml ÷ 5 = 11 teaspoons

Question **3** : 45 ml

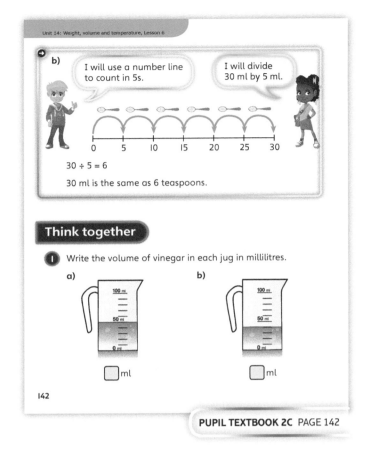

PUPIL TEXTBOOK 2C PAGE 142

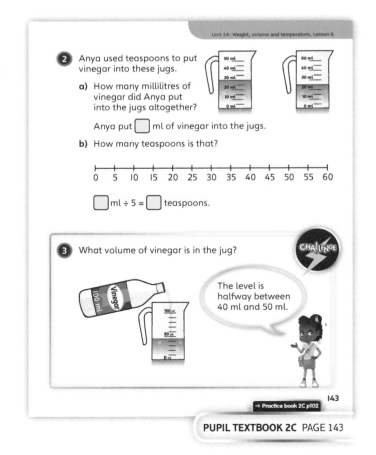

PUPIL TEXTBOOK 2C PAGE 143

Practice

WAYS OF WORKING Independent thinking

IN FOCUS Question **4** requires children to notice the subtraction (or part-whole) relationship between the level of water in the measuring cylinder before and after the water is poured into the glass.

Question **5** requires children to work backwards and establish the volume in the jug before water is poured out into the mug. Children are also expected to compare the volume in the jug before and after the beaker is emptied into it, in order to establish the capacity of each item.

STRENGTHEN To support children in answering question **4**, represent this problem practically, marking on the level of the water in the measuring jug before and after it has been used to fill the glass, using a marker pen, and illustrating how the scale on the jug can be used as a number line (you could empty the jug and turn it on its side to further emphasise this point). Children can therefore find the difference using the strategies they have already learned.

DEEPEN Encourage children to apply their measurement skills and knowledge of ml as a standard unit of volume to a range of increasingly complex situations. Provide children with a measuring jug and a range of containers and challenge them to devise a problem similar to the one in question **5**. Children can work in pairs and exchange questions.

ASSESSMENT CHECKPOINT Use question **3** to assess whether children can carry out basic calculations (in this case division) in the context of measuring volume in ml.

ANSWERS Answers for the **Practice** part of the lesson appear in the separate **Practice and Reflect answer guide**.

Reflect

WAYS OF WORKING Independent thinking

IN FOCUS This **Reflect** question draws children's attention to the different ways of accurately measuring volume using ml. For example, using measuring jugs and smaller items (such as teaspoons) that have a known capacity.

ASSESSMENT CHECKPOINT Use this question to assess whether children can explain how they can accurately measure capacity and volume, using both measuring cylinders and teaspoons or other measuring equipment.

ANSWERS Answers for the **Reflect** part of the lesson appear in the separate **Practice and Reflect answer guide**.

After the lesson ⏸

- Are children secure with the vocabulary millilitres, capacity and volume?
- How could you provide practical experience of measuring and calculating volume in other areas of the curriculum?

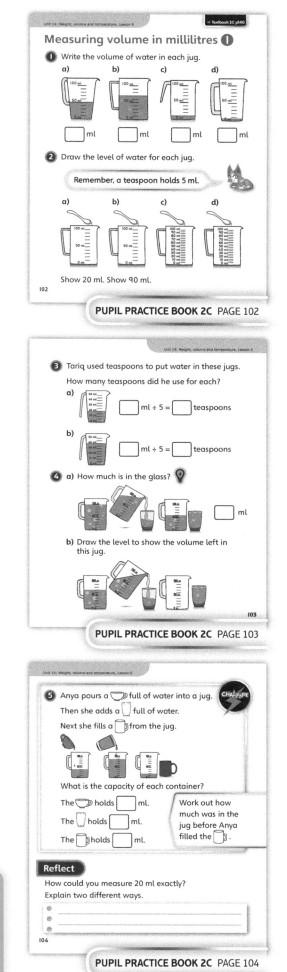

PUPIL PRACTICE BOOK 2C PAGE 102

PUPIL PRACTICE BOOK 2C PAGE 103

PUPIL PRACTICE BOOK 2C PAGE 104

Measuring volume in millilitres **2**

Learning focus

In this lesson, children will estimate and measure capacity and volume in ml. They will use scales that are marked in increments of 100 to link millilitres and litres (l).

Small steps

→ Previous step: Measuring volume in millilitres (1)
→ **This step: Measuring volume in millilitres (2)**
→ Next step: Measuring volume in litres

NATIONAL CURRICULUM LINKS

Year 2 Measurement – Weight, volume and temperature

Choose and use appropriate standard units to estimate and measure length/height in any direction (m/cm); mass (kg/g); temperature (°C); capacity (litres/ml) to the nearest appropriate unit, using rulers, scales, thermometers and measuring vessels.

ASSESSING MASTERY

Children can accurately measure capacities and volume using scales that are marked in increments of 100.

COMMON MISCONCEPTIONS

Children may count in 100s after 100, for example, they may count 98, 99, 100, 200, 300, 400... rather than 98, 99, 100, 101, 102... Address this misconception by using a range of number lines, including some marked in increments of 1 above 100 (101, 102, 103...) and others marked in increments of 100. Ask:
• *What numbers are missing between 100 and 200? Between 200 and 300?*

STRENGTHENING UNDERSTANDING

To support children in identifying the increments when counting in multiples of 100 ml, provide them with a number line that has multiples of 100 marked. Compare this against the scales on the measuring jugs, turning the measuring jugs onto their side to further emphasise the similarity and link between these two different representations.

GOING DEEPER

Children should begin to explore how else they can accurately measure volume. Ask: *If you didn't have a measuring jug, but knew that this bottle contained 100 ml, what volumes could you accurately measure?*

KEY LANGUAGE

In lesson: millilitres, ml, 100, 200, 300, 400, 500, 600, 700, 800, 900, 1,000, greater than, less than, more than, approximation, hundred, nearest to, capacity, volume, accurately

STRUCTURES AND REPRESENTATIONS

Number lines

RESOURCES

Mandatory: variety of measuring containers with scales marked in 100 ml increments

Optional: number lines

 In the eTextbook of this lesson, you will find interactive links to a selection of teaching tools.

Before you teach

• How successful were children at measuring mass in multiples of 100 g?
• Are children secure with using the standard unit of capacity or volume of millilitres and its associated symbol ml?

Discover

WAYS OF WORKING Pair work

ASK

- *What can you see in this picture?*
- *What are Jack and his dad using to measure the volume of the pasta sauce?*
- *What do you notice about the scale on the measuring jug?*
- *How could you work out what each line on the measuring jug stands for?*
- *What is the capacity of the different containers?*

IN FOCUS This section introduces children to measuring capacity in multiples of 100 ml, and requires them to use their knowledge of the number system and scales to work out the value of each interval on the scale shown on the measuring jug.

ANSWERS

Question ❶ a): Jack has made 800 ml of sauce.

Question ❶ b): There is too much sauce to fit in one 🍱 . It will fit in two 🍱 .

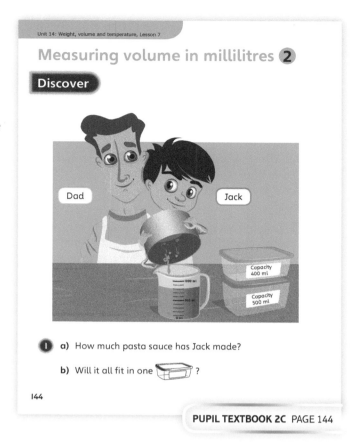

Share

WAYS OF WORKING Whole class teacher led

ASK

- *What does each interval on the measuring jug represent? How do you know?*
- Question ❶ a): *Can you count up in 100s?*
- Question ❶ b): *Is the volume of sauce greater or less than the capacity of the tubs shown? Could you use a number line or scale to help you check?*

IN FOCUS This lesson focuses on children counting in multiples of 100. Remind children of their work in Lesson 3, where they were introduced to counting in 100s in the context of mass and grams, to help them understand the link and relative sizes of ml and litres (which are explored further in Lesson 8).

Think together

WAYS OF WORKING Whole class teacher led (I do, We do, You do)

ASK

- Question **1** : *How can you work out the volume of orange juice? What does each mark on the scales stand for?*
- Question **2** : *Do any of the jugs have more than 500 ml in them? Do any have less than 300 ml?*
- Question **3** : *Which mark on the scale is the volume of liquid closest to?*

IN FOCUS Children are given further practice in this section at interpreting scales that are marked in 100 ml increments, and throughout this section they are exposed to a range of different ways that these scales can appear. Question **2** introduces children to the need to select items and volumes according to the task, and requires them to compare the different volumes in all three jugs.

STRENGTHEN Provide children with practical experience of measuring volume and reading scales that are marked in 100 ml increments. Use measuring jugs to recreate the contexts for questions **1** and **2** .

DEEPEN Children should be exposed to the need to make reasonable approximations when the volume of liquid lies between two marked increments on a scale. Question **3** provides children with the opportunity to practise this skill and builds on their work in Lesson 3 when approximating the mass of objects to the nearest 100 g. Provide children with measuring jugs, filled to various levels, and ask them to approximate the amount in each jug to the nearest 100 ml.

ASSESSMENT CHECKPOINT Use questions **1** and **2** to assess whether children are able to accurately read scales that are marked in increments of 100 ml.

ANSWERS

Question **1** a): 500 ml

Question **1** b): 500 ml

Question **1** c): 800 ml

Question **2** : Jug C

Question **3** a): 300 ml

Question **3** b): 🫖 is 900 ml to the nearest 100 ml.

🧃 is 400 ml to the nearest 100 ml.

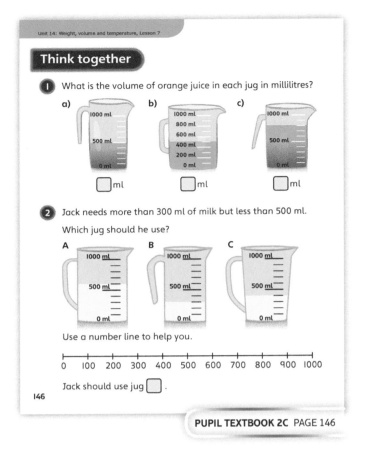

PUPIL TEXTBOOK 2C PAGE 146

PUPIL TEXTBOOK 2C PAGE 147

Practice

WAYS OF WORKING Independent thinking

IN FOCUS Question **3** exposes children to further reasoning based on the requirement for a specific volume of liquid. Children may state the jug that matches the exact volume when the question asks for 'more than' or 'less than'. Draw children's attention to this wording, for example, ask: *Does jug C contain more than or equal to 600 ml?*

STRENGTHEN To support children with selecting the most appropriate option in question **3**, encourage them to place each measuring jug on a number line, and use this number line to explore which jug best fits each statement.

DEEPEN Children should begin to consider how they could accurately measure volume or capacity without using a measuring jug. Question **4** introduces them to using fixed capacity containers (200 ml and 500 ml) to accurately measure volumes that are multiples or combinations of these amounts. Encourage children to find more volumes that they could accurately measure using these two bottles. For example, ask: *Can you list all the volumes below 1,000 ml that you could accurately measure?*

ASSESSMENT CHECKPOINT Use question **3** to assess children's understanding of the terminology 'more than' and 'less than' and their ability to make appropriate selections based on the criteria given.

ANSWERS Answers for the **Practice** part of the lesson appear in the separate **Practice and Reflect answer guide**.

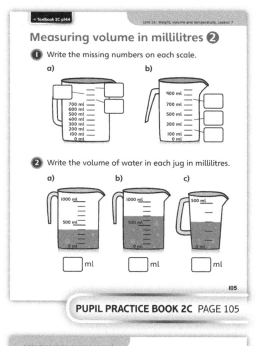

PUPIL PRACTICE BOOK 2C PAGE 105

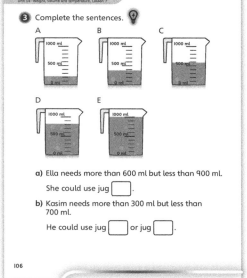

PUPIL PRACTICE BOOK 2C PAGE 106

Reflect

WAYS OF WORKING Pair work

IN FOCUS This activity invites children to use their knowledge of capacity to estimate the capacity of different containers through comparison.

ASSESSMENT CHECKPOINT Use this activity to assess children's ability to estimate volumes and their understanding of the relative sizes of the different capacities given.

ANSWERS Answers for the **Reflect** part of the lesson appear in the separate **Practice and Reflect answer guide**.

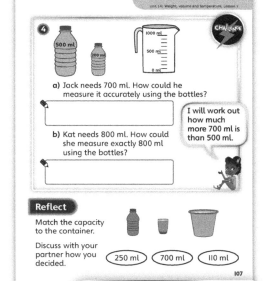

PUPIL PRACTICE BOOK 2C PAGE 107

After the lesson ⏸

- Are children secure at reading scales marked in increments of 100?
- Do children have a clear understanding of the relative sizes of different capacities and volumes? For example, do they understand that 600 ml is significantly (3 times) more than 200 ml?

Measuring volume in litres

Learning focus

In this lesson, children will be introduced to litres as a standard unit of measure, and will carry out a variety of calculations using litres.

Small steps

→ Previous step: Measuring volume in millilitres (2)
→ **This step: Measuring volume in litres**
→ Next step: Measuring temperature using a thermometer

NATIONAL CURRICULUM LINKS

Year 2 Measurement – Weight, volume and temperature

Choose and use appropriate standard units to estimate and measure length/height in any direction (m/cm); mass (kg/g); temperature (°C); capacity (litres/ml) to the nearest appropriate unit, using rulers, scales, thermometers and measuring vessels.

ASSESSING MASTERY

Children can use litres to accurately measure and compare volume and capacity for a range of real-life examples. Children can also make sensible approximations and estimates about volume and capacity based on their understanding of the relative sizes of millilitres and litres. Children can also carry out basic calculations involving litres.

COMMON MISCONCEPTIONS

Children may not have a clear understanding of the relative size of volumes and capacities measured in litres compared with those measured in millilitres. Provide children with practical experience of measuring volume and capacity in both litres and millilitres. Ask children to pour different volumes measured in millilitres into a 1 l container in order to see how much less the volume is than 1 l. Ask:
• *Is the volume more or less than 1 l?*

STRENGTHENING UNDERSTANDING

Children will benefit from plenty of practical experience of measuring in litres. Once children have some familiarity with the relative size of a litre, their estimating skills could be strengthened by asking them to first estimate the capacity before accurately checking it by measuring.

KEY LANGUAGE

In lesson: litre, l, capacity, volume, left, altogether, estimate, exactly, full, more than, less than, half as much as, *X* times as much

Other language to be used by the teacher: millilitres, >, <

STRUCTURES AND REPRESENTATIONS

Number lines

RESOURCES

Mandatory: a range of containers with a capacity of 1 l

Optional: a range of containers with litre capacities such as 1 l, 2 l, 5 l and smaller containers with capacities in millilitres such as 100 ml, 200 ml, 500 ml, Base 10 equipment, place value counters

 In the eTextbook of this lesson, you will find interactive links to a selection of teaching tools.

Before you teach

• Are children secure with the terminology of volume, capacity and millilitres from previous lessons in this unit?

Discover

Unit 14: Weight, volume and temperature, Lesson 8

WAYS OF WORKING Pair work

ASK

- *What can you see in this picture?*
- *What could the l stand for? What is it measuring?*
- *Do these objects have a bigger or smaller capacity than the ones you have seen in the past two lessons?*

IN FOCUS This section introduces children to the litre, and its symbol l, as a standard unit to measure capacity and volume for the first time. This section links to the work that children have previously done on using millilitres in lessons 6 and 7.

ANSWERS

Question **1** a): Kat can fill 4 large 🪣 .

Question **1** b): There are 13 l left in the 🛢 .

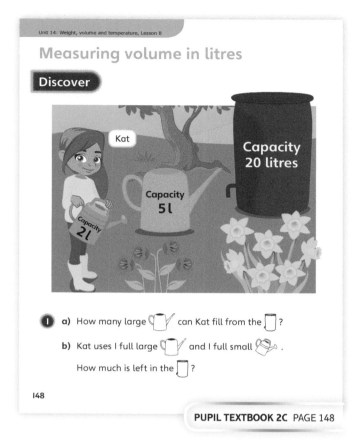

Measuring volume in litres

Discover

1. a) How many large 🪣 can Kat fill from the 🛢 ?

   b) Kat uses I full large 🪣 and I full small 🪣 . How much is left in the 🛢 ?

148

PUPIL TEXTBOOK 2C PAGE 148

Share

WAYS OF WORKING Whole class teacher led

ASK

- *What do you think litre means?*
- Question **1** a): *How did you work out how many watering cans Kat could fill from the large container? Did you use any methods or diagrams to help you?*
- *Is there another way you could have worked out how many watering cans could be filled from the large container?*
- Question **1** b): *How did you work out how much water was left in the large container? What did you need to work out first?*

IN FOCUS Children are asked to apply basic calculation and reasoning skills to solve problems involving litres. It is important that as part of this section children are introduced to the fact that a litre is a larger unit for measuring volume and capacity than millilitres. They should understand the volume of 1 l relative to volumes in millilitres that they have been using previously. This could be practically achieved by asking children to fill 100 ml containers until they have filled a 1 l container. The link to 1 l being the same as 1,000 ml could also be made at this stage.

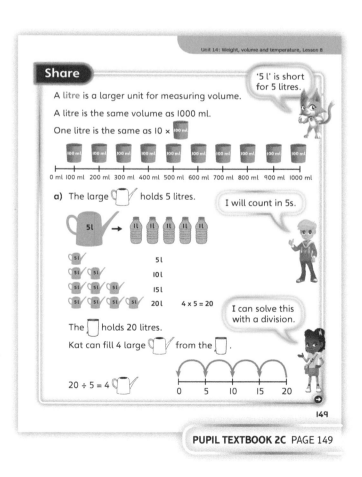

Share

'5 l' is short for 5 litres.

A **litre** is a larger unit for measuring volume.

A litre is the same volume as 1000 ml.

One litre is the same as 10 × [100 ml]

0 ml 100 ml 200 ml 300 ml 400 ml 500 ml 600 ml 700 ml 800 ml 900 ml 1000 ml

a) The large 🪣 holds 5 litres.

I will count in 5s.

5l → 1l 1l 1l 1l 1l

5l ✓   5l
5l 5l ✓   10l
5l 5l 5l ✓   15l
5l 5l 5l 5l   20l   4 × 5 = 20

I can solve this with a division.

The 🛢 holds 20 litres.

Kat can fill 4 large 🪣 from the 🛢 .

20 ÷ 5 = 4 🪣

0   5   10   15   20

149

PUPIL TEXTBOOK 2C PAGE 149

Think together

WAYS OF WORKING Whole class teacher led (I do, We do, You do)

ASK

- Question ❶ : *How can you work out the total volume of water used by the sunflower?*
- Question ❶ : *What operation do you need to use to work out how much water the tulip and the daisy had each day if you know the total they had in 5 days? Could you use a number line to help?*
- Question ❷ : *How big is this 1 l container? [Show children a 1 l container.] How many 1 l containers do you think would fill the bath? The washing bowl? The kettle?*

IN FOCUS In question ❷ , children are asked to estimate the volume of each object. In order to do this they need to use their understanding of the relative size of 1 l.

STRENGTHEN In order to help children have an accurate understanding of the relative size of a litre, it is important to provide practical experience of finding the capacity of a variety of large objects, and measuring out capacities in litres, for example by using multiple 1 l containers. This will help children when they need to estimate larger capacities.

DEEPEN Children should be able to apply increasingly advanced reasoning and logic to solve problems involving litres. Question ❸ presents a version of a 'classic' logic problem. ❸ a) requires children to realise that they can use the difference between the capacities of two containers to accurately measure the volume that is the difference between them (they can use an 8 l and a 5 l container to measure 3 l, because 8 − 5 = 3). Children will benefit from practical experience of doing this and attempting to solve this problem and the harder one in ❸ b).

ASSESSMENT CHECKPOINT Question ❶ will help you assess whether children are able to carry out basic calculations in the context of litres.

ANSWERS

Question ❶ : The total for the 🌻 is 25 l.

The 🌷 has 3 l of water each day.

The 🌼 has 1 l of water each day.

Question ❷ a): 100 l

Question ❷ b): 10 l

Question ❷ c): 2 l

Question ❸ a): Fill the 8 l 🪣 and then use it to fill the 5 l 🪣. The water remaining in the 8 l 🪣 will have a volume of 3 l.

Question ❸ b): Yes. Fill the 5 l 🪣. Pour all this water into the 8 l 🪣, which still has room for 3 l more. Refill the 5 l 🪣 and use it to top up the 8 l 🪣. 5 − 3 = 2, so 2 l will be left in the smaller 🪣.

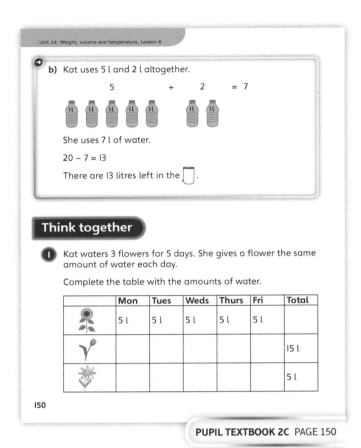

Practice

WAYS OF WORKING Independent thinking

IN FOCUS Question ② focuses on finding proportional relationships between capacities measured in litres, and on comparing capacities.

STRENGTHEN Encourage children to revisit the different methods and representations used throughout Year 2 in order to support them with their calculation skills within these questions. Ask: *How can you use a number line, Base 10 equipment or place value counters to help calculate the answers?*

DEEPEN Encourage children to continue to develop their logical reasoning skills using litres. Question ④ provides further opportunity to do this, and at a slightly deeper level than question ③ . In question ④ , children need to consider using multiples of one container (the 4 l container) to accurately measure other volumes. Children could also be asked to work out all the capacities under 20 l that they could accurately measure using the 7 l and 4 l containers.

ASSESSMENT CHECKPOINT Question ② will help you assess whether children can make proportional statements about volume measured in litres, including using the terms 'more', 'half as much' and 'X as much', and whether they can compare capacities. Question ③ will help you assess whether children are able to accurately estimate volumes, using their knowledge of the relative sizes of, and the relationship between, millilitres and litres.

ANSWERS Answers for the **Practice** part of the lesson appear in the separate **Practice and Reflect answer guide**.

Reflect

WAYS OF WORKING Independent thinking

IN FOCUS This activity draws on knowledge and understanding that have been developed both in this lesson and over the past three lessons.

ASSESSMENT CHECKPOINT Use this activity to assess whether children are confident with the vocabulary around volume and capacity, including the use of the standard units, millilitres and litres, and their symbols, ml and l. Assess whether children are able to explain different ways in which they can measure volume.

ANSWERS Answers for the **Reflect** part of the lesson appear in the separate **Practice and Reflect answer guide**.

After the lesson ⏸

- Are children confident at using both ml and l to measure and compare volume?
- How can you create opportunities in other subjects and throughout the school day for children to practise their capacity and volume measurement skills?

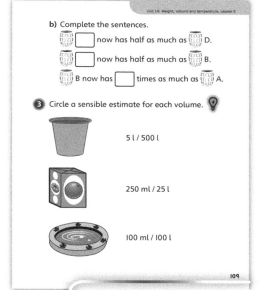

PUPIL PRACTICE BOOK 2C PAGE 108

PUPIL PRACTICE BOOK 2C PAGE 109

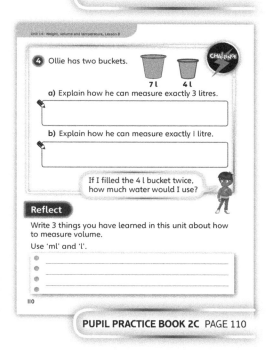

PUPIL PRACTICE BOOK 2C PAGE 110

Measuring temperature using a thermometer

Learning focus

In this lesson, children will read temperatures from a thermometer and use temperature to make simple comparisons and to carry out calculations.

Small steps

→ Previous step: Measuring volume in litres
→ **This step: Measuring temperature using a thermometer**
→ Next step: Reading thermometers

NATIONAL CURRICULUM LINKS

Year 2 Measurement – Weight, volume and temperature

Choose and use appropriate standard units to estimate and measure length/height in any direction (m/cm); mass (kg/g); temperature (°C); capacity (litres/ml) to the nearest appropriate unit, using rulers, scales, thermometers and measuring vessels.

ASSESSING MASTERY

Children can read temperature from a thermometer and use the unit degrees Celsius and its symbol °C. Children can use their knowledge of relative temperatures to begin to estimate temperatures, and can use the terms warmer and cooler to carry out simple calculations.

COMMON MISCONCEPTIONS

Children may not appreciate how warm or cold temperatures are. For example, they may estimate that the temperature outside is 70 °C. Ask:
• *What do you think the temperature is outside? What about inside? What could you use to help you tell the temperature?*

STRENGTHENING UNDERSTANDING

Discuss common temperatures with children. For example, the temperature at which water boils, the temperature in deserts, in their fridge, and so on. Plot these temperatures onto a large thermometer. This will help children gain a relative understanding of temperature.

To help support children in reading thermometers, make the link between a thermometer and a number line, lying a thermometer down horizontally if needed to help make this link.

GOING DEEPER

Encourage children to create their own comparisons about temperature, including using estimations rather than accurate measurements. For example, ask children to compare the temperatures at various points in the day, leading to statements such as: *It was warmer at playtime than it was before school, but playtime was cooler than lunchtime.*

KEY LANGUAGE

In lesson: temperature, thermometer, °C, degrees Celsius, warmer, warmest, cooler, coolest, estimate, more, less

Other language to be used by the teacher: greater than, less than, >, <

STRUCTURES AND REPRESENTATIONS

Number lines

RESOURCES

Mandatory: thermometers

Optional: number lines

 In the eTextbook of this lesson, you will find interactive links to a selection of teaching tools.

Before you teach ⏸

• What exposure have children had to discussing temperature before? Has this been a focus of any work in science lessons?

Discover

Pair work

ASK

- *What can you see in this picture? What is Eve holding in her hand?*
- *What do you think °C stands for? What does it measure?*
- *How can you work out where Eve lives?*
- *How can you work out where is 3°C warmer than Aberdeen? What operation should you use?*

IN FOCUS This part of the lesson introduces children to measuring temperature for the first time. They are likely to be familiar with the notion of measuring temperature from contexts outside of school (for example, weather forecasts and conversations at home). Measuring temperature builds on children's work on measurement and reading scales, however, unlike other measurements, temperature is something that children cannot physically see, yet they experience it on a daily basis.

ANSWERS

Question ❶ a): Eve lives in York.

Question ❶ b): Marta lives in Edinburgh.

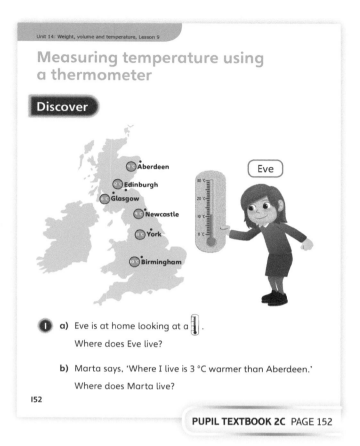

Share

Whole class teacher led

ASK

- *How did you work out where Eve lived?*
- *How did you read the thermometer?*
- *What unit do you measure temperature in?*
- *How did you work out the temperature where Marta lives?*
- *Does 'warmer' mean you have to count on or count back?*

IN FOCUS In this part of the lesson, children are introduced to reading thermometers for the first time. Make links to the vertical scales experienced in other types of measurement. Ask children to practically explore the temperature in their school, and explore weather forecasts to help them gain a better understanding of temperature.

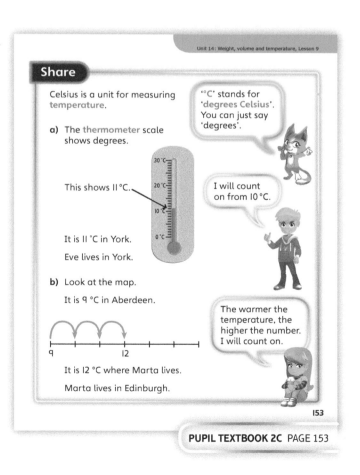

Think together

WAYS OF WORKING Whole class teacher led (I do, We do, You do)

ASK

- Question ❶ : *What numbers are marked on the thermometers?*
- Question ❶ : *What does each mark stand for?*
- Question ❷ : *Does 'warmer' mean the temperature is more or less?*
- Question ❷ : *How could you use a number line to help you solve these problems?*
- Question ❸ : *What is the normal summer temperature in the UK?*

IN FOCUS In question ❷ , children need to link 'warmer' to an increase in temperature (addition) and 'cooler' to a decrease (subtraction). They must also use temperature for comparison, using the terms 'cooler than' and 'warmer than'.

STRENGTHEN For question ❷ , encourage children to use number lines to help them calculate the differences in temperature. A thermometer scale can also be used as a vertical number line (or rotate it so it is horizontal) which may help keep the direct link to thermometers. For question ❷ c), encourage children to mark the temperatures in Penzance and London on a number line or thermometer and work out which temperatures from the map fall in between these two values.

DEEPEN Children should begin to develop an understanding of the relative warmth of different temperatures, which can be achieved by linking temperatures to common experience (for example, that 100 °C is the temperature at which water boils, 0 °C is when water freezes, 3 °C is the average temperature in a fridge). Children can then use this knowledge to match temperatures to various situations, and in question ❸ they are given the opportunity to do this in the context of temperature in the sun and shade. Ask children to investigate the usual summer temperature in the UK, and perhaps even use the temperatures on a weather forecast today to help.

ASSESSMENT CHECKPOINT Question ❶ should help you assess whether children are confident at reading the temperature from a thermometer.

ANSWERS

Question ❶ a): 10 °C

Question ❶ b): 15 °C

Question ❶ c): 22 °C

Question ❶ d): 9 °C

Question ❷ a): Glasgow

Question ❷ b): Swansea

Question ❷ c): Liverpool

Question ❸ : Thermometer A is in the shade. Thermometer B is broken. Thermometer C is in the sun.

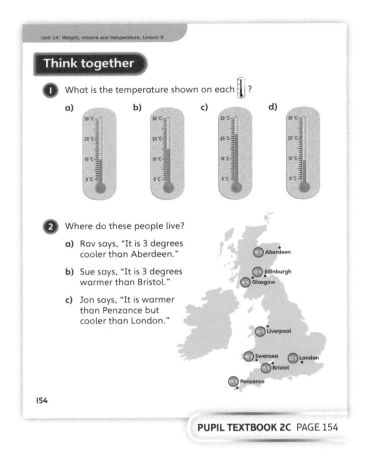

PUPIL TEXTBOOK 2C PAGE 154

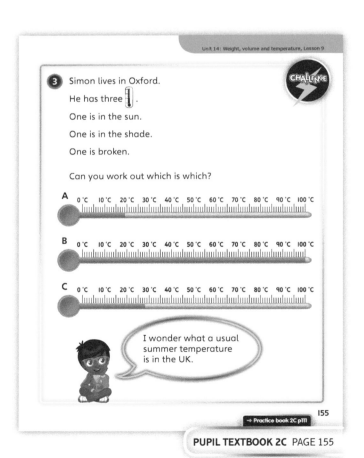

PUPIL TEXTBOOK 2C PAGE 155

Practice

WAYS OF WORKING Independent thinking

IN FOCUS Question ③ switches the focus from children reading thermometers to them marking given temperatures on thermometers. Whilst this is an unlikely situation to occur in real life, this will help children secure and apply their knowledge of reading thermometers.

Question ④ further develops children's ability to compare temperatures, and requires them to use the inverse relationship between warmer and cooler to help them calculate.

STRENGTHEN In question ②, it can help to make the link to ordering numbers (without the °C) and discussing how °C is just a unit, and therefore does not impact our ordering.

DEEPEN Children should begin to create their own comparison statements, using the terms 'warmer than' and 'cooler than'. Question ⑤ provides children with an opportunity to do this, using the map given in question ③.

ASSESSMENT CHECKPOINT Question ② will help you assess whether children are confident at understanding the relative warmth of different temperature values.

Question ④ will help you assess whether children are comfortable at comparing temperatures and using the terms warmer and cooler.

ANSWERS Answers for the **Practice** part of the lesson appear in the separate **Practice and Reflect answer guide**.

Reflect

WAYS OF WORKING Independent thinking

IN FOCUS This activity focuses on children using their knowledge of temperature to make estimations based on a given situation.

ASSESSMENT CHECKPOINT Use this activity to assess whether children have a relative understating of the warmth and coolness of temperature, and therefore are able to estimate temperatures in given situations.

ANSWERS Answers for the **Reflect** part of the lesson appear in the separate **Practice and Reflect answer guide**.

After the lesson ⏸

- Are children confident at reading thermometers and using the terminology degrees Celsius (°C)?
- How can you include discussion about temperature in your day-to-day classroom routines?

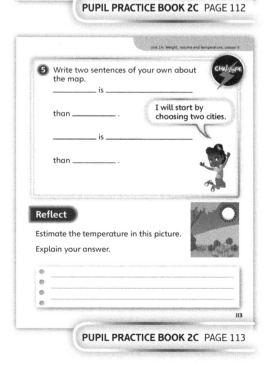

PUPIL PRACTICE BOOK 2C PAGE 111

PUPIL PRACTICE BOOK 2C PAGE 112

PUPIL PRACTICE BOOK 2C PAGE 113

Reading thermometers

Learning focus

In this lesson, children will apply their knowledge of counting in 2s, 5s and 10s to reading different scales on thermometers.

Small steps

→ Previous step: Measuring temperature using a thermometer
→ **This step: Reading thermometers**

NATIONAL CURRICULUM LINKS

Year 2 Measurement – Weight, volume and temperature

Choose and use appropriate standard units to estimate and measure length/height in any direction (m/cm); mass (kg/g); temperature (°C); capacity (litres/ml) to the nearest appropriate unit, using rulers, scales, thermometers and measuring vessels.

ASSESSING MASTERY

Children can accurately read the temperature from a range of thermometers that use different scales. Children can also compare two temperatures.

COMMON MISCONCEPTIONS

When comparing different temperatures taken on different thermometers with different scales, children often assume that the higher up the scale the reading, the higher the temperature. To help address this, ensure children are exposed to a range of thermometers that use different scales. Ask:
• *Where would you find 20°C on these two thermometers?*

STRENGTHENING UNDERSTANDING

To help support children, it is important that they have practical experience of using a range of thermometers that use different scales. Encourage children to measure the same temperature using the different thermometers and compare how the temperature is recorded on each. It is also important to retain the link between scales on a thermometer and number lines.

GOING DEEPER

Encourage children to use their real-world knowledge and experiences in order to make sensible predictions and estimations about the temperature in different scenarios.

KEY LANGUAGE

In lesson: temperature, hotter, hottest, cooler, coolest, scale, degrees Celsius, °C, interval

Other language to be used by the teacher: interval, greater, greatest, less, least, warmer, warmest

STRUCTURES AND REPRESENTATIONS

Number lines

RESOURCES

Mandatory: number lines, range of thermometers with different scales

 In the eTextbook of this lesson, you will find interactive links to a selection of teaching tools.

Before you teach 🕚

• Do children still have misconceptions about temperature and thermometers from the work in Lesson 9?
• If so, how can these be addressed?

Discover

WAYS OF WORKING Pair work

ASK

- *What can you see in this picture?*
- *What is the same and what is different about each thermometer?*
- *What do you notice about the scales on each thermometer?*
- *Why do you think we don't always use scales that count in 1s?*

IN FOCUS This part of the lesson exposes children to the use of different scales, and focuses on children being able to determine the scale used on each thermometer and using this knowledge to accurately read the temperatures from the thermometers.

ANSWERS

Question ❶ a): Baby Bear's 🍲 is 10 °C.

Question ❶ b): Daddy Bear's 🍲 is hotter (15 °C) than Mummy Bear's 🍲 (12 °C).

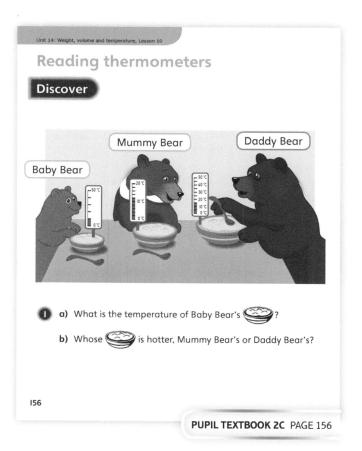

Reading thermometers

Discover

❶ a) What is the temperature of Baby Bear's 🍲?

b) Whose 🍲 is hotter, Mummy Bear's or Daddy Bear's?

156

PUPIL TEXTBOOK 2C PAGE 156

Share

WAYS OF WORKING Whole class teacher led

ASK

- *What did you notice about the different thermometers? What is the same? What is different?*
- *How did you work out what each mark on the different thermometers stood for? Can you explain to another pair what you did?*
- *What number knowledge did you use?*
- *Did you use any representations to help you work this out?*

IN FOCUS Accurately reading each scale closely links to children's knowledge of counting in 2s, 5s and 10s, and builds upon the work on reading scales as part of the capacity and mass elements of this unit. Children need to establish what each mark on the scale is worth, which they can do in a number of ways. For Baby Bear and Mummy Bear's porridge, children can use their knowledge of their 2 and 10 times-table, and for Daddy Bear's porridge, they can use their 5 times-table knowledge, or link the temperature to being halfway between 10 and 20 degrees.

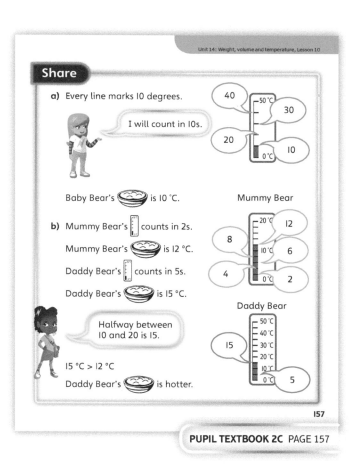

Share

a) Every line marks 10 degrees.

I will count in 10s.

Baby Bear's 🍲 is 10 °C.

Mummy Bear

b) Mummy Bear's ▯ counts in 2s.

Mummy Bear's 🍲 is 12 °C.

Daddy Bear's ▯ counts in 5s.

Daddy Bear's 🍲 is 15 °C.

Halfway between 10 and 20 is 15.

15 °C > 12 °C

Daddy Bear's 🍲 is hotter.

Daddy Bear

157

PUPIL TEXTBOOK 2C PAGE 157

Think together

Whole class teacher led (I do, We do, You do)

ASK

- Question **1** : *How can you work out the scale used by each thermometer? What is the value of each mark on each thermometer?*
- Question **2** : *Is it always, sometimes or never true that the thermometer with the highest line has the highest temperature?*
- Question **3** : *What do you know about what happens to water at different temperatures?*

IN FOCUS Question **2** involves children comparing temperatures, and addresses the common misconception that, when two different scales are used, the higher up the thermometer, the higher the temperature.

Question **3** can be linked to discussions in science about the boiling and melting point of water.

STRENGTHEN To support children in identifying the scales, orientate the thermometers horizontally, and make the link between the scales and a number line.

DEEPEN Children should be encouraged to use their knowledge of temperature to make sensible estimations for the temperature in different scenarios. For example, in question **3** , they should use their knowledge of the comparative temperature of boiling water, bath water and ice to help them make sensible approximations. Ask: *What would be a sensible temperature for bath water?*

ASSESSMENT CHECKPOINT Use question **1** to help you assess whether children are able to accurately use their number knowledge to identify the scale and value of each mark on the scale.

ANSWERS

Question **1** a): 10 °C

Question **1** b): 22 °C

Question **1** c): 35 °C

Question **1** d): 45 °C

Question **2** a): Thermometer A shows the hotter temperature.

Question **2** b): Thermometer A shows the hotter temperature.

Question **3** : 🫖 matches thermometer A

🧴 matches thermometer B

🛁 matches thermometer D

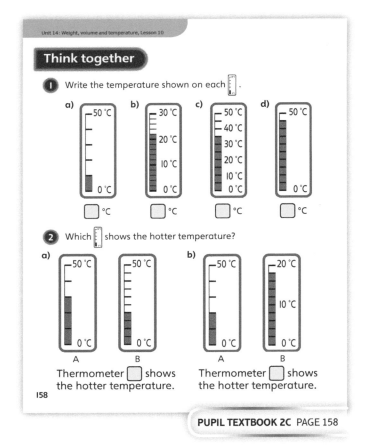

PUPIL TEXTBOOK 2C PAGE 158

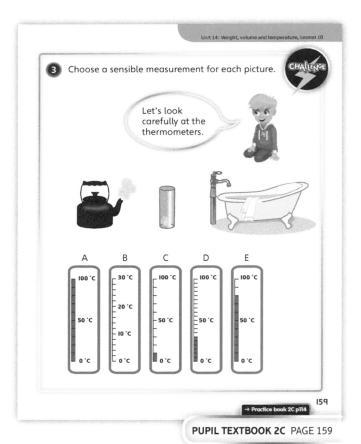

PUPIL TEXTBOOK 2C PAGE 159

Practice

→ Textbook 2C p156

WAYS OF WORKING Independent thinking

IN FOCUS Question **1** asks children to mark the same temperature on three different thermometers that use different scales. This will help to further draw children's attention to how the same temperature can appear differently on different thermometers, based on the scale used.

Question **3** switches the orientation of the thermometer and relies on children realising that the same skills apply despite a different orientation.

In question **4**, children should be encouraged to use their knowledge of approximate temperatures in different locations to check the reasonableness of their answers.

STRENGTHEN Encourage children to use number lines marked in different value jumps (for example, number lines that increase in 1s, 2s, 5s and 10s) to help them identify the value on the different thermometers throughout this section.

DEEPEN Children should continue to be asked to make sensible estimations based on their knowledge of temperature and the relative values of different temperatures. Question **4** provides further opportunity for children to develop this skill, this time with a wider range of situations. Encourage children to first order the pictures in relative 'warmth' before matching them to temperatures.

ASSESSMENT CHECKPOINT Use question **3** to assess whether children can use their knowledge of numbers to compare temperatures, and whether they have overcome the common misconception that the greater temperature in a pair will always be the temperature that is higher up the scale.

ANSWERS Answers for the **Practice** part of the lesson appear in the separate **Practice and Reflect answer guide**.

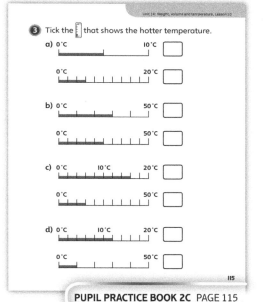

PUPIL PRACTICE BOOK 2C PAGE 114

PUPIL PRACTICE BOOK 2C PAGE 115

Reflect

WAYS OF WORKING Independent thinking

IN FOCUS This question helps children reflect on their learning and explain how they can recognise the value on different scales. Being able to explain is a key indicator that children are secure in a concept.

ASSESSMENT CHECKPOINT Use this question to assess whether children are secure at being able to identify the scale on a range of different thermometers.

ANSWERS Answers for the **Reflect** part of the lesson appear in the separate **Practice and Reflect answer guide**.

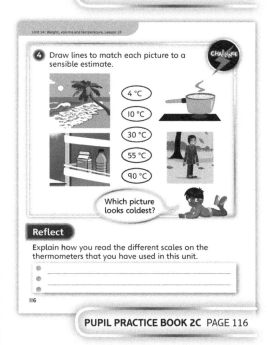

PUPIL PRACTICE BOOK 2C PAGE 116

After the lesson ⏸

- How can you apply the knowledge of temperatures and thermometers children have gained in this lesson to other areas of the school curriculum?

End of unit check

Don't forget the *Power Maths* unit assessment grid on p26.

WAYS OF WORKING Group work – adult led

IN FOCUS Question ➊ focuses on children being able to make connected chains of reasoning to find the mass of an object.

Question ➌ focuses on children being able to make sensible estimations based on their experiences and knowledge of measures.

Think!

WAYS OF WORKING Pair work or small groups

IN FOCUS This activity focuses on children being able to interpret a range of measurements and compare masses, then use this information to make chains of linked reasoning to deduce the mass of the different objects. Children will need to consider what information they have, and how the different measuring balances are linked, in order to solve the problem. With the third scale, they also need to realise that the mass of box B is 15 kg (20 kg minus the 5 kg weight that is on the same side as B) rather than 20 kg (the total mass of the two 10 kg weights that balance B and the 5 kg weight).

Encourage children to think through or discuss what information they knew and the steps they took to help solve the problem, before writing their answer in **My journal**.

ANSWERS AND COMMENTARY Children who have mastered this unit will be able to use the standard units to measure and solve problems relating to mass, volume, capacity and temperature. They will be able to order and compare using each type of measure, and will be able to make sensible approximations as to the mass, volume, capacity or temperature of different objects or real-life situations. Children will be able to reason using measures, including making chains of connected reasoning when ordering and comparing measures.

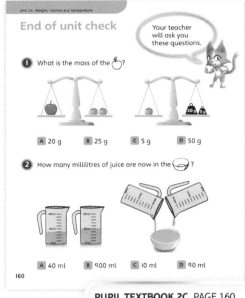

PUPIL TEXTBOOK 2C PAGE 160

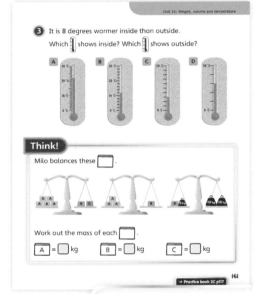

PUPIL TEXTBOOK 2C PAGE 161

Q	A	WRONG ANSWERS AND MISCONCEPTIONS	STRENGTHENING UNDERSTANDING
1	D	B suggests that children are not linking the information given in the two balance scales, and are assuming that the mass of one apple is the same as one (rather than two) satsumas. A or C suggests that children have not combined the two weights shown on the second scale.	If children are struggling to read scales accurately, link them to a number line, if possible manipulating them to 'turn them into' number lines. Also ensure that children have practical experience of measuring using a range of equipment with different scales. If children are struggling to make chains of reasoning, break the question into smaller steps, and ask: *What do you need to know first?*
2	D	A suggests that children have not combined both volumes from the two jugs. C suggests that children have accurately read both volumes from the scale, but have done a subtraction not an addition.	
3	A (inside) C (outside)	Children may reverse A and C, suggesting that they do not have a real-world understanding of different temperatures. Answers that do not have a difference of 8 °C suggest children have misread the scales or made a calculation error.	

My journal

Independent thinking

Box A = 5 kg   Box B = 15 kg   Box C = 10 kg

First I worked out the mass of Box B by subtracting 5 kg from 20 kg.

Then I worked out the mass of Box A by dividing 15 kg (the mass of Box B) by 3 (which is how many Box As balance Box B).

Next I worked out the mass of Box C by knowing that Box A is 5 kg, so 5 would be 25 kg, and then taking away Box B (15 kg): 25 – 15 = 10 kg.

If children struggle with this question it indicates that they are finding making chains of connected reasoning difficult and are not able to connect the information shown on the different balance scales. Ask questions to help them break down the question into its different parts. For example: *What do you need to know first? Which box can you work out the mass of without knowing the mass of any other box?*

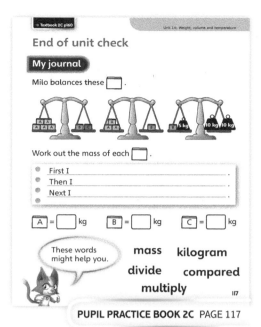

PUPIL PRACTICE BOOK 2C PAGE 117

Power check

Independent thinking

- *How do you feel about reading different scales?*
- *Are there some types of measurement that you feel better about using than others? Why?*
- *What could you do to improve?*

Power puzzle

Pair work or small groups

Use this **Power puzzle** to see whether children are able to accurately measure both mass and volume and make connections between different types of measure. This activity could be quite messy, so ensure that this is completed in an area where water spillage won't be a problem!

Children will find that, once the mass of the empty jug has been subtracted, the numeric values of the mass and volume measurements are the same in each case. For example, 50 ml of water has a mass of 50 g, 100 ml of water has a mass of 100 g and so on.

If children are able to complete this **Power puzzle**, it suggests that they are able to accurately measure mass and volume, and make connections between different type of measures.

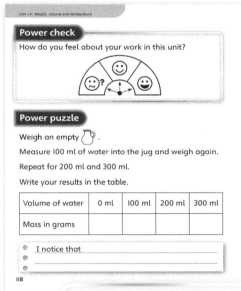

PUPIL PRACTICE BOOK 2C PAGE 118

After the unit ⏸

- Consider whether children have grasped the relationship between different types of measure.
- Did children understand that they should read a scale by the numbers marked on it, and not by how long it is?

Strengthen and **Deepen** activities for this unit can be found in the *Power Maths* online subscription.

Published by Pearson Education Limited, 80 Strand, London, WC2R 0RL.

www.pearsonschools.co.uk

Text © Pearson Education Limited 2017
Edited by Pearson, Little Grey Cells Publishing Services and Haremi Ltd
Designed and typeset by Kamae Design
Original illustrations © Pearson Education Limited 2017
Illustrated by Laura Arias, Fran and David Brylewski, Nigel Dobbyn and Nadene Naude at Beehive Illustration;
Emily Skinner at Graham-Cameron Illustration; Paul Higgins at Hunter Higgins Illustrations; and Kamae.
Cover design by Pearson Education Ltd
Back cover illustration © Will Overton at Advocate Art and Nadene Naude at Beehive Illustration.

Series Editor: Tony Staneff
Consultant: Professor Liu Jian

The rights of Tony Staneff, David Board, Jonathan East, Tim Handley, Julia Hayes and Timothy Weal to be identified as authors of this work have been asserted by them in accordance with the Copyright, Designs and Patents Act 1988.

First published 2017

2021
10 9 8 7 6 5

British Library Cataloguing in Publication Data
A catalogue record for this book is available from the British Library

ISBN 978 0 435 18978 5

Printed in Great Britain by Ashford Colour Press Ltd.

www.activelearnprimary.co.uk

Note from the publisher
Pearson has robust editorial processes, including answer and fact checks, to ensure the accuracy of the content in this publication, and every effort is made to ensure this publication is free of errors. We are, however, only human, and occasionally errors do occur. Pearson is not liable for any misunderstandings that arise as a result of errors in this publication, but it is our priority to ensure that the content is accurate. If you spot an error, please do contact us at resourcescorrections@pearson.com so we can make sure it is corrected.